Environmental Mediation

Other Titles in This Series

What Happened to Fairbanks?: The Effects of the Trans-Alaska Pipeline on the Community of Fairbanks, Alaska, Mim Dixon

Cultural Resources: Planning and Management, edited by Roy S. Dickens, Jr., and Carole E. Hill

The ELF Odyssey: National Security versus Environmental Protection, Lowell L. Klessig and Victor Strite

Social Impact Assessment Series
Charles P. Wolf, General Editor

Environmental Mediation: The Search for Consensus
edited by Laura M. Lake

The inevitable policy dilemmas that accompany attempts to implement environmental policy decisions can lead to judicial review or, alternatively, can be channeled into administrative processes that directly involve opposing interest groups. In this first effort to compare the two approaches, the authors draw attention to the potential institutional repercussions of reliance on only one technique. Their case studies suggest that mediation is a feasible--and significant--alternative to litigation in solving environmental disputes.

Laura Lake, adjunct assistant professor of political science at the University of California, Los Angeles, was previously assistant program officer in the Office of Resources and the Environment at the Ford Foundation.

Environmental Mediation:
The Search for Consensus

edited by Laura M. Lake

Westview Press / Boulder, Colorado

Social Impact Assessment Series

Published in 1980 in the United States of America by
    Westview Press, Inc.
    5500 Central Avenue
    Boulder, Colorado 80301
    Frederick A. Praeger, Publisher

Library of Congress Cataloging in Publication Data
Main entry under title:
Environmental mediation, a search for consensus.
    (Social impact assessment series ; no. 3)
    Includes bibliographies.
    1. Environmental law--United States--Addresses, essays,
lectures. 2. Compromise (Law)--United States--Addresses,
essays, lectures. 3. Actions and defenses--United States
--Addresses, essays, lectures. 4. Arbitration (Administrative law)--United States--Addresses, essays, lectures.
5. Judicial review--United States--Addresses, essays,
lectures. I. Lake, Laura M. II. Series.
KF3775.A75E57   346.73'046   79-28445
ISBN 0-89158-587-7

Composition for this book was provided by the editor.
Printed and bound in the United States of America.

Contents

Tables and Figures

Tables

Figures

Preface

This book analyzes the role of administrative
and judicial authority in environmental decisionmaking, and examines six case studies of
environmental mediation in the United States.
Environmental mediation, the use of neutral third
parties to help disputants negotiate an administrative, rather than judicial settlement,
represents an experimental conflict resolution
process which can serve as an alternative to
citizen lawsuits. For environmental policy implementation has frequently resulted in
administrative breakdowns and judicial intervention, two phenomena which indicate significant
institutional stress and adaptation, and suggest
the need for new procedures which permit diverse,
competing interest groups to accommodate their
demands regarding natural resource and energy
policy.

Environmental policy implementation involves
a highly fragmented intergovernmental
administrative system in local disputes over dams,
power plants, highways, shopping centers,
factories and ski resorts. Locked into bitter,
lengthy battles are local and national groups
(environmental, business, labor, civic, health and
local residents) which differ over the
distributional impacts of regional and site-
specific implementation decisions. Fundamentally,
these are political disputes which have technical
elements. Yet the judiciary has emerged as the
critical implemention institution and has
displaced the executive through the development of
substantive judicial review. Although this
institutional change has not been met with
equanimity by all members of the federal bench, it
has fundamentally altered environmental policy

implementation and retarded the search for consensus among competing groups by maintaining adversarial relationships.

As legal precedents becomes rarer and the scope of judicial review is narrowed by the Supreme Court (e.g., Vermont Yankee v. NRDC, 1978), the need for alternative processes to develop a consensus for local and regional disputes over resource allocation will increase. Experiments such as those described here have been initiated to find such alternatives to judicial decisionmaking which involve the use of mediators to facilitate consensus among competing interest groups and government agencies. While the track record of this experimental field is short and the road is rocky, these experiments suggest that a limited but significant alternative to litigation is feasible. Such consensus-building processes may restore administrative authority to environmental agencies which are currently challenged by the courts over their use of administrative discretion.

Most of the case studies were presented at an American Association for the Advancement of Science Symposium on Environmental Mediation, Denver, Colorado, 1977. They illustrate the problems encountered in changing adversarial relationships to negotiating relationships, and indicate the importance of developing face-to-face opportunities for dialogue between disputants and socialization, so that they are able to develop their own settlement, rather than have one imposed by the courts.

To keep the panel of environmental mediators from becoming too euphoric about the prospects for conflict resolution, four discussants were invited to review the case studies and to formulate their assessments of the state-of-the-art of environmental conflict resolution. Their remarks, primarily on the problems of technical information in decision-making, difficulties in selecting negotiation participants, and doubts about the legitimacy of compromise for many environmental disputes, are incorporated into the third chapter.

Finally, the American Association for the Advancement of Science's Committee on Science and Public Policy sponsored this symposium. The contributors to this volume provided draft papers which I have edited, and received extensive editorial assistance from Charles P. Wolf. I assume full responsibility for the analysis of the field of conflict resolution in general, and of the

six case studies published here.   Thus, for
example, in the first three chapters, I have
employed a generic term, <u>environmental mediation</u>,
to encompass a variety of conflict resolution
techniques defined in Chapter 3.   The intention of
such liberties is to facilitate an overview of the
field.

L.M.L.

About the Contributors

Peter B. Clark is a professional environ-
mental mediator located in Boston. He was formerly
Executive Director of the Center for Energy Policy,
Inc., and spent several years in Latin America and
Africa as a research economist for the World Bank.
He received his Ph.D. in Economics from the
Massachusetts Institute of Technology.

Gerald W. Cormick and Leota K. Patton are
Director and Assistant Director, respectively, of
the Office of Environmental Mediation, Institute
of Environmental Studies, University of
Washington, Seattle. Together with Jane McCarthy,
Cormick pioneered in the successful mediation of
the Snoqualmie flood control dam dispute in 1974.
His background is in labor mediation and sociology
(he holds a Ph.D. from the University of Michigan).
Before his current environmental mediation work,
he mediated prison, school, racial, and hospital
conflicts around the United States. Ms. Patton
holds a degree in Forestry from Yale, and has
worked in several developing nations prior to her
mediation activities.

Laura M. Lake is Adjunct Assistant Professor
of Political Science at the University of
California, Los Angeles, The conflict avoidance
project described in Chapter 7 was conducted in
collaboration with colleagues from the Environmental Science and Engineering Program at UCLA;
Chapter 9's analysis of the West Side Highway was
written while she was an Assistant Program Officer,
Office of Resources and the Environment, The Ford
Foundation, New York City. She received her Ph.D.
in Political Science from Tufts University.

Donald B. Straus is President of the Research
Institute of the American Arbitration Association,
and former President of the American Arbitration

Association. He thus brings to environmental conflict resolution a lifetime of experience in the field of arbitration and mediation.

Paul Wehr is an Associate Professor of Sociology, University of Colorado, Boulder, and directs an environmental conciliation project for the Rocky Mountain Region. His special interest in environmental conciliation is based on years of peace research. He holds a Ph.D. in Sociology.

DISCUSSANTS

The following persons served as symposium discussants:

David Fradin, Vice President, Environmental Balance Association of Minnesota;

Helen Ingram, Associate Professor, University of Arizona and Resources for the Future, Washington, D.C.

William C. Pendleton, Program Officer, The Ford Foundation, New York City; and

Christopher Wright, Staff Member, Carnegie Institution, Washington, D. C.

1
Environmental Conflict and Decisionmaking

Laura M. Lake

INTRODUCTION

This book examines the problems posed for
public decisionmakers and interest groups as they
grapple with regional and site-specific disputes
over dams, highways, shopping centers, wilderness
designations and other "environmental" conflicts.
This genre of dispute is associated with preemptive
federal legislation passed during the early 1970s
such as the National Environmental Policy Act of
1969 (NEPA), the Clean Air Act Amendments of 1970,
and the Clean Waters Act Amendments of 1972. These
statutes articulated national goals, set ambitious
deadlines for compliance with national standards,
and produced profound impacts on environmental
policy implementation decisions. In particular,
there were four major impacts:

1. Changes in intergovernmental relations;
2. Innovations in the participatory process;
3. Developments in the scope of judicial
   review (resulting in changes in
   institutional authority); and
4. The emergence of new processes for
   bargaining to resolve environmental
   disputes.

This fourth impact, the development of
environmental conflict resolution processes, is
the focus of the six case studies presented in this
book. In order to place these experiments in
environmental mediation in perspective, however,
all four impacts are analyzed in this book.
By and large, the federal statutes of the
early 1970s were symbolic gestures toward very
concrete environmental problems.(1) The gap

1

between the rhetoric of the laws and the reality of implementation thus presents a major challenge to public administrators.(2) They must weigh the value of amenities and public health against social, economic and political values. In addition to the skill and wisdom required for these social choices, administrators in all federal agencies must comply with the procedural guidelines for public participation and preparation of environmental impact reports to comply with NEPA. Thus agency missions may be blocked, diverted or stalked by environmental procedures. For agencies which perceive themselves to be only tangentially involved with the natural environment (Department of Defense, Federal Highway Administration, etc.), this is an unwelcome change. In particular, the requirement for public comment included in NEPA is often obtained through vituperative public hearings. No agency seeks public criticism willingly.(3)

From past experience, one would expect administrators to respond to these new procedural demands by making incremental adjustments to their established routines. Many agencies did initially attempt to comply with NEPA and related environmental statutes through incremental, token formal compliance and held hearings after commitments had been made, or buried readers in huge impact reports prepared in technical language to stave off lay readers.(4) Thus environmental protection and industrial interest groups concerned about federal regulations have successfully utilized the courts to block projects due to procedural errors--sloppy administration.

Since token, incremental compliance resulted in litigation, agencies learned to be procedurally careful. Environmental litigation then focused on the substantive aspects of environmental law enforcement: are projects necessary? Was the assessment conducted by qualified personnel, etc. However, I believe that substantive judicial review on the merits of an agency decision threatens the traditional authority of administrators.(5) It indicates erosion of judicial restraint. Chapter 2 reviews the development of substantive judicial review and its institutional implications.

It will be shown in Chapter 2 that prospects for expanded substantive judicial review are limited. As precedents become rarer, environmental disputes destined for the courts for

substantive cause will require alternative dispute
resolution processes. These conflict resolution
processes are generally termed <u>environmental
mediation</u>, and are illustrated through six case
studies involving neutral third parties who
facilitate negotiated compromises between feuding
interest groups. Since environmental mediation
may be an important alternative to litigation, it
is important to carefully characterize the role of
the courts as well as the nature of environmental
disputes before analyzing the six case studies of
environmental mediation published in this book.

Throughout this book my objective is to
examine the decisionmaking process itself and not
to evaluate the outcomes of this process, i.e.,
changes in environmental quality. It is assumed
that the implementation process profoundly shapes
final outcomes.(6) This volume, however, is
limited to examining how policy implementation at
the local and regional level affects
intergovernmental relations, institutional
authority and local interest group behavior.

Environmental mediation involves local and
national environmental interest groups which
attempt to influence the allocation of natural
resources, energy policy, pollution abatement and
the preservation of a healthy and aesthetically
pleasing environment. These distributional
decisions involve political as well as legal
considerations and thus it is necessary to analyze
the administrative/political system at the local,
state and federal levels in order to understand the
impacts of the implementation process on existing
institutions. Through such analysis one can better
understand the functioning of contemporary
federalism.

The implementation of environmental policy
centers on bureaucratic politics of both public and
private decisionmakers. This became apparent when
Section 102 of the National Environmental Policy
Act of 1969 (NEPA) required that environmental
impact statements be filed for projects receiving
federal subsidies which had significant impacts on
the natural environment. This law was designed to
protect the natural environment from governmental
actions which would harm it, such as massive public
works projects. Thus unlike earlier regulatory
legislation, this act represents an unusual curb on
government by the government, rather than
regulation of corporate interests.(7)

3

Environmental impact reports exposed for the first time both public and private priority--setting processes. Subsequent NEPA and related environmental litigation highlighted the differences between administrative and legal processes, since the decision to litigate results in the transfer of the decisionmaking process from the operating agency to the Justice Department or to state attorneys general who then assume the authority to determine procedure and to formulate the terms of settlements.(8)

Analytical Framework

For students of bureaucratic politics and interest group behavior, the existence of two competing decisionmaking loci within governmental agencies, often lawyers and engineers, present a useful vantage point from which to analyze the differences in institutional decisionmaking. Depending upon which political strategy is selected by interest groups (lobbying, testifying, letter-writing, litigating, etc.), either general counsel or administrators will shape the questions to be resolved by either judges or executives. Since litigation has become a common strategy of public interest groups, it is important to determine why interest groups decide to litigate, and ascertain what, if any, the differences are between administrative and judicial decision-making. What are the consequences of litigation for interest groups and for federal and state courts, executives and legislatures? Finally, what are the consequences of environmental mediation for these institutions and for interest groups?

Few policy analysts have considered these questions because the field of environmental policy implementation rapidly evolved into the practice of environmental law, and thus lawyers, intent on the development of precedents and procedural regularity, failed to consider the institutional impacts of expanded judicial roles on the quality of decisions and on the authority on administrators.(9)

Local environmental disputes over projects such as power plants or ski resorts can be viewed as "agenda-setting processes" within the federal system which illustrate "the ways in which groups articulate grievances and transform them into viable issues that require decisionmakers to

4

provide some sort of ameliorative response."(10)
The six case studies published here provide
examples of this process, particularly
institutional and intergovernmental relations.

Use of the term agenda-setting here,
describes the process of decisionmaking which
involves groups, and not the ideologies of
disputants. For unlike traditional interest group
bargaining models of pluralism,(11) environmental
disputes frequently involve the courts to channel
conflict into an adversarial process which does not
require consensus or negotiation. However,
environmental advocates do assume that public
participation in governmental decisions will alter
final decisions, and thus are in agreement with the
faith in representation held by pluralists; i.e.,
they equate access with power.(12) They also
assume that decisionmaking is rational. These
beliefs tend to obscure the vote-counting
proclivities of public officials when evaluating
interest group testimony, and ignore the
nonrational aspects of decisionmaking.(13)
Finally, the limited ability of environmentalists,
a minority within society, to represent "the"
public, creates a flaw in the representational role
claimed by many environmentalists.(14)

Until recently, environmental disputants
viewed bargaining and negotiating with abhorrence.
They desired participation, but did not value compromised settlements, the bulwark of pluralism.
Similarly, bureaucrats engaged in environmental
disputes resented public criticism by environmentalists, and resisted the value preferences
articulated in NEPA. These attitudes are changing.
Environmentalists, as evidenced by the experiments
described in this book, are willing to negotiate in
certain instances, and bureaucrats are interested
in seeking more effective ways to involve the
various interests involved with environmental
decisionmaking. The innovations in conflict
resolution studied here are thus timely
developments.

CHARACTERIZING ENVIRONMENTAL DISPUTES

Defining the characteristics of environmental
disputes is an important prerequisite to understanding the challenges of environmental policy
implementation for a fragmented federal
government. Though environmental policy shares

5

many of the problems confronted by other public areas, such as civil rights, consumer rights and welfare rights, it also has unique features which make implementation particularly cumbersome and difficult. Local environmental disputes involve a mix of resident and nonresident interests: local, county, state and federal officials (elected and appointed), technical consultants to public officials and to interest groups, public interest law firms, and local residents. Fundamentally, these disputes are political, i.e., they center on the authoritative allocation of resources(15) and vividly illustrate "who gets what, when and how"(16) regarding major public and private investments and regulatory decisions.

One of the most useful ways of determining what the distributional impacts of environmental decisions may be through case studies of local and regional environmental and energy conflicts such as those presented in this symposium. These cases can be analyzed to determine their intensity, duration, and the extremity of action as well as their impacts on the governmental process.(17) It is particularly helpful to employ "community power structure" analyses(18) to identify the overt and covert influentials in each of these disputes. In this way, one can trace the distributional impacts associated with the projects.

When one does apply this approach to environmental disputes, one often finds that but for the right to sue provided by federal and state statutes, environmental politics would exclude environmental protection groups and local residents from the political bargaining process. Until the early 1970s, pluralism did not work for environmentalists because their electoral power was diffuse and they were unable to litigate their claims.(19) In addition, the traditional bureaucratic response of incrementalism does not always apply to environmental decisionmaking, since the physical damage from a project may be irreversible.(20) Thus unlike a social or economic policy which can be reformulated and renegotiated over time, the implementation of environmental policy at the local level poses particularly difficult problems for bureaucrats. In these dilemmas, the only aspect of bureaucratic incrementalism and muddling through which still works for a while, at least, is delay. Even delay can create problems if it permits damage to the environment, e.g., continued pollution, timber cutting of virgin forests, or development in wilderness. We shall return to the role of delay in environmental disputes shortly.

Having said that pluralism did not work for environmental protection groups, I wish to modify this statement: it may begin to work for them now that they have established a political strategy which others may wish to avoid--litigation. But let us continue to examine why pluralism has not worked well for environmentalists within the administrative decisionmaking system by characterizing environmental disputes.

Socio-Economic Characteristics

Although environmental disputes do not often involve large numbers of active participants and the membership of most environmental protection groups is frequently middle class, well-educated persons,(21) the interests they represent are often collective interests concerned with the management of natural resources, pollution control and energy policy. It is important to acknowledge the variety of interests sheltered under the umbrella of the "environmental movement," because these groups range from urban pollution control organizations to sport fisherman and hunters. In addition, local groups opposed to projects often claim to be environmentalists.(22) The environmental movement ought not to be viewed as a monolith of shared objectives and solidarity.

Aside from this quasi-elitist character of environmental interest group membership, environmental conflicts have other characteristics which distinguish them from other social disputes. They often center on collective interests and common goods, but the notions of common goods and their sound management are not as firmly rooted in our political, legal and economic systems as are those of private property rights and individual due process.(23) Thus environmental protection groups face the problem of trying to defend the interests of those who do not assign the same priority to these issues or acknowledge the legitimacy of regulating common goods.

Delay

The longevity of environmental disputes is great and taxes the stamina and resources of project advocates and opponents alike. For example

7

the Snoqualmie Dam dispute (Chapter 4) began in 1959 and was resolved in 1974. This slow pace of environmental policy implementation is due in part to the multiple decisionmakers and publics who are (potential or actual) parties to a dispute. It is also related to the strategy of delay employed by industries seeking to delay enforcement of laws through voluntary compliance, or to delay the enforcement of pollution abatement laws through litigation,(24) and to environmentalists seeking to block the construction of projects. The organizational costs of delay are greatest for volunteer, ad hoc local organizations, which run the risk of collapsing long before a final decision is reached.

The use of delay strategies by environmentalists has placed them in a negative role vis-à-vis industry and government. They are usually consulted only after a decision has been reached and placed in the awkward position of saying "no" to most proposals. This negative stance is actually the opening round for determining how much flexibility there is for modifying the project. But environmentalists often feel that unless they take an absolute stand against a project and invoke threats of litigation, their positive suggestions will be ignored or they will be coopted by agencies.(25) They also typically lack the resources to develop constructive alternatives for project modifications.

Legitimacy of Environmental Values

The legitimacy of environmental values and of environmental laws also influence the weight assigned by public officials to environmental interest group demands. Early research in the field of civil rights implementation indicates that it is difficult for public officials to bow to small numbers of activists representing values not recognized as legitimate by the local community.(26) In environmental disputes, it is not usually that environmental values are not considered legitimate; rather, they are subordinate to other concerns such as revenue for local government, jobs for residents, and profits for local businesses. In addition, the legitimacy of some environmental demands is suspect when environmentalists are not members of the

8

community, just as many of the early civil rights
workers were Northerners who were considered to be
outside agitators.(27)

Environmental values also suffer reversals in
public opinion. For example, in 1976 the voters of
California rejected a nuclear power plant
moratorium referendum, but in March 1978, the
voters of Kern County, California, rejected by a
two-to-one margin a proposal to site a large
nuclear power plant to serve Los Angeles, over a
hundred miles away.(28) The result of continued
negative votes will be to leave the state in the
awkward position of having to determine if nuclear
power plants will be accepted anywhere, and perhaps
forcing communities to accept power plants, both
conventional and nuclear. One key to this dilemma
is identified in Chapter 7: most communities in
California appear to be willing to carry their
share of power plant impacts if demand is
demonstrated for local consumption, but they do not
want to become pollution sinks for other
communities. Nevertheless, there is the prospect
of increased tension between local governments and
the state government over the siting of such public
facilities.

Technical Uncertainties

There are technical aspects of environmental
disputes which often intimidate generalist politicians so that they defer essentially political
decisions to technically trained bureaucrats who
do not view their jobs as social impact analysts,
but rather, prefer to treat the design and
implementation of a project as a purely technical
exercise. This bureaucratic response is not unique
to natural resource and environmental quality
administration, for as Peter Rossi has noted,
education and public health administrators have
also masked their decisions in technical
terms.(29) As a result of the technical elements
in environmental disputes, scientific and
technical expertise become political resources
necessary to interact with project proponents
(both public and private); however, this expertise
is not evenly distributed within society or between
interest groups.(30)

Issues in Dispute: The Primary
of Substantive Concerns

9

Environmental disputes are often substantive conflicts over the merits of a project rather than over procedural issues (due process). Examination of the case studies in this book provide some evidence of the primacy of substantive issues in environmental disputes. Procedural issues do develop, but as strategies to obtain access to the courts, rather than as ends in their own right. I believe that when disputes involve substantive rather than due process issues, they ought to be decided by administrators or legislators. This point will be developed in Chapter 2.

Turning to the case studies, with one exception, Donald Straus' case study of coastal zone planning (Chapter 6), all of the case studies center primarily on substantive issues. Straus' study also focuses on substantive matters, but simultaneously fulfills federal requirements for public participation, a due process objective. The substantive issues which surface in these cases include:

1. The desire to obtain federal subsidies for local communities.
2. Concerns about urban sprawl (air quality, aesthetics, etc.).
3. Desires for recreational and wilderness opportunities.
4. Fears of health problems from automobile and power plant pollution.
5. Concern for reliable energy supplies and for economic stability.
6. Desire for equity between communities impacted by projects which benefit other communities (power plants, highways, etc.).

We conclude that the case studies involve substantive interest group objectives and that administrative procedures are the most appropriate method of resolving such disputes. These case studies illustrate how substantive issues can prompt groups to seek judicial relief if they find legal cause (either procedural or factual errors) if administrators reject their demands.

Intergovernmental Relations

Intergovernmental relations were abruptly altered by federal preemption in the environmental policy field in 1969 with the passage of NEPA and the Clean Air Act Amendments of 1970.(31) Subsequently, national standards and regulations were established for water quality, noise, pesticides, toxic substances and other environmental hazards. The six case studies in these proceedings will be analyzed to determine how intergovernmental relations were altered by the policy implementation process, particularly, whether: (1) state sovereignty decreased (i.e., if the governors' authority to veto projects and regulatory decisions was reduced); (2) new relationships developed between local and federal governments; and (3) new types of intergovernmental conflict emerged.

Intergovernmental conflict has surfaced between the states and the federal government through a series of constitutional law cases and through regulatory decisions.(32) Federal-state conflict usually develops over the state's need for revenue to administer federally-mandated programs and to construct facilities required by federal laws, such as sewage treatment plants. In addition, local communities fear loss of jobs and revenue to other states which may not be as aggressive in enforcing federal laws. The tensions generated by air and water quality control are especially great because these programs require state and local enforcement of federal laws. The federal response to this dilemma has been to involve the states in the development of their own implementation plans, and to provide federal grants for regional planning and construction of facilities.(33)

Other aspects of federal-state conflict are illustrated by the six case studies, which indicate that planning and evaluation of site-specific projects occurs at the local level in consultation with federal authorities, in effect, relegating the states to a grant disbursement role for the federal government. For example, residents of Seattle were concerned about a large highway creating air pollution levels which would violate federal air quality standards (Chapter 4); and power plant siting and operation in California and New England had to comply with federal standards (Chapters 7 and 8). Similarly, the Forest Service was directly involved in the decisionmaking process of the Town of Eagle, Colorado (Chapter 5); and highway planning in New York City involved consultations between local interest groups and senior federal officials regarding the alternative

11

uses of federal grants (Chapter 9). Close consultation between local and federal agencies is the pattern of project review which emerges from these cases.

The case studies provide further insight into intergovernmental relations by illustrating the key role played by country governments in land-use planning. Snohomish and King Counties (Washington) were involved in developing easements and land purchases to guarantee the dam dispute settlement (Chapter 4); and King County officials were also concerned in the Interstate 90 dispute to balance the interests of urban dwellers with suburban commuters (Chapter 4). Eagle County, Colorado, played a pivotal role in regard to the ski resort proposal (Chapter 5), and in California, counties are closely involved in zoning for major facilities such as power plants (Chapter 7).

Intergovernmental conflict also involves local regional conflicts, and intra-county disputes such as highway route selection (Chapter 4 and 9); intercounty disputes over the costs and benefits of power plant siting (Chapter 7); and multistate regional conflict regarding unfavorable energy rates for New England vis-à-vis the rest of the nation (Chapter 8).

To summarize this analysis of recent trends in intergovernmental relations:

1. State sovereignty has decreased significantly, as measured by gubernatorial authority to veto energy and environmental projects proposed by state and local governments, or required by the federal government.
2. County and local governments follow federal guidelines and have established direct contacts with regional federally-mandated planning organizations and with federal regional offices to review proposals.
3. County governments maintain important decisionmaking roles in environmental policy implementation.
4. Environmental policy implementation has stimulated intergovernmental conflict: central-city-versus-suburb; county-versus-county; and regional-versus-national.

State Sovereignty

Until the late 1960s, states retained substantial authority over natural resources and pollution control policy based on their constitutional policy powers to protect the health and general welfare of their citizens.(34) Preemption of this state authority by the federal government has not only negated the states' final authority over such regulatory matters, as air and water quality, nuclear power and energy policy; it has also created new political institutions such as the Office of Management and Budget "A-95" regional clearinghouses which coordinate federal grant programs and develop regional land-use plans (e.g., under PL 92-500, Section 208).(35) These clearinghouses facilitate new lines of communication and review procedures involving local governments and federal regional offices.

At the same time that the federal government was encroaching upon state sovereignty, it was also becoming sensitive to local communities' concerns about federal projects and of the possibility that municipalities and local interest groups might use federal environmental laws to block federal projects. This phenomenon is illustrated in Chapter 5, in which the U.S. Forest Service decided not to approve a request to develop a ski resort until it learned the wishes of the local community.

The veto authority of state governors is a useful indicator of state sovereignty. From Chapters 4 and 9 one learns that projects involving federal subsidies (highways and dams) can still be vetoed by governors, but the other cast studies show dwindling gubernatorial veto authority:

-- Chapter 5 shows an ambiguous role for the governor of Colorado: the major veto power is the county. The governor can, however, withhold services which might be necessary for the project such as road improvements and water diversion projects, and federal agencies might veto the project as a political courtesy.

-- Chapter 6 involves a federally mandated coastal zone planning program involving public participation in New Jersey. While the substance of the plan is still under the governor's control, the planning process must be completed and must involve the public.

13

-- According to Chapter 7, the Governor of California can veto power plants, but all power plant decisions must also conform with federal air and water quality standards and must be reviewed by federally-mandated regional planning organizations.
-- In Chapter 8, the intergovernmental relations described involved New England governors who faced a federal order to change power plant fuels from oil to coal and to simultaneously comply with federal air quality standards.

This review of case studies thus indicates substantial changes in state sovereignty. However, the relationship between states and the federal government is in a state of flux. While environmental statutes of the early 1970s preempted considerable state authority, recent court rulings have favored state authority.(36)

LITIGATION AND ALTERNATIVE POLITICAL STRATEGIES

Environmental laws have occasionally been invoked for reasons not related to environmental damage, such as fear of low income housing, fear of lowered property values,(37) fear of lost revenue for local government, etc., because these nonenvironmental issues do not otherwise have legal standing as cause for litigation.(38) The decision to litigate, however, means forfeiting the focus of attention on such substantive concerns, and turning the deliberations into technical contests of finding and disclaiming, procedural errors. Litigation this converts value conflicts into procedural disputes. Nevertheless, litigation offers positive attributes and these, in combination with the failures of administrative procedures, contribute to the selection of litigation as a political strategy.

The attributes of litigation include:(39) speed of relief, visibility,(40) legitimacy, political efficacy, opportunity for cross-examination, technical factfinding, avoidance of frivolous cases, settlements (pretrial),(41) impartiality, creation of precedents, and appeals procedures. These advantages make litigation an attractive political process when administrative remedies fail, since courts require exhaustion of remedies before accepting cases. Thus litigation signifies a breakdown in the administrative-political process and signals political desperation,(42) for those wealthy enough to obtain counsel. The act of suing may itself secure a settlement out of court, as discussed in Chapter 2.

Since litigation is a political strategy of desperation, let us examine the major causes for this course of action.

1. Federal and state environmental statutes grant access for judicial review only after a decision has been reached by agencies; the public's rights are limited to advisory comments on the adequacy of the document reviewing the project plan, and not on the justification of the project. Only recently has there been a suggestion in some states that adequate environmental impact reviews must also include information on the socioeconomic impacts of projects, and not just on the project's damage to local flora and fauna.(43) This is particularly important because many environmentally damaging projects are justified on the basis of unsubstantiated claims of employment and local prosperity. There is thus a need to clarify what types of jobs are likely to occur if a project is approved, and if the local labor pool will be eligible for recruitment.

2. Public participation has been achieved primarily through public hearings. These hearings are not the basis for decisionmaking, however. Rather, project plans are placed on the docket as a fait accompli by agency managers who challenge the technical competence of laymen to find fault with their documents. These agencies have missions to defend are not neutral hearing officers.(44) Yet as noted earlier, the major concerns of the environmentalists and local residents may basically concern whether there should be a project at all, not alternative ways in which it might be carried out.

3. Most local governments are not staffed adequately to perform the type of reviews described in the first point above, and this has created a complaint that there are no personnel available to conduct environmental impact sutides which include socioeconomic analyses, and that it would be too costly to hire such persons. This problem results

in demands from municipalities to the states that they clarify exactly what the state will accept as adequate environmental impact studies.(45)

4. Environmental disputes can be precipitated by interagency conflict. For example, the Peripheral Canal project in California involves a conflict between California's Department of Water Resources and the Federal Bureau of Reclamation regarding water quality standards for the Sacramento Delta region. The state wants to maintain the ecosystem of the Delta while the Bureau wants to assure farmers of water for irrigation.(46) Thus analysis of interagency and intergovernmental conflict is crucial for understanding natural resources and pollution control policy implementation.

5. The time frame of elected officials may be shorter than the duration of many environmental disputes, since these can continue for twenty years or more. It is therefore likely that elected officials will delay taking positions and hope that they will no longer be in office when the crunch comes to decide, or when a project they supported produces problems.

6. Local officials may face implementation dilemmas. For example, implementating civil rights laws and court orders during the 1960s meant in the South that the officials had to ". . . take considerable risk...(and) be willing to alienate the 'rednecks,' to run the danger of social or even physical attack."(47) Environmental policy implementation may on occasion require similar political courage.

7. There have been few opportunities for sharing and delegating the authority for project review with the public. The merits of such a delegation are debatable, since, as noted on the previous point, there are some laws which are not popular to enforce, but need to be implemented. Our constitution does not provide for federal referenda, but at state and local levels, referenda and initiatives may be utilized to delegate decisionmaking back to the electorate. For example, in Kern County, California, a county-wide referendum defeated a plan of a nuclear power plant to serve the City of Los Angeles.(48) The petition initiative has been used in several states to determine popular views toward nuclear power; e.g., in California and Arizona the voters supported nuclear power during 1976 initiatives.

16

The six case studies included in this book represent novel experiments to involve the public in decisionmaking so that its quality is improved. The ultimate responsibility for these decisions will rest with elected officials, however. Figure 1-1 summarizes the primary strategies available to environmental protection interest groups and to citizens to influence environmental policy decisions.

Limited Lobbying

Foremost among the reasons for environmental protection groups utility of litigation is that their resources to lobby the executive and legislature are quite limited, as noted in Figure 1-1. The limits to lobbying are rooted in attitudinal and in financial dilemmas: many environmental groups feel that political decisionmaking is corrupt, that agencies are captives of vested interests, and thus that lobbying is futile.(49) In addition to limited financial resources, public interest environmental organizations have been greatly constrained from lobbying by the Internal Revenue Service Act of 1969, which prohibited the expenditure of "substantial" amounts of money by tax-exempt organizations for the purpose of lobbying. In addition, this law made it illegal for tax-exempt foundations to award grants to organizations which expended substantial funds lobbying. This restriction was lifted in 1976 when the IRS Act was amended to permit more extensive lobbying.(51) Lobbying is also limited by structural factors, particularly fragmentation of the decisionmaking system. Although fragmentation provides multiple access points and generates additional information for decisionmaking,(52) the transaction costs of utilizing multiple access points are high for small, volunteer, ad hoc organizations.(53) The fragmentation of decisionmaking also creates many veto powers, but restricts the ability of any one person to guarantee that a project can be approved. This is a double-edged sword: in cases of preserving wilderness or enforcing pollution abatement laws, fragmentation induces unacceptable delays. When environmentalists seek to block construction so that costs increase to the point where a project is jeopardized, however, fragmentation is an asset.

Figure 1-1. Alternative Strategies for Environmental Interest Groups to Influence Decision-Making

INSTITUTION	ACCESS MODE	POSSIBLE OUTCOMES AND LIMITATIONS
Executive	Hearings	Play-off interagency and intergovernmental conflict, introduce technical information and evidence of broad support for group's position. Limitations: volunteers distrust administrators and have limited resources to testify at a large number of hearings which we are advisory and are not the basis for decision-making.
	Lobbying	Attempt to persuade elected officials to reject agency recommendations. Utilize media, petitions, form coalitions, etc. Also lobby staff during project design and planning. Limitations: It is unlikely that an official will reject staff recommendations; volunteer lobbyists are not as skillful as professional, full-time lobbyists, and frequently environmentalists neglect administrative lobbying.50
	(Third Party Intervention)	Negotiate voluntary compromise through (third party intervention) which must be implemented by an elected official. Limitations: environmental mediators are not plentiful, the process is new and therefore not always considered, and independent sources of funding (neutral intervenors) are scarce. In addition, compromise may not be appropriate for disputes involving due process.
Legislative	Lobbying	Lobby to clarify policy intentions of legislature (state or federal) and to encourage legislative oversight of implementing agencies. Limitations: there is danger that the legislature may decide to rescind earlier statutes protecting the environment (e.g., Trans Alaska Pipeline). In addition, there are still limitations on the amount of money which tax exempt organizations may use for lobbying and few groups can afford professional lobbyists.
Judicial	Seek Injunction File Amicus Curiae Briefs, Develop Litigating Strategy	Group must have financial and legal resources. Limitations: legal processes are slow, costly and difficult for ad hoc groups to sustain. Suits may result in dismissal, pre-trial settlement, or go to trial and result in an injunction; remand to the agency or remand to the legislature. Amicus curiae briefs are a form of judicial lobbying but require a permanent litigating organization, as does the development of a litigating strategy.

18

But delay costs accrue to environmentalists as well in their pursuit of staying power.

It is also important to remember that access to many decisionmakers does not automatically provide influence, since elected officials must also consider how legitimate the group's concerns are perceived by the community and how many votes the membership can mobilize. A small group is not a significant threat unless their concerns are considered to be legitimate by the rest of the community.(54) Consequently,(55)

> . . . successful litigation is seen as providing legitimacy equal to and independent of any moral pressure that extrajudicial activities might engender. Consequently, such legitimacy is achieved even when the plaintiff's moral position is supported by only a small part of the community.

However, the decision to litigate can also raise interest groups' expectations and may encourage them to refuse to negotiate with administrators, only to find later that they either lost the case or that the case is remanded back to the agency for further action.

In addition to the concerns of legitimacy and electoral strength, political executives and their staffs must also consider the economic losses incurred if a project is rejected (loss of federal or state subsidies, new revenue, jobs, etc.), or if a pollution control law is enforced (polluter threatens to move, taking jobs and revenue with it). Finally, environmental issues may have a low priority for local officials--there may be crises or other higher priority issues to attend to--or they may not personally find the problem of interest. Local officials may also find that their staffs are not properly trained to evaluate projects and to advise them on the problem, and therefore avoid taking positions which challenge their weakness.

Looking at Figure 1-1 again, it seems obvious why environmental protection groups utilize a one-stop decisionmaking process for a highly fragmented political system: they believe, as Joseph Sax asserts, that litigation changes "the balance of power (through) the development of a scheme of enforceable legal rights, backed by judicial power."(56) Judicial power is a weak form of power for statutory, nonconstitutional issues,

however, since at any time legislatures may bow to
current public demands and rescind judicial review
of statutes. For example, Congress has amended the
Endangered Species Act and rescinded judicial
review for the Trans Alaska Pipeline.

More realistic, I believe, is Stuart
Sheingold's observation that "although the legal
approach may not promise a convenient solution, it
does specify the issues simply and directly, thus
promising maximum understanding for minimum
expenditure of intellectual energy"(57) There are
risks and problems associated with litigation
which must be weighed by environmentalists before
selecting the court as the final decisionmaking
arena, however.

Problems of Litigation

Some of the limitations of litigation are
noted in Figure 1-1, particularly the problems of
regarding financial ability to sue, and the slow
pace of decisionmaking if the court decides to
grant a temporary injunction. More important, is
the failure of many lawsuits to address the merits
of the project which are of concern to local
residents and environmentalists and industry. For
with the selection of litigation as a strategy,
individuals with substantive expertise are
displaced by attorneys who seek to build legal
cases on procedural error. Since, as we shall show
shortly, many environmental cases concern
substantive problems such as damaging a wilderness
area or fears of increased air pollution, the
procedural (due process) focus of lawsuits (which
is the appropriate scope for judicial review)
neglects the substantive political issues in
dispute:(58)

> There is a general obstacle to judicial
> innovation in certain kinds of policy
> arenas--particularly those involving the
> allocation of economic resources. These
> matters are most appropriately dealt with by
> marginal utility calculations, which focus on
> the consequences of individual decisions. In
> contrast, judges tend to be tied to the
> procedural absolutes which are bound up in a
> regime of rules with its attendant emphasis on
> vindicating rights and enforcing obligations
> irrespective of the consequences. (Original
> emphasis.)

In addition to the problems of deciding a case regardless of the consequences, there are problems associated with proving factual errors and causal relationships for projected damage:(59)

> Frequently, standards and regulations are directed not at alleviating existing hazards, but at minimizing the potential risks of secondary and tertiary adverse environmental impacts, and must necessarily be based on inferences drawn from incomplete scientific data . . . .
>
> It is often difficult to establish cause-in-fact existing concepts of cause are temporal limitations and limitations of range of permissible inferences. For example, injunctive relief cannot be obtained without a demonstration of imminent irreparable injury; this reqauires a showing that the anticipated harm is immediate and practically certain to occur . . . .
>
> A sanction imposed in the absence of a causal relationship between the prohibited activity and posited adverse consequences would be arbitrary and hence unconstitutional.

The expertise required to inquire into causality itself can become a problem, since experts in the adversary system can be used as "hired guns" to make the most persuasive case, rather than to ascertain the truth of their allegations.(60) Thus arguments over alleged factual errors can obscure the political value conflicts as much as emphasis on procedural errors.

Factual disputes can be the very essence of substantive concerns in environmental conflicts, however. For example, the Reserve Mining (1976) case hinged on probablistic risk assessments that anthibloe fibers from taconite tailings posed a health hazard, although epidemiological data to substantiate this claim were unavailable.(61)

In the process of litigation other more subtle changes occur: environmental interest group leaders are displaced as the spokesmen for their interest groups and attorneys from national public interest law firms become the group's de facto spokesmen, articulating the local group's legal demands. These lawyers may not be the most effective representatives for their

21

interests.(62) Moreover, the role of the leader as representative, articular of demands and maintainer of group cohesion may be diminished by this new spokesman. As a result of dependence upon lawyers, to represent the interests of local organizations during negotiations, the leaders of these groups are increasingly unaccustomed to directly participating in face-to-face negotiations, or in formulating concessions and demands.(63) While local leaders are permitted to testify at public hearings, they are rarely offered the opportunity to discuss their concerns with opponents. Such face-to-face discussions socialize disputants and enable a common basis for negotiation to be developed. Thus even if an interest group might want to compromise with an agency or an industry, it is not accustomed to directly negotiating with them and does not trust or respect the individuals involved on a personal basis.

In spite of these defects in litigation as a political strategy, public interest lawyers have been successful in developing judicial review to serve environmental interest groups. Chapter 2 analyzes these developments.

INCREASED ACCESS TO THE COURTS AND PARTICIPATORY INNOVATIONS

Access to decisionmakers does not guarantee influence and can instead raise expectations beyond the actual ability or willingness of government officials to meet demands.(64) In fact, it has been suggested that "the more government operates by the spreading of access, the more public order seems to suffer."(65) While public order remains intact, the requirements for public involvement in environmental decision-making have indeed changed the bargaining process:(66)

The zone of viable negotiation, which can be controlled exclusively by the professionals as long as conflict can be narrowly contained, diminishes substantially when the bargaining area is forced to absorb a high influx of amateur advocates. When the nonprofessional enters into a conflict situation, he introduces many of the elements that the professional is committed to ignore . . . .

22

As a consequence, system instability dramatically increases while the prospects of a compromise solution achieved by professionals within a collegial atmosphere visibly evaporates.

It is the professionals' narrowness which often prompts environmentalists to enter the policy implementation process as adversaries. Unfortunately, the adversary process, unlike the collegial system, seeks to prove the other side wrong, rather than to generate a consensus for a feasible solution,(67) and in the course of pursuing litigation objectives, the roles of environmental interest group leaders are changed.

This section will determine if environmental litigation increased in frequency after NEPA's passage in 1969, and if interest groups developed innovations in the participatory process to more effectively utilize environmental litigation as a political strategy.

Innovations in the Participatory Process

Associated with the increase in environmental lawsuits are several innovations in the participatory process which enable environmental interest groups to more effectively utilize judicial access. This section reviews the participatory innovations initiated by environmentalists and administrators since 1970 in response to increased demands for public involvement in environmental decisionmaking.

The establishment of public interest law firms(68) such as the Natural Resources Defense Council, the Environmental Defense Fund and the Sierra Club Legal Defense Fund, provided a permanent litigating ability for environmental groups in the United States. These firms also provide continuity between cases, and develop a litigation strategy. Public interest law firms are tax-exempt organizations which are supported by membership dues, court-awarded fees, and grants from private foundations. These firms develop their litigating strategies by selecting cases which are likely to set precedent; with limited resources they cannot provide environmental "legal aid" (across the board).

In order to increase their effectiveness, environmental law firms practice "judicial lobbying" by filing amicus curiae briefs and by

23

coordinating their cases with those of other
environmental law firms. The use of amicus curiae
briefs to lobby the courts was first utilized in
the civil rights litigation of the 1950s(69) and
has been quite useful to the environmental firms as
a tactic to conserve their limited resources while
showing support for the issues involved in
particular cases.

Through litigation, environmentalists were
able to extend the scope of environmental protection statutes to private actions in several states,
so that the influence of environmental protection
groups has extended beyond a review of governmental
decisionmaking to a close scrutiny of private
developers' plans. In several states,
environmental statutes explicitly require that
developers provide environmental review statements
for their projects.(70) It has been this expansion
of judicial review into private projects which has
caused industry and developers to oppose environmental impact review processes which permit
environmentalists to challenge non-publicly
financed projects such as the $500 million Dow
Chemical plant proposed for Northern
California.(71)

Another innovation in litigation was the
development of class action suits which permitted a
few individuals to represent the interests of a
large class of individuals. Furthermore, these
suits did not always require that the plaintiffs
have immediate personal interests in the
complaint.(72)

In order to handle the factual disputes in
environmental decisionmaking the courts developed
their own methods for obtaining expert advice.
Thus one of the innovations which is increasingly
used in environmental litigation is the appointment of court masters and referees to report to the
judge, rather than the traditional practice of
having the adversaries provide technical experts.
For example, in the Reserve Mining case, the court
appointed a master to make a recommendation on the
epidemiological problems.(73) Litigation has also
involved environmental mediators, as in the
Interstate 90 dispute when the case was remanded
back to the lead agency with instructions to
formulate a plan which would address the concerns
of the affected communities (see Chapter 4).

In response to these changes in litigation,
administrative efforts have been made to develop
constructive roles for environmental intervenors

24

to avert unnecessary litigation. For example, the Council on Environmental Quality has proposed a new set of guidelines for implementing NEPA which include page and time limits for the preparation of environmental impact statements, requirements that mitigating measures be identified early in the planning process and, most importantly, stipulations that the public be involved early in the planning process before a decision is reached.(74) These changes manifest a new concern that the review process not be abused by administrators seeking to inundate the public with massive tomes of environmental impact data because they fear intervenors' lawsuits over procedural shortcomings. "Ultimately, of course, it is not better documents, but better decisions that count," and this is the objective of the Council's new guidelines.(75)

At the state level, California has also revised its CEQA review procedures by placing a one-year time limit on the review process (Assembly Bill 884). The governor has established an Office of Permit Assistance within the Office of Planning and Research to assist in the implementation of this new law, and if necessary, to expedite the permit review process when several agencies are involved.

The establishment of new administrative agencies also indicates a governmental response to environmental policy implementation. After 1970, a panology of environmental and science policy agencies was created, including the Council on Environmental Quality, the Environmental Protection Agency, the National Oceanographic and Atmospheric Administration, and the Department of Energy (formerly the Energy Research and Development Administration). Congress has also gotten into the spirit of science policy analysis by establishing the Office of Technology Assessment which provides independent analyses of policy questions including energy and environmental safety issues. In addition, the recently formed Congressional Budget Office analyzes economic performance so that the legislature is not dependent upon the Office of Management and Budget for analysis. These legislative agencies in effect challenge the executive's hegemony over information and analysis, and add a new wrinkle to the policy implementation process. Thus as the judiciary increasingly considers administrative problems,

25

the legislature has emulated the executive's analytic capacities.(76)

Finally, although requirements for public participation were originally greeted with little enthusiasm by administrators who feared subjecting their agency missions to public criticism,(77) new efforts are underway to modify public participation procedures.(78) In this way, it is expected that administrators will be able to retain their authority over decisionmaking and avoid costly litigation delays. The costs of intervention in administrative proceedings for environmentalists can reach ". . . tens of thousands of dollars . . . (and) prolonged, multiple party proceedings cost even more."(79) Indeed, these costs were factors in the initial preference for litigation for groups with limited financial resources. Thus as environmental interest groups begin to intervene in administrative rulemaking decisions and lobby more frequently, funding their involvement will present a problem. Several federal agencies are starting to subsidize public interest representatives in their rulemaking activities to avoid last-minute challenges.(80)

To summarize this brief review of participatory innovations, it is clear that environmental groups have developed new techniques to utilize judicial access more effectively. More recently, however, these groups are turning to political processes for relief. Simultaneously, agencies are trying to reduce the chances of litigation by testing new participatory techniques, including environmental mediation processes analyzed in Chapter 3.

REFERENCES

1. Helen Ingram, "The Political Rationality of Innovation: The Clean Air Act Amendments of 1970," in Ann F. Friedlaender, ed., Approaches to Controlling Air Pollution (Cambridge: MIT Press, 1978), pp. 12-56.

2. Ibid., p. 13.

3. Burton Weisbrod, et al., Public Interest Law: An Economic and Institutional Analysis (Berkeley: University of California Press, 1978), p. 157.

4. Eugene Bardach and Lucian Pugliaresi, "The Environmental Impact Statement vs. The Real

World," <u>The Public Interest</u>, No. 49 (Fall, 1977), p. 24.

5. Daniel P. Moynihan, "Imperial Government," <u>Commentary</u>, Vol. 65, No. 6, (June 1978), pp. 25-32; Nathan Glazer, "Should Judges Administer Social Services?" <u>The Public Interest</u> (Winter 1978), pp. 64-80.

6. Jeffrey Pressman and Aaron Wildavsky, <u>Implementation</u> (Berkeley: University of California Press, 1973); Martha Derthick, <u>New Towns in Town</u> (Washington, D.C.: The Urban Institute, 1972); Donald Van Meter and Carl Van Horn, "The Implementation of Intergovernmental Policy," in C.O. Jones and R. Thomas, eds., <u>Public Policy Making in a Federal System</u> (Beverly Hills: Sage Publications, 1976), pp. 39-62; Lettie Wenner, <u>One Environment Under Law</u> (Pacific Palisades: Goodyear Publishing Company, 1976), p. 20.

7. David Vogel, "Promoting Pluralism: The Public Interest Movement and the American Reform Tradition," paper delivered at American Political Science Association Meeting, New York, September 1978.

8. Laurin Wollan, "Lawyers in Government," <u>Public Administration Review</u> (March/April 1978), p. 106; Charles Corkin II, "Comment," in Friedlaender, <u>op</u> cit., p. 195.

9. Glazer, <u>op</u> cit., pp. 66-67.

10. Roger Cobb and Charles Elder, <u>Participation in American Politics: The Dynamics of the Agenda-Building Process</u> (Boston: Allyn and Bacon, 1972), p. 13.

11. Charles Lindblom, <u>The Intelligence of Democracy</u> (New York: The Free Press, 1965); David Truman, <u>The Governmental Process</u> (New York: Alfred Knopf, 1965).

12. Vogel, <u>op</u> cit.

13. Ingram, <u>op</u> cit.

14. Vogel, <u>op</u> cit.

15. David Easton, <u>A Systems Analysis of Political Life</u> (New York: John Wiley and Sons, 1965), pp. 86-96.

16. Harold Lasswell, <u>Politics: Who Gets What, When, How</u> (New York: Meridian Books, 1958).

17. Lester Milbrath, <u>Political Participation</u> (Chicago: Rand McNally, 1965), p. 6.

18. Willis Hawley and Frederick Wirt, <u>The Search for Community Power</u> (Englewood Cliffs: Prentice-Hall, 1968).

19. Robert Dahl, <u>Democracy in the United</u>

States (Chicago: Rand McNally, 1971).

20. Walter   Rosenbaum, The Politics of
Environmental Concern (New York: Praeger, 1977),
p. 97.

21. Rosenbaum, op cit., pp. 74-75; Marjorie
Hershey and David Hill, "Is Pollution 'A White
Thing'?   Racial   Differences   in   Preadults'
Attitudes," Public Opinion Quarterly (Winter
1977-1978), pp. 430-458.   A recent survey by
environmental protection by the poor and urban
residents in addition to the expected middle class
support (see "Public Support for Environmental
Protection Remains Strong," Science, Vol. 203,
January 12, 1979, p. 154.

22. Bardach and Pugliaresi, op cit.;
Michelle White, "Self-Interest in the Suburbs: The
Trend Toward No-Growth Zoning," Policy Analysis
(Spring 1978), pp. 185-203.

23. Richard B. Stewart, "Paradoxes of
Liberty, Integrity and Fraternity: The Collective
Nature of Environmental Quality and Judicial
Review of Administrative Action," Environmental
Law, Vol. 11, 1977, p. 470; and J. H. Dales,
Pollution,   Property   and   Prices   (Toronto:
University of Toronto Press, 1968), pp. 61-76.

24. Christian Hill, "Turning the Tables:
Businesses are Finding Environmental Laws Can Be
Useful to Them," Wall Street Journal, June 9, 1978,
pp. 1, 13.

25. Cynthia Enloe, The Politics of Pollution
in a Comparative Perspective (New York: David
McKay, 1975), pp. 188-189; Rosenbaum op cit., p.
73; Bardach and Pugliaresi, op cit., p. 35.

26. Harrell Rodgers and Charles Bullock, Law
and Social Change (New York: McGraw Hill Book
Company, 1972), p. 188; Enloe, op cit.,
pp. 156-168.

27. Rodgers and Bullock, op cit.

28. "Kern County Voters Oppose A-Plant:
Referendum Fails 2 to 1," Los Angeles Times, March
9, 1978, Part II, p. 9.

29. Cobb and Elder, op cit., p. 121.

30. Weisbrod, op cit., pp. 156-157;
Lindblom, Intelligence of Democracy, p. 298.

31. Jeffrey Kessler, "The Clean Air Act
Amendments of 1970: A Threat to Federalism?"
Columbia Law Review, October 1976, pp. 990-1028.

32. Philip Soper, "Constitutional Power of
the Federal Government," in Erica Dolgin and Thomas
Guilbert, eds., Federal Environmental Law (St.
Paul: West Publishing Company, 1974), pp. 78-99;

28

Arthur Murphy and Bruce LaPierre, "Nuclear 'Moratorium' Legislation in the United States and the Supremacy Clause: A Case of Express Preemption," Columbia Law Review, April 1976, pp. 392-456; Robert Thomas, "Intergovernmental Coordination in the Implementation of National Air and Water Pollution Policies," in Jones and Thomas, op cit., p. 129.

33. Thomas, op cit., pp. 130, 131, 146.

34. Reference 31 supra.

35. William Hillhouse II, "The Federal Law of Water Resources Development," in Dolgin and Guilbert, op cit., pp. 897-898:

The Intergovernmental Cooperation Act of 1968 requires that, to the extent practicable, affected federal agencies and departments shall have the opportunity to review 'Federal programs . . .' 42 U.S.C. s. 334 requires review of applications for federal loans or grants to assist in carrying out water development projects by an area-wide agency designated to perform metropolitan or regional planning. The Office of Management and Budget has promulgated regulations contained in Circular A-95, concerning this type of review and coordination.*** Circular A-95 also affects the federal agencies which have direct responsibility for the development of public works . . . .

36. Kessler, op cit.

37. White, op cit.

38. Harold Leventhal, "Environmental Decision-Making and the Role of the Courts," University of Pennsylvania Law Review, January 1974, pp. 509-555.

39. Laura M. Lake, "Environmental Mediation: An Effective Alternative?" Issue Paper prepared for Resolve Conference on Environmental Mediation, Reston, Virginia, January 11-13, 1978, p. 2. (Mimeographed.)

40. Joseph Sax, Defending the Environment (New York: Alfred Knopf, 1971), p. 189.

41. Robert K. Huffman, "The Opportunities for Environmentalists in the Settlement of NEPA Suits," Environmental Law Reporter, 1974, pp. 50001-50020.

42. Stuart Sheingold, The Politics of Rights (New Haven: Yale University Press, 1974), p. 95.

43. Ralph Catalano and Joseph DiMento, "Local Government Responses to State Environmental Impact Assessment Requirements: An Explanation

and Typology," <u>Environmental Law</u>, Vol. VII (1976), pp. 25-50.

44. Weisbrod, <u>op</u> <u>cit</u>., pp. 157-158.

45. Catalano and DiMento, <u>op</u> <u>cit</u>.

46. John Hart, "One System, Many Masters," <u>Cry California</u> (September 1977), pp. 2-23.

47. Rodgers and Bullock, <u>op</u> <u>cit</u>., p. 42.

48. Reference 28, <u>supra</u>.

49. Jeffrey Berry, <u>Lobbying for the People</u> (Princeton: Princeton University Press, 1977).

50. Laura M. Lake, <u>Massachusetts: A Case Study of the Politics of the Environment</u> (unpublished Ph.D. Dissertation, Tufts University, 1972), pp. 151-152, 158, 159.

51. Robert Hyslop and Walter Ebel, "Public Interest Lobbying and the Tax Reform Act of 1976," <u>Environmental Law</u> (Winter 1977), pp. 283-292.

52. Robert Bish and Vincent Ostrom, <u>Understanding Urban Government</u> (Washington, D.C.: American Enterprise Institute, 1973), p. 93.

53. Enloe, <u>op</u> <u>cit</u>.

54. Rodgers and Bullock, <u>op</u> <u>cit</u>.

55. Frank Upham, "Litigation and Moral Consciousness in Japan: An Interpretive Analysis of Four Japanese Pollution Suits," <u>Law and Society Review</u> (Summer 1976), p. 616.

56. Sax, <u>op</u> <u>cit</u>., p. 83.

57. Sheingold, <u>op</u> <u>cit</u>., p. 49.

58. <u>Ibid</u>., p. 111.

59. Marcia Gelpe and Dan Tarlock, "The Uses of Scientific Information in Environmental Decision-Making," <u>Southern California Law Review</u> (1974), pp. 373, 375.

60. Ralph Kasper, <u>et</u> <u>al</u>., <u>Implementing Technology Assessment</u> (Washington, D.C.: George Washington University, 1974), p. 269; Jerome Frank, "The Fight Theory Versus the Truth Theory," in Walter Murphy and C. Herman Pritchett, <u>Courts, Judges and Politics</u> (New York: Random House, 1974), p. 360.

61. James Krier and Richard B. Stewart, <u>Environmental Law and Public Policy</u> (tentative revised edition, 1976), p. IV78. (Mimeographed.)

62. Weisbrod, <u>op</u> <u>cit</u>., p. 156.

63. Tom Alexander, "A Promising Try at Environmental Detente for Coal," <u>Fortune</u>, February 13, 1978, pp. 94-102; and Enloe, <u>op</u> <u>cit</u>., p. 163.

64. William A. Gamson, "Rancorous Conflict in Community Politics," in Hawley and Wirt, <u>op</u> <u>cit</u>, p. 252; Ralph Nader, "Consumerism and Legal

Services: The Merging of Movements," <u>Law and Society Review</u>, Vol. 11, 1976, p. 248.

65. Theodore Lowi, <u>The End of Liberalism</u> (New York: W.W. Norton & Company, 1969), pp. 292, 299.

66. Kasper, <u>op</u> <u>cit</u>., p. 281.

67. Sally K. Fairfax, "A Disaster in the Environmental Movement," <u>Science</u> (February 17, 1978), pp. 743-748.

68. Weisbrod, <u>op</u> <u>cit</u>., entire.

69. Robert Rabin, "Layers for Social Change: Perspectives on Public Interest Law," <u>Stanford University Law Review</u>, Vol. 28, pp. 207-261.

70. Catalano and DiMento, <u>op</u> <u>cit</u>., p. 33: 'The reaction of local government officials (to the <u>Friends of Mammoth</u> decision, 1972) was virtually one of despair, particularly since few local governments had even implemented CEQA (California Environmental Quality Act of 1970) to their own public works projects by the data of the decision.' in Donald Hagman, <u>Urban Planning and Land Development Law</u>.

71. Marvin Braude, "Will We Now Drown in Paper Pollution," <u>Los Angeles Times</u>, March 27, 1978, VI, pp. 1, 3.

72. Dolgin and Guilbert, <u>op</u> <u>cit</u>.

73. Gelpe and Tarlock, <u>op</u> <u>cit</u>.; Krier and Stewart, <u>op</u> <u>cit</u>.

74. Charles Warren, <u>Memorandum on Draft Regulations to Implement the National Environmental Policy Act of 1970</u>, <u>Environmental Law Reporter</u>, December 16, 1977, pp. 1291-1311.

75. <u>Ibid</u>.

76. Moynihan, <u>op</u> <u>cit</u>.

77. Weisbrod, <u>op</u> <u>cit</u>, p. 156.

78. For example, <u>Environmental Impact Assessment Review</u> (MIT), No. 1 (December 1977); National Academy of Public Administration, <u>Public Participation in Energy Related Decision-Making</u> (Washington, D.C.: National Academy of Public Administration), 14 pp. (Mimeographed.)

79. Ernest Gellhorn, "Public Participation in Administrative Proceedings," in Marian Blissett, ed., <u>Environmental Impact Assessment</u> (New York: Engineering Foundation, 1976), p. 210.

80. Weisbrod, <u>op</u> <u>cit</u>., p. 498.

2
Judicial Review:
From Procedure to Substance

Laura M. Lake

INTRODUCTION

We know that environmental disputes have unique characteristics, but this alone does not explain why environmental policy implementation has resulted in judicial involvement in substantive decisionmaking and why traditional administrative procedures used to negotiate decisions have been by-passed. Indeed, it has been suggested that the major share of post-1970 environmental policy implementation has involved the judiciary.(1) This chapter examines the origins of judicial access for environmentalists and the reasons why litigation is increasingly drawn into substantive review, as indicated by recent trends in environmental litigation. In order to ascertain the current status of judicial review, we will analyze several leading decisions of the United States Circuit Courts of Appeals and recent Supreme Court decisions on environmental litigation. It will be shown that new access to the courts has resulted in transfer of authority to the courts from the executive. The institutional implications of this phenomenon are discussed.

In reality, the debate over procedural versus substantive judicial review is an institutional conflict over judicial versus administrative discretion in deciding site-specific political conflicts and general regulations, such as banning a pesticide. More broadly, the debate poses the question of where judicial review fits into the policy implementation process, and when does it usurp the role of congressional policymaking and administrative discretion.(2) It is useful to explore the institutional relationships which are threatened by expanded judicial review.

An important element in this institutional
conflict is whether one views environmental
disputes as political or legal disputes:(3)

> (A) fundamental false pretense is the idea
> that a dispute between, say, the Disney
> Corporation and the Sierra Club is a legal
> dispute in any basic sense. . . . But
> the . . . outcome of the case and thereby
> fragments of public policy, will . . .
> depend on a kind of trick: whether an
> administrator followed to the courts' satis-
> faction procedures for drawing up a non-
> building report on environmental impact;
> or . . . whether legislation authorizing a
> particular agency allows courts to issue the
> type of injunction necessary to remedy the
> administrators' acknowledged misstep.

This statement makes several points which are
relevant to this inquiry. Substantive judicial
review competes with congressional policymaking by
producing fragments of public policy, in response
to the targets of opportunity selected by
environmental interest groups.(4) Several of
those who advocate substantive judicial review
recognize that this poses a constitutional
conflict between Congress and the courts, and
suggest that in cases involving major policy
decisions, substantial controversy or large
amounts of money, the final decision be remanded to
Congress.(5) There is, however, a problem with
remanding cases to Congress:(6)

> Even assuming that courts would refrain from
> remanding an excessive number of cases to
> Congress so as to bypass volatile questions,
> there could be no practical assurance that
> Congress would act on a remanded case. In
> such an event, the agency proposal could be
> stalled, not for lack of merit, but for
> congressional inattention. Finally, there is
> the possibility that this "remand" approach
> may allow successive Congresses to cut away
> quietly at the policies behind NEPA on a case-
> by-case basis.

Precedents for this behavior by Congress already
exist, since Congress exempted the Trans Alaska
Pipeline from judicial review and nuclear power
plan licensing.(7) But there is a more fundamental

reason for opposing judicial intervention into Congressional policymaking, the doctrine of limited judicial review: "if a legislature chooses to confer a power--be it a power to build roads or to license the use of the public domain--on an administrative officer, there is simply no basis for the exercise of the power by the court."(8) It appears that the Supreme Court supports this concept in its recent Vermont Yankee Power Corporation v. NRDC (1978),(9) discussed shortly.

Despite these issues of constitutional incursions by the courts, advocates of substantive judicial review argue that without such review administrative decisions would run amuck, that judicial review represents the only check against non-elected civil servants.(10) Such arguments, however, neglect alternative political pressures which can be brought to bear upon reluctant bureaucrats. For example, Congressional oversight, administrative lobbying and interest group campaign endorsements of elected officials can be used to develop influence on environmental decisions. These advocates of judicial review in administrative matters expect to reach bureaucracy through the courts and object to judicial restraint because "litigation in which courts limit themselves to a correction of legal failings . . . fails to focus upon the real underlying problem--the attitude, rather than the legality of administrative behavior."(11) While one can empathize with this frustration, it seems too much to expect of litigation that it undertake to change attitudes. "The fact is, that adjudication as a technique of altering social behavior has not been very successful where the principles themselves are seriously opposed," such as school desegregation, voter registration and school prayer.(12)

Victory in the courts may be only a partial success, for the case may be remanded back to the agency for procedural corrections. Such remands are common and serve to remind us that judicial relief for environmental conflicts is a procedural and not substantive victory:(13)

> Environmentalists see citizen litigation as a potentially powerful tool for forcing reluctant administrators to implement many anti-pollution laws that are on the books. . . . (However), the requirement to take the environmental impact statement

34

seriously can do no more than force
administrators to consider--or at least
receive--all of the factors. The final
decision remains theirs, and the work of the
courts is thus confined to opening the
administrative process and or delaying the
inevitable.

When procedural victories involve long delays
they can cause the abandonment of projects and
thereby serve as useful strategies. In order to
determine the reason for abandonment, however, it
is necessary also to consider delays and costs
associated with engineering and construction
problems which are independent of litigation.
Permanent abandonment of major projects is rare.
Projects are often resurrected during new
administrations, by a committed agency staff.
Feigned abandonment is a more typical result of
litigation.

GREAT EXPECTATIONS: THE COURTS AND THE PUBLIC

The provision of procedural rights in
environmental policy implementation raised public
expectations regarding the benefits of judicial
remedies for environmental disputes, and prompted
the response of federal courts to expand the
standards for judicial review into substantive
matters, replacing their discretion for that of the
administrators. Since members of the bench are not
immune to public expectations, it is helpful to
review public expectations of judicial relief
before reviewing leading decisions of the federal
bench and assessing the institutional changes
which have resulted from the broadening of judicial
review. This section thus sets the social context
of judicial review deliberations.
The courtroom has become the center arbiter of
many social, economic and political disputes in the
United States. Not all judges agree that they
ought to embrace requests for expanding judicial
review into substantive decisionmaking, and
several have recently suggested that alternative
dispute settlement procedures ought to be
developed to relieve the courts of this burden.(14)
Perhaps the most eloquent of the voices calling for
judicial restraint is that of Judge Shirley
Hufstedler of the Ninth Circuit Court of
Appeals:(15)

Federal judges are the congressionally favored catchers of . . . hot potatoes. They do not have to run for office and are therefore presumed to have asbestos fingers. Should Concorde landings prevail over enemies of noise pollution? Why not let the courts decide. The federal courts are already running ailing railroads . . . and they are supervising mental hospitals, prisons, and school systems. . . .

What's wrong is that judicial systems are not designed to handle the massive influx of cases. . . . Federal judges have no bureaucracies to tap with trivial exceptions, no experts to help them who are not suplied by the litigants as witnesses. The average personal staff of a federal judge is one secretary and two law clerks. . . .

Ultimately, Americans will simply have to learn that justice does not rest with the courts, but in the minds and hearts of us all.

Public expectations of the value of judicial victories are also contributing factors to the selection of litigation as a political strategy, for many people who believe in the efficacy of judicial victories have ". . . exaggerated expectations about the political impact of judicial decisions."(16) This can partially be explained by the sense of political efficacy the public experiences through the litigation process.(17)

Citizen contact with executive and judicial agencies of government is increasing at the same time as legislators become isolated from personal contact with their constituents and electoral participation becomes meaningful primarily in a symbolic sense. Involvement in litigatiion usually is intensive and involves a crisis. For those portions of the population who become involved, court proceedings constitute a highly visible and personally significant segment of the governmental system.

These expectations of political efficacy, coupled with frustration with alternative political arenas, summarized earlier in Figure 1-1, present a

36

challenge to the judiciary. The next section
examines the mixed response of the bench to this
challenge to enforce environmental policy
statutes.

DEVELOPMENT OF JUDICIAL ACCESS

Pre-1970 environmental lawsuits were often
litigated as "nuisance" suits. Environmental
statutes passed between 1969 and 1972 shifted the
burden of proof for damage from the plaintiff to
the defendant, thereby dramatically enhancing
litigation as a strategy for environmentalists.(18) In this way it became the
obligation of polluters or developers to prove that
they were not harming the environment. Although it
is a common assessment in environmental juris-
prudence that "without NEPA (a citizen) is legally
powerless,"(19) the development of environmental
procedural rights has been based on the
Administrative Procedure Act of 1946 (APA) and not
on NEPA per se.(20) For example, in Citizens to
Preserve Overton Park v. Volpe (1971), the basis
for litigation was not a violation of NEPA but
rather, a violation of the APA, because as the
Supreme Court stated, the Federal Highway
Administration had overstepped its jurisdiction
and therefore violated the APA.(21)
Since the APA is the basis for much environmental litigation, it is worthwhile to review
briefly the procedural requirements placed on
agencies by this law:(22)

The reviewing court shall--

   (2)   hold unlawful and set aside agency
         action, findings, and conclusions found
         to be--

      (A) arbitrary, capricious, an abuse of
          discretion, or otherwise not in
          accordance with law;

      (B) contrary to constitutional right,
          power, privilege or immunity;

      (C) in excess of statutory juris-
          diction, authority, or limitations,
          or short of statutory rights...

(F) unwarranted by the facts to the extent that the facts are subject to trial de novo by the reviewing court.

Judicial review based on the APA supplemented specific environmental statutes which provided for citizen standing in litigation (NEPA; Clean Air Act Amendments of 1970 and Clean Air Act Amendments):(23)

Section 102(2)(c) of the National Environmental Policy Act (1969) requires opportunity for citizen review of "environmental impacts" prepared by federal agencies and permits citizens to sue to ensure that agencies properly prepare such material.

Section 505(a) of the Federal Water Pollution Control Act Amendments (1972) permits citizen suits against any public or private party violating provisions of its major section.

Section 304 of the Clean Air Act (1970) empowers citizens to seek compliance with basic regulatory features of the act when violations are discovered.

One of the procedural requirements associated with NEPA has been public participation--which, however, is not mentioned in NEPA. Rather, it is recommended in Council of Environmental Quality guidelines for implementing NEPA; and mandated by Executive Order 11514. NEPA itself only requires that the public have access to documents prepared for environmental impact statements and have the opportunity to comment on those reports (oral testimony is optional).(24) The much-heralded NEPA proclaims national environmental goals, but the brunt of their implementation rests with these other laws and agency discretion.(25) Essentially, this law has been used to derive new procedural requirements for environmental decisionmaking which have only recently been rejected by the Supreme Court (Vermont Yankee v. NRDC (1978), which declared that NEPA does not require adjudicative procedures by administrative agencies to comply with NEPA (this decision is discussed in this chapter). In addition to procedural rights, the derivation of substantive rights is based on interpretations of how far the courts must go into the

record in order to determine if there has been a
violation of the APA or environmental
statutes.(26)

We have discussed the environmental rights
developed through litigation; now we will examine
the extent to which access to the courts has
increased the use of litigation for environmental
disputes. In addition, we will determine if the
nature of these lawsuits has changed from procedural concerns to substantive issues, thereby
pressing the courts to develop a broader scope for
judicial review.

Although the number of environmental disputes
has increased dramatically since 1970,(27) the
number of environmental lawsuits during this
period has only gradually increased. This is
because litigation is costly(28) and also because
many groups do not have good legal counsel or
cases.(29) These observations are borne out by
recent surveys of the impacts of environmental
litigation. For example, the Council on Environmental Quality conducted a survey in 1975 to
determine the effects of NEPA on court
caseloads:(30)

> The survey shows that in 5.5 years from
> January 1, 1970 to June 30, 1975, there were
> 654 cases completed or pending in which a NEPA
> issue was alleged by an environmental,
> business, labor, or other party to the
> litigation. Of these 654 cases, 363 were
> brought on the ground that an impact statement
> was required. This litigation record
> contrasts with the tens of thousands of
> federal administrative actions taken in the
> same period. (More than 30,000 actions were
> assessed by federal agencies in FY 1975 alone
> to determine whether they would cause
> significant environmental effects.) Most of
> the other 291 cases challenged the adequacy of
> an impact statement that had been prepared.
> This figure contrasts with the 6,000 impact
> statements that were prepared during the same
> period; at most, approximately 5 percent of
> the actions was challenged in court.

The survey thus shows that substantive issues were
involved in approximately half of the NEPA cases
and that substantive cases regarding the adequacy
of the impact statements increased by five percent
during this time.(31)

39

A more specialized litigation survey revealed that the APA was used in 1967 to block 23 out of 65 nuclear power plants, and 23 out of 125 conventional power plants.(32) At the state level, a survey was conducted by the California Office of Planning and Research to determine the effects of the California Environmental Quality Act of 1970 (CEQA) on court caseloads. This 1976 survey found that less than one percent of the total environmental impact reports and "negative declarations"(33) were litigated.(34) The study provides particularly useful information because it distinguishes between cases settled before and after trial (33 percent of the 244 cases were settled before going to trial). Although this study found that there has been only a slight increase in the number of cases filed since 1971, there has been a significant shift in the basis for judicial review from procedural to substantive issues:(35)

> The prevailing cause of action in CEQA cases has changed since 1971. In 1971 and 1972 suits involving a failure to file an EIR (Environmental Impact Report) accounted for 83 percent of all CEQA cases initiated in those years (47 out of 57 cases filed). In 1975, the "no EIR" cause of action decreased significantly to 21 percent of all cases filed that year (14 out of 69 cases). During this same period, cause of action involving the adequacy of EIR's rose from 12 percent of all cases filed in 1971 and 1972 (7 out of 57 cases), to 50 percent of all cases filed in 1975 (34 out of 69 cases).

These surveys indicate that both NEPA and CEQA litigation involve substantive review in at least half of the cases, that caseloads are slightly increasing, and that only a small percentage of all environmental impact reviews are challenged in the courts. In addition, a majority of litigation in the United States is settled before trial.(36) These small percentages of challenges can be misleading, however; many of these cases set precedents which apply to other similar situations, e.g. Friends of Mammoth (1972) which opened all private projects to environmental reviews in California.(37)

The statistics also fail to convey the large amount of money and political controversy

40

associated with these disputes, and assume that each is like the others, i.e., that a lawsuit over a town dump is the equivalent of the impacts of off-shore oil drilling. Such oversimplifications of litigation trends overlook the precedents set by these cases, as noted above, and also the headlines which increasingly challenge the values espoused by environmentalists, particularly when a major industrial firm claims that it is not able to locate a plant in a state because of environmental controls and reviews.(39) To assume that because only one or five percent of the environmental impact statements are challenged means that there is no significant problem is erroneous. For example, the Trans Alaska Pipeline controversy not only involved large amounts of money but eventually resulted in congressional action (PL 93-153) to exempt the Supreme Court's judicial review of the project's environmental impacts.(39) Similar actions have been taken by Congress when environmental reviews jeopardized favored projects.(40) Indeed, revised guidelines (the third set since 1970) for the implementation of NEPA have recently been issued by the Council on Environmental Quality because of the frustration with the process which is raplidly losing its substantive value and strangling agencies in procedural red tape.(41)

We have seen that until recently the trends in environmental litigation were toward substantive review. Although significant public controversy has resulted from the use of litigation as a political strategy, the number of lawsuits continues to be quite small. As a tactical strategy, the quest for substantive judicial review has failed in several areas, e.g., water resources, and recently, several public interest law firms have turned to supplementary tactics such as administrative and legislative lobbying.(42)

A review of the definitions of compliance with environmental statutes developed by different members of the federal bench helps to explain the interpretations of institutional authority which underlie the scope of judicial review. Rather than assuming unanimity within the bench, it is important to consider the arguments raised by opposing members of the judiciary to justify judicial review. It ought to be noted that unlike compliance with constitutional law, judicial review of statutory compliance is usually confined to protecting constitutional rights (procedural review), and not to the merits of the decisions made. Furthermore, provisions for judicial review are provided in each statute and can be rescinded at any time by the legislature. Thus the development of substantive judicial review is based on a weaker foundation, as compared with traditional due process concerns.

At a minimum, the environmental impact statement requirements of NEPA are the equivalent of a public disclosure law.(43) Others, however, consider them to be a good deal more: "a mandate to the agencies to consider environmental factors as coequal with traditional technical and economic factors in the planning process."(44) The determination of compliance with these statutes has provided the basis for expanded judicial review. Traditionally, compliance with substantive decisions was considered to be within the realm of administrative discretion; newer interpretations by the courts have transferred this compliance determination to the courts.

Compliance with federal statutes has usually involved the judicial determination of reasonable and good faith actions by administrators.(45) In the environmental policy implementation process, which depends upon state enforcement of local violations of federal standards, the states have generally relied upon voluntary compliance with the law,(46) hereby prompting environmental interest groups to litigate in order to force compliance. Initially these lawsuits involved procedural concerns based on the APA, but subsequently the majority of the Circuit Courts of Appeals adopted a broader view of judicial review, "extending judicial inquiry to the limits permitted by the Administrative Procedure Act. Only the Fifth Circuit has narrowly restricted its scope of review" to procedural requirements.(47)

In numerical terms, approximately one-half of the NEPA related lawsuits reviewed by the Council on Environmental Quality in 1975 were based on allegations of substantive error, i.e., inadequacy of the environmental impact statement.(48) It is not clear, however, that NEPA was intended to establish such substantive discretion for the courts: Figure 2-1 summarizes leading cases of the

Figure 2-1. Federal Circuit Courts of Appeals Leading Decisions Regarding the
Scope of Judicial Review for Environmental Law Enforcement

CIRCUIT COURT	BROAD/NARROW SCOPE OF REVIEW	LEADING DECISIONS
District of Columbia	Broad	Calvert Cliffs Coordinating Committee v. ABC (1971): reverse a district courts substantive decision if it can be proven that the actual balance of costs and benefits struck was arbitrary, or clearly gave insufficient weight to environmental factors. See also Concerned About Trident v. Schlessinger (1976).
First	Broad	Silva v. Lynn (1973) and NRDC v. EPA (1973): review is based on arbitrary and capricious actions by administrators.
Second	Narrow	Scenic Hudson v. Federal Power Commission (1971): "To read these cases as sanctioning a new standard of judicial review for findings on matters of environmental policy is to misconstrue . . . the holdings in the cases . . . (453 F. 2nd at 468-69).
Third	Broad	Concerned Residents of Buck Hill Falls v. Grant (1976): adequacy of the cost-benefit analysis was considered by the court.
Fourth	Broad	Ely v. Velde (1971): "To enable a court to ascertain whether there has been a genuine, not prejunctory compliance with NEPA, the /agency/ will be required to explicate fully its course of inquiry, its analysis and its reasoning" (451 F. 2nd 1130).
Fifth	Narrow	Pizitz v. Volpe (1972): no substantive rights are created by NEPA; however, Save Our Ten Acres v. Kreger (1973) and EDF v. Corps of Engineers (1974) state that the agency must review significant impacts, implying that the court can identify the significant impacts which are alleged to have been neglected.
Sixth	Narrow	Overton Park v. Volpe (1971): the Secretary of Transportation must provide a record of standards use for informal decision-making.
Seventh	Broad	Sierra Club v. Froelkhe (1973): inadequacy of benefit-cost analysis.
Eighth	Broad	EDF v. Corps of Engineers (1972): NEPA created substantive and procedural rights; however, this case was decided on traditional procedural grounds of "arbitrary, capricious, and abuse of discretion" in agency conduct.
Ninth	Narrow	Jicarilla Apache Tribe v. Morton (1973): courts may not substitute their judgment for that of the administrator.
Tenth	Narrow	National Helium v. Morton (1973): no required format for public participation.

Circuit Courts of Appeals and characterizes their bases for judicial review. All of the decisions cited (which are merely illustrative rather than exhaustive) are based on procedural grounds; substantive review is a by-product of determining if there has been adequate procedural action, i.e., if there has been an arbitrary or capricious decision, or an abuse of discretion.

At the heart of the debate over the expansion of judicial review is the definition of compliance. The decisions discussed in Figure 2--range from narrow definitions of what constitutes procedural compliance, to quite broad assertions of the creation of substantive rights. At the "conservative" end of this spectrum, the Ninth Circuit Court of Appeals directly addressed the question of substantive rights, and decided that no substantive rights were created by NEPA. In the middle of this range of judicial decisions is the Fifth Circuit Court of Appeals which in EDF v. Corps of Engineers (1974) was somewhat indecisive regarding substantive rights, but insisted that agencies must review significant environmental impacts, and assumed that the courts were in a position to recognize significant (substantive) impacts. Somewhat also in this middle range of judicial opinions are several circuits which interpret procedural compliance to include substantive aspects of the environmental impact statement, e.g., the adequacy of a cost-benefit analysis in Concerned Residents of Buck Hill Falls v. Grant (3 Cir., 1976). At the "liberal" end of the scope of judicial review spectrum are the Eighth, First and District of Columbia Circuit Courts of Appeals, which advocate substantive review.

The District of Columbia Circuit Court of Appeals has a particularly important role in environmental law, since it has jurisdiction over federal agencies located within the District of Columbia.(49) Indeed, several of its members have been leading exponents of judicial review of environmental decisions. Their definitions and explanations for judicial review, however, are varied.

Judge Harold Leventhal promulgated the "hard look doctrine," one of the earliest standards for judicial review of environmental decisions, in Greater Boston Television Corp. v. FCC (D.C. Cir., 1970):(50)

> The court must study the record attentively,
> even the evidence on technical matters, to
> satisfy itself that the agency has exercised a
> reasoned discretion with reasons that do not
> deviate from or ignore the ascertainable
> legislative intent. The court is not to make
> its own findings, or select policies.

In addition, he distinguished between the
obligations posed by NEPA for nonenvironmental
agencies and for agencies with primarily environmental protection missions. For the
nonenvironmental agencies, he suggested that NEPA
required them to seriously consider environmental
values at least equally with other values; and for
environmental agencies, that they weigh heavily
the socioeconomic values involved with environmental decisions.(51)

Chief Justice Bazelon of the District of
Columbia Circuit Court of Appeals has been
considered an advocate of substantive judicial and
procedural review. Depending upon which decision
one cites, his views have come to mean many
different things to environmental law scholars.
For example, Robert Jordan cites EDF v. Ruckelshaus
(1971) to indicate that Judge Bazelon advocates
substantive judicial review.(52) Reviewing a
subsequent decision of Bazelon's, International
Harvester v. Ruckelshaus (1973), Grant Thompson
interprets his position as limiting judicial
review to guarantee "reasoned decision-making" and
not substantive review.(53) Since these opinions
are so important to our inquiry into judicial
review, it is worthwhile to examine Judge Bazelon's
own words in both decisions.

In EDF v. Ruckelshaus (1971), he "emphasized
that the primary function of courts is to 'protect
these interests from administrative
arbitrariness,'" and went on to explain,(54)

> We stand on the threshold of a new era in the
> history of the long and fruitful
> collaboration of administrative agencies and
> reviewing courts. For many years, courts have
> treated administrative policy decisions with
> great deference. . . . On matters of
> substance, the courts regularly upheld agency
> action. . . . Courts occasionally asserted,
> but less often exercised, the power to set
> aside agency action on the ground or a crucial
> factor had not been considered. Gradually,

however, that power has come into more frequent use, and with it, the requirement that administrators articulate the factors on which they base their decisions.

Strict adherence to that requirement is especially important now . . . courts are increasingly asked to review administrative action that touches on fundamental personal interests in life, health, and liberty. These interests have always had a special claim to judicial protection, in comparison with the economic interests at stake in a rate-making or licensing proceeding.

This position was further clarified by Judge Bazelon's opinion in International Harvester v. Ruckelshaus (1973)(55)

I cannot believe that Congress intended this court to delve into the substance of mechanical, statistical, and technological disputes in this case. Senator Cooper, the author of the judicial review provision, stated repeatedly that this court's role would be to "determine the question of due process."

Thus Thompson's initial interpretation of Judge Bazelon's reservations about substantive review are supported by the 1973 decision.

Judge J. Skelly Wright, a fellow member of the District of Columbia Circuit Court of Appeals disagrees with Judge Bazelon:(56)

(Judge Bazelon's) approach mandates that the courts prescribe precise and formal methods for bureaucratic policy-making. This mandate assumes an expertise in administrative science which duty on the bench simply does not confer. . . .

Substantive review is an inquiry into the realities of the rule-making process, not an occasion for pretending that agencies are some species of lower court. . . .

Section 553 (APA) thus opens a broad window on the rule-making process, surely broad enough to reveal any unfairness to the public committed by the rulemaker. At the same time,

the window is not so large as to invite a
judicial breaking and entering.

In his review of judicial procedural inquiries,
Judge Wright suggests that rulemaking procedures
utilized by administrative agencies are substantially different from adjudicatory procedures
and that this is the fundamental reason why the
courts should not impose adjudicatory procedures
on administrative decisionmaking, nor delve into
the discretionary substance of cases:(57)

> An adjudication applies a preexisting legal
> standard to a small set of controverted facts
> to determine whether a particular individual
> should receive a benefit or a penalty. An
> adjudication is fair to the individual only if
> the facts are accurately found. . . . But it
> makes no sense to speak of a rule as being
> fair or unfair to an individual in this
> objective sense of accuracy. A rule allocates
> benefits and penalties among large classes of
> individuals accordng to a specific normative
> standard, and the fairness of such an alloca-
> tion is ultimately a political or philo-
> sophical question. Thus, in the rulemaking
> context, fairness is not identified with
> accuracy, and procedures designed to maximize
> accuracy at the cost of all other values are
> simply inappropriate. . . . To adopt maximum
> procedures in all cases . . . we would obtain
> administrative paralysis. The inherent
> virtues of rule-making--expedition,
> flexibility to experiment, a sensible balance
> between expertise and broad public
> participation--would be forfeited.

We have dwelt upon Judge Wright's analysis
because it summarizes critical arguments for
maintaining judicial restraint when confronting
environmental agency rulemaking, and because the
Supreme Court, in two major recent uanimous decisions (two members did not participate), cites
Judge Wright's article.(58) For example, in
Vermont Yankee Nuclear Power Corp. v. NRDC (1978),
the Court declared that:(59)

> Nuclear energy may some day be a cheap, safe
> source of power or it may not. But Congress
> has made a choice to at least try nuclear
> energy, establishing a reasonable review

47

process in which courts are to play only a limited role. The fundamental policy questions appropriately resolved in Congress and in the state legislatures are <u>not</u> subject to reexamination in the federal courts under the guise of judicial review of agency action. Time may prove wrong the decision to develop nuclear energy, but it is Congress or the States within their appropriate agencies which must eventually make that judgment. In the meantime courts should perform in their appointed function. <u>NEPA does set forth significant substantive goals for the Nation, but its mandate to the agencies is essentially procedural</u> . . . . It is to assure a fully informed and well-considered decision, "not!" necessarily a decision the judges of the Court of Appeals (D.C. Cir.) or of this Court would have reached had they been members of the decisionmaking unit of the agency. . . . <u>A single alleged oversight on a peripheral issue, urged by parties who never fully cooperated</u> or indeed raised the issues below, <u>must not be made the basis for overturning a decision properly made</u> after an otherwise exhaustive proceeding. (Emphasis added.)

This decision stresses the authority of administrators to set substantive policy, and notes the negative role--"parties who never fully cooperated"--of environmental interest groups. It suggests a test of good faith public participation.

The substantive goals of NEPA cited by the Court refer to the policy goals of NEPA, that is, that agencies take "a hard look at environmental values during decison-making.(60) Thus the Court emphasizes procedural rights, agency flexibility, and definitively rejects the notion of substantive environmental rights created by NEPA. This decision signals the need to develop alternative administrative procedures for resolving environmental conflicts; environmental mediation may be one such alternative.

We have found that the scope of judicial review has been broadened through new interpretations of procedural compliance by the District and Circuit Courts of Appeals. The trend toward substantive review and the creation of substantive rights now seems to be stemmed by the Vermont Yankee v. NRDC (1978) decision. The Court's reasons, as described in this decision, are based on the desire to maintain flexibility in rulemaking proceedings by not imposing adjudicative procedures on agencies:

> A false impression has become widespread that the most crucial administrative function is that of informal adjudication.

> Informal adjudication is not the most vital portion of the administrative process. Discretionary action is, and informal adjudication is only a small portion of discretionary action.(61)

The erosion of agency discretion through environmental litigation is a serious matter. It affects the ability of agencies to function satisfactorily and is discussed in the following section.

INSTITUTIONAL IMPACTS OF
SUBSTANTIVE JUDICIAL REVIEW

We noted in Chapter 1 why plaintiffs seek judicial relief; how and why courts accept these cases will not be reviewed. (To a great extent the debate over substantive review has taken place within the legal community. Nonsense! Social scientists have not considered judicial intervention a significant factor in policy implementation until fairly recently.(62)) Yet the institutional aspects of judicial intervention are so great, that they deserve very close scrutiny by social scientists.

The decision to accept a case is made by the judiciary, and judicial review is thus a self-legitimizing process.(63) Judges frequently respond to situations in which the laws are vague, contradictory, or in which unsatisfactory social results will occur from the law's application. At what point the balancing of equities becomes substantive decisonmaking and encroaches upon Congress and administrative agencies is debatable, however. Administrators are inclined to think that when the balancing involves "factual decisions bearing on enforcement," judicial review is inappropriate.(64)

> The issue becomes one of the power to decide. Environmentalists feel that they have lost

49

too often in the administrative process, and therefore prefer an expansion of judicial intervention. The agencies obviously prefer to be the ultimate arbiters, citing their statutory missions and their expertise.

Placing the ultimate power in the hands of agencies may not be so much a question of expertise rather, the power rests there because Congress has "conferred the power on the executive branch and thought it proper to confer discretion in the exercise of that power."

When NEPA litigation finally reaches the substantive merits, the agency involved should be free to make the ultimate choice among alternatives, subject to those political influences to which it responds.(65)

Environmental policy implementation thus involves fundamental constitutional relationships between the three branches of government. The analysis presented here points toward a reaffirmation of the role of administrative discretion to make flexibile, expeditious, informed and equitable decisions. While there has been a transfer of some decisionmaking authority from the executive to the judiciary through the development of substantive review, and some erosion of principle, recent decisions of the Supreme Court(66) suggest that this trend is reversing.

While there has been increasing concern over judicial intervention into social policy (integration, welfare, prisons, etc.), environmental litigation has not been included in this assessment because it is not a field based on constitutional rights, but rather, statutory rights to procedural fairness. The justification of the courts to go into the details of integration plans, for example, was to safeguard fundamental constitutional rights (equal protection) and even in these situations, critics such as Nathan Glazer and Donald Horowitz have argued, judicial intervention into substantive issues is not warranted.

Substantive judicial review which does not involve constitutional matters, particularly weak. This is why environmental lawyers are increasingly discussing the desirability of a constitutional amendment to provide environmental rights. The precedent exists at the state level, e.g.,

Massachusetts passed an amendment to the state constitution in 1970 to provide for an environmental bill of rights.(67) Without such constitutional action, environmentalists are engaged primarily in substantive decisionmaking without rights other than due process.

Even with constitutional environmental rights, there are problems associated with substantive judicial review, since judges often become involved in the minutiae of administrative decisionmaking. Glazer thus distinguishes between rights-pronouncing decrees (procedural review) and administrative-intervention decrees (substantive review) in matters of constitutional interpretation. Procedural reviews concern rights, while substantive review shift attention "from rights to policy with no relation to rights, which ignores the large impact of a decision."(68) Substantive review places the judiciary in an active, general public problem-solving role, rather than a specific private rights-protecting role.(69)

In approaching problem-solving, administrators utilize a broader framework for decisionmaking which takes into account the larger impacts of site-specific decisions, since they are accustomed to allocating resources among competing programs and are aware of the implications of major new programs for existing programs.

The origin of expanded judicial review in policy implementation is school desegregation and civil rights litigation.(70) The courts had to devise detailed plans to minimize administrative discretion which would be used by local and state officials to defy desegregation. The institutional changes which resulted from this involvement in administrative problem-solving are only now starting to be questioned and understood. Of concern are the legitimacy and capacity of the courts to make substantive public policy decisions and to commit public resources to programs activities designated by judges. These substantive actions changes traditional <u>judicial rights and remedies</u>:(71)

> The form of relief does not flow ineluctably from the liability determination, but is fashioned <u>ad</u> <u>hoc</u>. Relief is not a terminal, compensatory transfer, but an effort to

51

devise a program to contain future consequences in a way that accommodates the range of interests involved.

Essentially, judicial activism intervenes in the administrative chain of command, separating the operating bureaucracy from executive control; it is more than an expansion of traditional activities; it displaces executive authority.(72) Recently a number of scholars have become concerned about this incursion into executive authority. For example, Daniel P. Moynihan observes,

Such a role for the courts, pursued through decrees in class-action suits, is unprecedented and raises serious concerns of legitimacy.

A court without an elaborate bureaucracy to fuzz the results and conceal its mistakes will soon be judged no court at all, but merely a panel of well-intentioned amateurs exposed to all the world as bumblers.(73)

Horowitz similarly notes that "there is a difference between a fresh perspective and an ignorant one."(74)
Substantive judicial review of environmental decisionmaking has resulted in "a reluctance to downgrade the non-critical issues" lest they provide the basis for litigation. This leads to time-consuming costly studies which are not particularly instructive to decisoin-makers.(75) Institutionally, this hesitancy to make judgments regarding enviroinmental tradeoffs produces a standoff between the executive and the judiciary: "each becomes more capable of thwarting the others' purposes, and probably more disposed to do so." (Original emphasis.)(76) The only parties to benefit from this situation appear to be members of the legal profession. Surely this small circle of beneficiaries hardly warrants the major institutional changes incurred.
The expansion of judicial review from procedural to substantive matters was not achieved through an act of Congress. It was the result of judicial activism. The institutional implications of this assertion of judicial authority into administrative discretion are significant: administrative authority (discretion) is reduced, and the policy objectives of Congress are held

52

hostage in a jurisdictional struggle between the executive and the judiciary.

Finally, there are differences between administrative and judicial decisionmaking systems which affect the outcomes.(77) Policy choices and problem-solving by judges is likely to be quite different from implementation through administrative processes. At stake are the legitimacy and capacity of the courts to assume such a large role in policy implementation, as opposed to a small role as catcher of occasional hot potatoes.

REFERENCES

1. H.J. Young, "Implementation of NEPA for Electric Power," in Marland Blissett, ed., Environmental Impact Assessment (New York: Engineering Foundation, 1976), p. 74.

2. J. Woodford Howard, Jr., "Adjudication Considered as a Process of Conflict Resolution: A Variation on Separation of Powers," Journal of Public Law, Vol. 18 (Spring 1969), pp. 339-370; Donald Horowitz, The Courts and Social Policy (Washington, D.C.: The Brookings Institution, 1977).

3. Karen Orren, "Standing to Sue: Interest Group Conflict in the Federal Courts," American Political Science Review (September 1976), pp. 740-741; Malcolm Baldwin, ed., Law and the Environment (New York: Walker and Co., 1970).

4. Thomas P. Jahnige and Sheldon Goldman, The Federal Judicial System (New York: Holt, Rinehart and Winston, 1968), p. 302.

5. Theodore Lowi, The End of Liberalism (New York: W.W. Norton & Co., 1969), p. 298; George Coggins, "Some Suggestions for Future Plaintiffs," Kansas Law Review, Vol. 24 (1976), p. 307.

6. Steven O. Rosen, "Cost Benefit Analysis, Judicial Review and the National Environmental Policy Act," Environmental Law, Vol. 7 (1977), p. 380.

7. Coggins, op cit., p. 307.

8. Louis Jaffe, review of Sax (Defending the Environment) in Louis Jaffe and Laurence Tribe, Environmental Protection (Chicago: Bracton Press, 1971), p. 661.

9. Vermont Yankee Power Corporation v. NRDC, et al., 38 CCH. S. Ct. Bull. p. B 1471 (April 1978).

10. Reference 5 supra.

11. Joseph Sax, Defending the Environment (New York: Alfred Knopf, 1971), p. 135.

12. Howard, op cit., p. 365.

13. Stuart Sheingold, The Politics of Rights (New Haven: Yale University Press, 1974), pp. 121-123, 130.

14. See opinion of Warren Burger, in Aberdeen and Rockfish Ry. Co. v. SCRAP, 93 S Ct. 1, 7, 2 Environmental Law Reporter, 20481, 20494 (1972); see also Mr. Burger's comment before the American Arbitration Association, November 1968, in Odom Fanning, Citizen Action (New York: Harper and Row, 1975), p. 218.

15. Shirley Hufstedler, "Americans Simply Expect Too Much of Their Courts and Judges," Los Angeles Times, October 117, 1977, pp. 1, 4.

16. Sheingold, op cit., p. 95.

17. Herbert Jacob, "Judicial and Political Efficacy of Litigants," in Joel Grossman and Joseph Tannenhaus, Frontiers of Judicial Research (New York: John Wiley, 1969), p. 271.

18. Raphael Kapser, et al., Implementing Technology Assessments (Washington, D.C.: George Washington University Program of Policy Studies in Science and Technology, 1974), p. 127; Lettie Wenner, One Environment Under Law (Pacific Palisades: Goodyear Publishing Co., 1976), p. 9.

19. Coggins, op cit., p. 307.

20. Sally K. Fairfax, "A Disaster in the Environmental Movement," Science (February 17, 1978), pp. 743-748.

21. Grant Thompson, "The Role of the Courts," in Dolgin and Guilbert, eds., Federal Environmental Law (St. Paul: West Publishing Company, 1974), pp. 199-200, 232.

22. Kenneth Culp Davis, Administrative Law (St. Paul: West Publishing Company, 1977), pp. 653-654.

23. Walter Rosenbaum, The Politics of the Environment (New York: Praeger, 1977), p. 73.

24. James Curlin, "The Role of the Courts in the Implementation of NEPA," in Blissett, op cit., p. 27.

25. Burton Weisbrod, et al., Public Interst Law: An Institutional and Economic Analysis (Berkeley: University of California Press, 1978), p. 193.

26. Ibid., pp. 195-217.

27. Thomas N. Gladwin, "The Management of Environmental Conflict: A Survey of Research Approaches and Priorities," paper delivered at

Resolve Conference, Reston, Virginia, January 1978, p. 3. (Mimeographed.)

28. Weisbrod, op cit., pp. 152, 193; Steven Ebbin and Raphael Kapser, Citizen Groups and the Nuclear Power Controversy: Uses of Scientific and Technological Information (Cambridge: MIT Press, 1974), pp. 255, 265.

29. For example, out of 215 non-pending California Environmental Quality Act (CEQA) cases in 1970, 71 cases (33 percent) resulted in pre-trial dispositions. California Office of Planning and Research, California Environmental Quality Act Litigatiion Survey (Sacramento: Office of Planning and Research, April 1976), p. 10. (Mimeographed.)

30. Council on Environmental Quality, Seventh Annual Report of the Council on Environmental Quality (Washington, D.C.: U.S. Government Printing Office, 1977), pp. 124, 125.

31. Ibid.

32 Gary Neustadter, "The Role of the Judiciary in the Confrontation with the Problems of Environmental Quality," UCLA Law Review (May 1970), p. 1100.

33. A "negative declaration" is a "statement of record, for all non-exempt projects found to be without potential or real significant adverse environmental impact." Office of Planning and Research, The California Environmental Quality Act: A Review (Sacramento: Office of Planning and Research, March 1976), p. 17. (Mimeographed.)

34. CEQA Litigation Study, op cit., p. 17.

35. Ibid.

36. Howard, op cit., p. 360.

37. Frederick R. Anderson, NEPA in the Courts (Washington, D.C.: Resources for the Future, 1973); Geoffrey Wandesford-Smith and Laurence D. Baxter, "Implementation and the Strategic Retreat on Objectives: Environmental Impact Assessment Legislation in California," paper delivered at Annual Meeting of the American Society for Public Administration, Atlanta, Georgia, April 1977. (Mimeographed.)

38. Marvin Braude, "Will We Now Drown in Paper Pollution," Los Angeles Times, March 27, 1978, Part VI, pp. 1, 3.

39. Henry Myers, "Federal Decisionmaking and the Trans-Alaskan Pipeline," Ecology Law Quarterly, Vol. 4, 1975, p. 941.

40. Coggin, op cit., p. 312.

41. Charles Warren, Memorandum on Draft
Regulations to Implement the National
Environmental Policy Act of 1970, Environmental
Law Reporter, December 16, 1977, pp. 1291-1311.
42. Weisbrod, op cit., p. 215.
43. Curlin, op cit., p. 27.
44. Ibid.
45. Ibid., p. 28; Wenner, op cit., p. 70;
Robert Jordan III, "Alternatives under NELPA:
Toward an Accommodation," Ecology Law Quarterly
(Fall 1973), pp. 747-748.
46. Ibid.
47. Thompson, op cit., pp. 211-215.
48. Council on Environmental Quality, op
cit.
49. Thompson, op cit.
50. Harold Leventhal, "Environmental
Decisionmaking and the Role of the Courts,"
University of Pennsylvania Law Review, Vol. 122,
No. 3(January 1974), p. 511.
51. Ibid., p. 531.
52. Jordan, op cit.
53. Thompson, op cit.
54. Ibid.
55. Walter Gellhorn and Clark Byse, Administrative Law (Mineola, New York: The Foundation
Press, 1974), p. 466.
56. J. Skelly Wright, "The Courts and the
Rulemaking Process: The Limits of Judicial
Review," Cornell Law Review (March 1974), pp. 389,
390, 392, 395.
57. Ibid., pp. 379, 388.
58. Reference 9 supra.
59. Reference 9 supra, pp. B1481-1482.
60. Leventhal, op cit.
61. Kenneth Culp Davis, Discretionary
Justice (Urbana: University of Illinois Press,
1977), p. 21.
62. Nathan Glazer, "Should Judges Administer
Social Services?" The Public Interest, No. 50
(Winter 1978).
63. Martin Shapiro, The Supreme Court and
Administrative Agencies (New York: Free Press,
1968), p. 34.
64. James Krier and Richard B. Steward,
Environmental Law and Public Poilcy (tentative
revised edition, 1976), pp. IV-88.
(Mimeographed.); United States Attorney General,
Report of the President, Acting through the
Attorney General, On the Feasibility of
Establishing an Environmental Court System

(Washington, D.C.: U.S. Government Printing Office, 1973), p. B-11-12.

65. Jordan, op cit., p. 757.

66. Reference 9 supra.

67. Laura M. Lake, "Massachusetts: A Cast Study of the Politics of the Environment," (unpublished doctoral dissertation, Tufts University, 1972).

68. Glazer, op cit.

69. Horowitz, op cit., pp. 6, 9.

70. David L. Kirp, "School Desegregation and the Limits of Legalism," The Public Interest, No. 47 (Spring 1977).

71. Abram Chayes, "The Role of the Judge in Public Law Litigation," Harvard Law Review, Vol. 89, No. 7 (May 1976), pp. 1293-1294.

72. Glazer, op cit.

73. Daniel P. Moynihan, "Imperial Government," Commentary, Vol. 65, No. 6 (June 1978), pp. 27, 28.

74. Horowitz, op cit., p. 31.

75. Eugene Bardach and Lucian Pugliaresi, "The Environmental Impact Statement vs. the Real World," The Public Interest, No. 49 (Fall 1977), pp. 27, 35.

76. Moynihan, op cit., p. 31.

77. Horowitz, op cit., p. 297.

3
Characterizing Environmental Mediation

Laura M. Lake

INTRODUCTION

In the changing milieu of environmental policy implementation involving intergovernmental conflict and institutional authority changes, environmental mediation represents a political process which allows for more effective public involvement in certain types of environmental decisions.(1) By political process, I wish to distinguish mediation from processes involving the courts. Mediation requires authorization by implementing public officials, either through the appointment of the mediator, or the formal acceptance of the mediation group's recommendations.

Environmental mediation can supplement unwieldly public hearings by convening small bargaining groups and by providing interest group leaders with a socializing experience among their opponents. During these bargaining sessions the interest groups' objectives and priorities can be ascertained, and a measure of responsibility for developing a consensus is assigned to these groups. Thus environmental mediation techniques involving mediators, conciliators and dispute resolution personnel (defined shortly) represent a shift in environmental policy implementation from adversarial to consensual processes, and from judicial to administrative procedures.

Negotiation does not lend itself to a broad range of disputes, however. It is an important process for situations in which

> two (or more) parties combine their conflicting points of view into a single decision. It is a positive-sum exercise,

since by definition both parties prefer the agreed outcome to the status quo (i.e., to no agreement) or to any other mutually agreeable outcome.(2)

The broad, institutional issues involved with dispute resolution processes are the focus of this discussion; this is not a primer on how to mediate.(3) Two other caveats are also in order before we characterize the mediation process: the mediation techniques described here are exploratory, and in several cases represent ongoing efforts. Furthermore, compromise may not be possible in many environmental disputes; the bargaining processes described here may only be appropriate for a small number of disputes.(4) Nevertheless, these case studies permit us to examine environmental policy implementation processes at the state and local levels, intergovernmental relations, interagency conflict and interest group perceptions of issues in conflict.

The six case studies of environmental mediation in this book share several common elements: problems in selecting representatives for negotiations so that interests are adequately covered; limited legitimacy of compromise as an objective for environmental decisionmaking. The case studies also illustrate new roles for public involvement which may provide alternative sources of access to decisionmakers and avoid costly litigation. In addition, these intervention-negotiation processes may provide solutions for interagency conflicts which cannot be litigated and often lack arrangements to negotiate between different branches of the same administration.(5) Finally, environmental mediation processes provide a socialization process for disputants which is often lacking in public hearings and to some extent, in litigation.

Origins of Environmental Mediation

Mediation has been used to resolve international and domestic conflicts for many years.(6) The most established area of conflict resolution in the United States is in the labor-management field, which has helped to develop mediation, conciliation and arbitration skills and techniques to resolve disputes over contracts, benefits and working conditions. During the mid-1960s several

59

experiments were initiated to extend these
techniques to social conflicts over schools,
prisons, hospitals, race relations and other
community conflicts.(7) Environmental mediation
is the most recent extension of these techniques.
Using mediation skills developed in both labor and
community conflict resolution, Gerald Cormick and
Jane McCarthy successfully resolved the Snoqualmie
Dam dispute described in Chapter 4 in 1974. That
same year, Donald Straus attempted to mediate the
West Side Highway dispute in New York City without
similar success (Chapter 9). The experiment did
persuade him that the field was promising, however.
Both of these two initial case studies were based
on the premise that environmental disputes are not
zero-sum dilemmas. Rather,(8)

> the adversary posture of energy versus
> environment is utter nonsense--we must have
> both or we will have neither. The question is
> not one versus the other, but a question of
> what accommodations we must make to have both,
> and not 'neither.'

Terminology

Several different techniques are employed in
the case studies which follow. Thus some care is
required in defining these approaches and in
explaining their use. Environmental mediation,
conciliation and dispute reeducation in planning,
are all used in different ways in this volume.
Here is a brief glossary of mediation terms as used
here:

MEDIATION refers to a site-specific dispute
resolution process which results in a written
settlement statement. Cormick and Patton provide
two examples of this technique in Chapter 4, the
Snoqualmie Dam dispute and the Interstate 90
dispute. They believe that this technique is best
employed after a dispute has reached an impasse,
but only if there is some flexibility available for
bargaining. The mediator helps the disputants to
formulate their concessions and settlement plan
and does not decide what the settlement will be.

CONCILIATION refers to site-specific
conflict-reducing processes which involve neutral
third parties who seek to clarify issues and
concerns, but not necessarily to resolve the
dispute. In Chapter 6 Paul Wehr describes a
project to minimize conflict over a proposed ski

resort in Eagle, Colorado. His objective is to reduce tensions and to help the local government respond to the challenges of reviewing the ski resort proposal in a balanced, informed way.

CONFLICT REDUCTION technique involve third parties who convene meetings of opposing interest groups to develop a consensus over the parameters for planning and project review before site-specific decisions are reached. Donald Straus, Laura Lake and Peter Clark describe three different versions of non-site-specific planning and decisionmaking processes which involve mediators.

All of these processes are non-judicial, voluntary, political procedures which require approval and cooperation from public officials in order to implement the recommendations of the consensus-negotiating group. The mediator has no authority to decide any issue,(9) and serves at the pleasure of the sanctioning public officials and the disputants. Thus the techniques of mediation are substantially different from the better-known process of arbitration, which involves the third party as the decisionmaker, and grants the arbitrator the authority to impose a legally binding settlement on the disputants.

Arbitration is frequently used in contractual disputes involving two parties and results in a binding settlement, whereas environmental disputes often involve many parties and the implementation of a compromise settlement involves public officials. It is possible, however, that in certain cases which lack solid legal foundations, disputants might choose arbitration, but the benefits of negotiating a settlement, rather than having one imposed, are not derived through arbitration.

The linkage with political officials is a critical factor, as shown in the West Side Highway dispute (Chapter 9), which did not develop a consensus partially because the parties to the mediation experiment did not believe that the group's recommendations would be accepted by the officials with authority to implement the recommendations (the governor and the mayor of New York City) because there had been no communication between these officials and the mediator. Similarly, in Chapter 6, Eagle County officials withdrew their endorsement of the conciliation project, and in Chapter 8, the Federal Energy Administration retroactively withdrew its support

61

for the New England Energy Policy Council's efforts to obtain a consensus on how best to comply with its order to convert 75 oil-burning power plants to coal. These weak political linkages suggest that successful mediation efforts, ' such as those described in Chapter 4, require formal authorizations and regular briefings with political officials to assure eventual implementation.

THE NEED FOR SOCIALIZATION AMONG DISPUTANTS

It was noted in Chapter 1 that among the major impacts of environmental litigation has been the displacement of interest group leaders as the negotiators for their organizations, and the decrease in opportunities for opposing group leaders to socialize, a process which is a prerequisite for future bargaining and consensus. The need for such opportunities to socialize among political opponents in the environmental field is great; many American communities have experienced severe frustration as they sought to defend their perceptions of local and regional interests against others (corporations, the federal government, environmentalists, and other states). Thus an interesting result of the recent National Coal Policy Study was the response of participants to their counterparts, i.e., the development of mutual respect among staunch opponents.(10) Another example of the socialization of opponents is provided by the statewide workshop on power plant siting (Chapter 7). Several participants in this workshop have subsequently contacted me and told me of the rapport and comraderie which was established between participants and helped them interact on other issues.

Environmental mediation also promises to be helpful in resolving interagency conflicts. In a recent study of the "Institutional Barriers to Wastewater Reuse in Southern California," conducted for the Interior Department, I found that interagency conflict over public health standard-setting practices, local-state conflicts over funding and setting the price of reclaimed water at the local level, and concerns over the management of reclaimed water as a growth-limitation strategy, were perceived as major obstacles to increased wastewater reuse by local and regional officials. These views were

62

obtained at workshops convened as dispute reduction experiment. The conclusion of this study was that environmental mediation would be helpful in resolving water pricing disputes and in developing equitable public health standards,(11) and that environmental mediation may be a useful technique to facilitate policy implementation. Similarly, federal officials have welcomed the potential for negotiations not only with environmental interest groups, but also with other agencies, so that agencies involved in a dispute do not wind up embarrassed if the conflict escalates into a crisis which requires the involvement of the President or the Office of Management and Budget.(12). For example, the Carter Administration's coal policy creates a conflict for the Department of Energy and the Environmental Protection Agency: increased coal usage generates problems for enforcing air quality standards.

While one should not be overly optimistic about the number of disputes which might be resolved though environmental conflict resolution processes, it is important to recognize the value of the residual social benefit of political efficacy developed through these processes, which remains after the problem has been resolved. The goodwill developed can be tapped when the next dispute arises.

REPRESENTATION IN NEGOTIATIONS

As noted already, several laws passed around 1970 required that agencies adopt public participation procedures.(13) Most agencies have met this requirement by holding rulemaking or "notice and comment" public hearings,(14) however, in which there is little or no dialogue or questioning, simply the presentation of prepared (or extemporaneous) testimony by individuals and interest groups which manage to free-up staff or members to attend the hearing (often with little advance notice). Thus there is often the suspicion that such hearings are pro forma compliance with public participation regulations and have little bearing on the agency's deliberations. The final result of these hearings is that a group of self-elected individuals represent the public; other individuals and groups either lack the resources or the interest to participate in hearings, even though they may be affected by the agency's decision.(15)

While public hearings perform procedural functions which create expectations of public involvement, they result frequently in frustration and futility for testifiers. This in turn creates feelings of political alienation and a breakdown of the sense of community.(16) Litigation has permitted interest groups to overcome the futility of public hearings by granting them another access point to decisionmaking, but it does not restore the sense of community. Obviously, balanced representation in decisionmaking is not any easy achievement. Yet the shortcomings of mass public access (public hearings) warrant attempts to obtain an approximation of balanced interests in order to develop a community-based consensus with which major segments of the community are willing to live. This consensus should supplement the formal hearings, and can involve non-residents who have an interest in recreation, conservation or exploitation within the neighborhood. In this way, environmental mediation processes can help to mitigate the political alienation generated by public hearings, provide a measure of self-determination to communities embroiled in environmental disputes, and simultaneously, serve to constructively advise public decisionmakers, who in the final analysis, are the ultimate responsible implementation agents.

Selection Techniques

In selecting interest group leaders for environmental mediation negotiations, the mediator has the ability to seek not only the representatives who are overtly associated with the project--the types who show up at hearings--but also those who are usually not present at hearings but who exert influence covertly. These are often community leaders who are consulted before a sensitive political decision is made.(17) Unlike two-party labor-management dispute settlement processes, equitable representation in environmental disputes poses a major challenge for mediators: the interests are diffuse, sometimes participants are only indirectly involved in the dispute, and there are multiple groups claiming to represent the same general interests, but with slightly different objectives and interests (e.g.,

hunters and wilderness preservationists). From
this universe of parties and interests, the
mediators must select a small number of
participants who will adequately represent all of
the parties. Any bias in selecting participants
can sabotage the successful implementation of the
dispute settlement plan, or even the development of
a consensus among opposing groups. For example, in
the West Side Highway dispute in New York City
(Chapter 9), several neighborhood block
associations were not involved in the mediation
sessions. These groups eventually filed suit to
stop the highway; their participation might have
made the experiment a success, and their absence
certainly contributed to its failure.

Exclusion from these administratively-
sanctioned dispute settlement processes might
provide legal cause for litigation--for example,
by violating state "sunshine" laws which require
government meetings to be open to the public, (all
of the experiments described here are confidential
processes). In addition, it will be very
important to develop selection criteria so that
participation in these negotiations is not
arbitrary or capricious. If non-judicial dispute
settlement processes are to become viable
alternatives to environmental litigation, it will
be necessary to regularize equitable, feasible
selection criteria so that the results of
negotiations are not invalid because of arbitrary
or capricious exclusion of parties.

Lessons from Administrative Law

The experience of administrative law proceedings provides a model for selecting
participants for negotiating settlements.(18)
Participants must be "responsible" and
"representative spokesmen" and should not be
involved if their interests are already
adequately represented in the administrative
hearing.

One possible exception to allowing public
intervenors unlimited participation is in
settlement negotiations. Informal negotiations might be hampered by the participation
of additional parties, and settlement is a
legitimate objective. The public
intervenor's interest would be arguably
protected in most situations by allowing the

intervenor to study the result and comment upon any proposed settlement prior to its acceptance by the agency. Exclusion of an intervenor from settlement negotiations raises the possibility, however, that the agency and the other parties may freeze him out and settle the case to his disadvantage. Public intervenors could of course challenge such settlements, and challenging should prompt scrutiny of the settlement, including a hearing if any factual issue remains in doubt.(19)

In a similar vein, it has been suggested that a proliferation of participants should not be permitted by agencies if this delays or disrupts proceedings.(20) The involvement of out-of-state parties to a dispute also presents some difficulty: national corporations, federal agencies, and national environmental protection groups may be silent or active parties to a dispute, and efforts should be made to involve them either directly or indirectly. Yet even with a gubernatorial authorization to mediate a dispute, the mediator may have difficulty bringing out-of-state parties to the bargaining table. In matters of unique national resources such as the Redwoods or the Alaskan wilderness, local decisionmakers are particularly loath to permit national environmental groups to participate in decisionmaking. In such instances, there is a national tradeoff between local economic interests which favor development and the concern of the rest of the nation that unique resources not be squandered for short-term economic gain. Equitable decisionmaking requires that outside interests, environmentalists, or business, be involved in national-local decisions such as these. Making the interests at stake explicit is a step in developing criteria for balancing local and federal interests.

A critical selection factor facing environmental mediation is whether or not the disputants perceive delay to be in their favor. As long as they seek delay, they are unlikely to enter into negotiations in good faith. Thus while selecting participants for negotiations, the mediator must also determine the motivations of the participants.

Case Study Selection Techniques

A number of different selection techniques were employed in the case studies reported in this book. Gerald Cormick and Leah Patton (Chapter 4) utilize the nomination of community influentials by knowledgeable informants to select participants. This "reputational" technique widely used since Floyd Hunter's pioneering study of community power structure,(21) has the advantage of involving persons who are either covertly or overtly involved in leadership positions and are able to "sell" negotiated settlements to broad constituencies. The problems associated with this approach are that in a large community it may be difficult to identify such influentials; newcomers are excluded who might later seek to block settlement implementation; and the selection process results in possible images of backroom elitism.

Paul Wehr (Chapter 5) conducted a "value survey" of 400 residents of Eagle, Colorado to determine what the interests of the community were before selecting representatives to speak for those interests. In this way he enhanced the probability that the participants would be representative of community interests and also able to keep the number of participants small. There is no guarantee that these representatives will have the stature to sell a settlement to the community, however.

Donald Straus' case study (Chapter 5) was designed to serve as a public participation process and thus used the "open door" technique for large public meetings. As a result, the number of participants was too large to permit socialization; the participants were self-selected; and there was no agreement that they were interested in developing a consensus, the precondition for negotiation.

Laura Lake (Chapter 7) developed a typology for selecting dispute avoidance/reduction participants for regional planning which involved five to ten leaders of interest groups which had been active in the energy policy field. Each regional workshop group was asked in advance to indicate if there were other groups in their region which had been overlooked and whose absence from the workshop would create an imbalance of views. In addition to sectoral representation (business, environment, public health, civic, local government), participants were also selected to represent communities with different levels of experience with power plants (no plant, proposed plant, existing plant) in order to sample a broad range of experience with power plant siting.

In Chapter 8 Peter Clark selected participants on the basis of two criteria: official positions as state decisionmakers or technical experts; and interest group leaders (New England influentials). The organizational aegis for his project was the New England Energy Policy Council, a blue-ribbon organization of regional influentials, much like the influentials involved in the Snoqualmie dam dispute. Within the coal project, Clark divided participants into two groups: technical and policy. The technical task force developed a data base while the policy action group made political recommendations based on the technical information and analysis of the technical task force.

Finally, participants in the West Side Highway mediation experiment (Chapter 9) were selected by a neutral person, Christopher Wright, and a party to the negotiations, the Regional Plan Association, and not by the mediator, Donald Straus. Mr. Straus did not select participants because he was not at that time familiar with the dispute. This situation seriously diminished his independence, since as one commented after the experiment terminated, they were not sure that he was aware of missing parties, or truly neutral.

With exception of the coastal zone planning case study of Donald Straus (Chapter 6), all of the cases share the common selection principle of keeping the number of face-to-face participants small while maintaining a balance among competing interest groups. Since none of the experiments-- again excepting coastal zone planning, were designed as public participation activities, the mediators were free to select small numbers of participants. Large numbers of participants should be avoided because of the greater difficulty in reaching consensus. On the other hand, public access through public hearings must be continued because administrative fairness demands that public notice and comment be permitted for all decisions--environmental mediation is not public participation and should not be substituted for it.

Although in each of the case studies in this book the mediator selected the participants in concern with the disputants, it is preferrable in future negotiations that the participants identify those persons who are necessary for the development

68

and implementation of a negotiated settlement,
thereby enhancing the mediator's neutrality. The
mediator, of course, must verify the
representativeness of participants to ascertain
whether important parties are "shut out" from
negotiations.(22)

THE ROLE OF TECHNICAL INFORMATION IN
ENVIRONMENTAL CONFLICT RESOLUTION

Each of the case studies which follow this
chapter illustrate how technical information and
expertise are used in environmental decisionmaking to resolve disputes. It has been noted
earlier that technical disputes are often
associated with environmental litigation.(23) In
addition to resolving disputes, these case studies
focus on how mediators can educate disputants with
different levels of information and expertise, and
how such information bears on formulating
concessions.

In order for participants in a dispute to
evaluate the options available to them, a certain
amount of information and technical education is
required. This information is needed after the
group has agreed on shared concerns and a desire to
reach a consensus, however. Thus, Chapter 6
illustrates the problems of providing a large
amount of technical information on the coastal zone
to participants in the absence of a particular
issue, desire for a settlement, etc. Likewise,
Chapter 7 illustrates how the public is hesitant to
play "what if" in the abstract, and is accustomed
to dealing with immediate decisions, usually in a
negative, critical role, rather than a positive
role of suggesting what they would like to see
happen. Without constructive guidance from a
diverse set of interests, administrators are
unlikely to develop mitigating measures which
might make projects acceptable in the future. For
example, in Chapter 7, it was learned that water
consumption was consistently perceived by interest
group leaders to be a very critical criterion in
selecting power plant technologies; even a "clean"
power plant might be rejected if it consumed a
large amount of water for cooling purposes. On the
other hand, Chapter 4's case study of the
Snoqualmie Dam dispute illustrates how technical
information can be used to develop new project
alternatives acceptable to all of the major

disputants. Rather than giving the Snoqualmie Dam participants a short course on dams, Gerald Cormick devoted the initial phase of mediation to ascertaining the objectives of the disputants. Only then was the Corps of Engineers brought in to present technical information on dams and on alternative sites which might meet the group's criteria.

Without denigrating the role of environmental experts, the policy implementation process is a political process which must concentrate first on the values in conflict. Technical experts should not be used as a substitute for political commitment from the participants to seek a settlement. Unless the value basis of the conflict is acknowledged and incorporated into administrative procedures, the role of the technical expert will be that of the tail wagging the dog. In disputes such as nuclear power, technical information may be essentially irrelevant. The dispute centers on individuals' willingness to take risks and on their time frames for environmental impacts.

How much technical information is necessary for sound environmental decisionmaking? This is not a new problem; as Charles Lindblom has noted, political decisionmakers are accustomed to making decisions under conditions of uncertainty, and therefore consider only the most significant factors.(24) The challenge posed for environmental decisionmakers is that they may not accurately gauge which factors are significant to interest groups, and will not have the opportunity to undo damage after a project is underway, since many environmental impacts are irreversible, or take centuries for recovery. Environmental conflict resolution processes may help decisionmakers identify what is perceived to be significant by interest groups and enable them to become more aware of the risks assumed in decisionmaking.

The political decisions faced in environmental disputes are what amount of risk and damage is society willing to accept in return for a benefit, who will benefit and who will pay the costs. Technical expertise can only answer portions of these questions; they cannot resolve a political decision of balancing competing interests under conditions of uncertainty.

Christopher Wright noted during the symposium that the dispute avoidance experiments described in Chapters 6 and 7 might generate greater conflict by educating interest groups about the

70

implications of a policy for their interests. In addition, he observed that mediation techniques are educational, but present a challenge to the mediator because participants have great differences in knowledge. He stressed that the disputes are based on value differences rather than technical disputes, per se. The challenge is to know when there is indeed a technical issue. In the absence of good fatih on the part of participants, technical information and education only serve to fuel the dispute.(25)

THE LIMITS OF COMPROMISE

In this final section of this chapter the problems of coopting legitimate conflict through negotiation processes is discussed. When is it inappropriate to resolve a dispute through compromise, and what is the role of conflict in decisionmaking?

These six initial experiments in environmental dispute resolution revealed a hesitancy on the part of small, ad hoc environmental groups to participate in negotiations. For this reason it is important that non-judicial dispute resolution processes not replace public hearings, so that smaller groups which may distrust the bargaining process retain their constitutional right to due process and be permitted to comment on administrative actions.

The dangers involved in seeking compromise include the potential of coopting emerging interest groups; the abuse of the mediation process as a delay tactic; and the assessment by the mediator that the case should not be negotiated either because compromise is not feasible or because it would bypass existing laws, violate procedural rights, or foreclose a legal precedent. While negotiation processes can be important in developing a sense of political efficacy for local residents or interests groups which might otherwise feel unfairly treated by public officials, as Helen Ingram noted during the symposium, premature compromise may result in easy but unwise settlements:

From my background as a water resources policy person, I thank God for radicals and conflict, and I get very worried about pushing early consensus because at least in traditional

71

water politics, consensus came from giving
everybody something to the detriment of the
whole environment. When one reads about
mediation cases where the compromise was to
build both a highway and the railroad /Chapter
4/ one gets a little worried that we may wind
up doing exactly that: redistributive
politics rather than redefining issues.
Sometimes, open, unresolvable conflict that
comes to an absolute deadlock is the only way
to do that education. Preferences come along
by redefining an issue another way.

People who have more power tend to be more
willing to address tradeoffs. If you really
have nothing but your radicalism to make
certain that you get a fair date in court,
then willingness to sit down in a low temper-
ature arena with a third party and take the
risk of not knowing what the result is going
to be--that's really asking quite a lot.

These observations address the quality of the
decision, the definition of issues, and the reasons
for refusing to negotiate. Very often local
land-use disputes are redistributive disputes in
which the local community wants to receive some
benefit in return for the burdens of, for example,
siting a public facility, or not exploiting a local
natural resource. Compromise can be inappropriate
when it involves the relaxation of a legal right or
environmental or pollution control standards.
Gerald Cormick noted during the symposium that
mediation should not be used to reject or to
compromise an environmental law simply because
local interests find it objectionable.
    Finally, it is important to examine what a
"fair date in court" requires and implies. Small
ad hoc groups may not be able to pay an attorney
and may not have a justiciable case. If they are
able to secure places on court dockets, there is
only fifty-fifty chance of winning, and winning may
only involve a remand to the agency to correct an
error, not the abandonment of a project. If the
group is concerned with a procedural right, then
certainly litigation is the only feasible
solution. In addition, mediation sessions do not
provide the important visibility which litigation
can provide a small group. If the dispute involves
substantive issues within the realm of
administrative discretion, however, then an

invitation to participate in voluntary negotiations is not such an unfair alternative for small groups with limited resources. In addition, many small reform groups suffer from being placed in the position of constantly upholding legal standards and opposing projects. As Cormick observed, establishment groups frequently seek to squelch community conflict through negotiation. This requires mediators to be particularly careful not to accept cases which serve to crystallize issues and are signs of a vital public spirit, and to accept cases which are dysfunctional conflicts, not serving any purpose.

To summarize the abuses of environmental mediation noted in this discussion, the following potential misapplications of mediation were identified:

1. Delaying decisionmaking through a lack of good-faith bargaining.
2. Avoiding public criticism of administrative or private corporate decisions by substituting environmental mediation for public hearings.
3. Coopting emerging groups into bargaining before they have had a chance to articulate their demands publicly.(26)
4. Seeking compromise when a legal right or a legislated standard is involved.

Environmental mediation processes are executive-administrative rather than judicial decisionmaking techniques and are only appropriate for substantive decisionmaking, not for protecting rights. Viewed as a limited process, environmental mediation may improve the quality of environmental decisionmaking by identifying mitigating measures, creating political efficacy for participants, and securing administrative decisions that reflect more equitable choices.

REFERENCES

1. Resolve Center for Environmental Mediation, Environmental Mediation: An Effective Alternative? (Palo Alto, California: Resolve, 1978), pp. 17-19.
2. I. William Zartman, "Negotiation as a Joint Decision-Making Process," Journal of Conflict Resolution (December 1976), p. 622.

3. See, for example, Clark-McGlennon Associates, Draft Guidelines for Identifying, Managing and Resolving Environmental Disputes (New York: American Arbitration Association, August, 1978).

4. Margot Hornblower, "Mediation Studies as a Way to Resolve Environmental Disputes," Washington Post, January 13, 1978, p. A-7.

5. James Wilson and Patricia Rachal, "Can the Government Regulate Itself?" The Public Interest, Vol. 46, Winter 1977, pp. 4-14.

6. Ford Foundation, Conflict Resolution and Regulation: Another Look (New York: Office of Reports, The Ford Foundation, September 1977).

7. Ibid.

8. Donald Straus, No Winners--Only Losers or Mutual Victories (New York: American Arbitration Association, 1978), p. 2. (Mimeographed.) Laura M. Lake, "Mediating Environmental Disputes," Ekistics (September 1977), pp. 164-170.

9. "The mediator's 'power' may largely derive from the simple fact that he is there and that his help is badly needed." Lond Fuller, "Mediation--Its Forms and Functions," Southern California Law Review, Vol. 44 (1961), p. 315; and Jackson Baur, "Mediating Environmental Disputes," Western Sociological Review, Vol. 8, No. 1, (1977), pp. 16-24.

10. Reference 1, supra.

11. Laura M. Lake, The Politics of Delay: A Decade of Intergovernmental Environmental Policy Implementation (in preparation).

12. Cynthia Enloe, Environmental Politics from a Comparative Perspective (New York: David McKay, Co., Inc., 1975), pp. 177-178.

13. Bruce Bishop, "Public Participation in Environmental Impact Assessment," in Marlan Blissett, ed., Environmental Impact Assessment (New York: Engineering Foundation, 1976), pp. 219-236.

14. Kenneth Davis, Administrative Law (St. Paul: West Publishing Co., 1977), pp. 241-269; Walter Gellhorn and Clark Byse, Administrative Law (Mineola, New York: Foundation Press, 1974), pp. 731-752.

15. E.E. Schattschneider noted in Semi-Sovereign People (1960) that "the flaw in the pluralist heaven is that the heavenly chorus sings with a strong upper class accent. Probably 90 percent of the population cannot get into the pressure system,'" quoted in Cobb and Elder,

Participation in American Politics: The Dynamics
of Agenda-Building (Boston: Allyn and Bacon,
1972), p. 21.

16. William A. Gamson, "Rancorous Conflict
in Community Politics," in Willis Hawley and F.
Wirt, The Search for Community Power (Englewood
Cliffs, New Jersey: Prentice-Hall, 1968), p. 252;
Ralph Nader, "Consumerism and Legal Services: The
Merging of Movements," Law and Society Review, Vol.
11, 1976, p. 248.

17. Matthew Crenson, The Unpolitics of Air
Pollution (Baltimore: Johns Hopkins University
Press, 1971), p. 177.

18. Gellhorn, op cit., pp. 207-209.

19. Ibid.

20. Ibid.

21. Floyd Hunter, Community Power Structures: A Study of Decision-Makers (Garden City, New
York: Doubleday, 1953).

22. Clark-McGlennon, op cit.

23. Dan Turlock and Marcia Gelpe, "The Uses
of Scientific Information in Environmental
Decisionmaking," in Southern California Law
Review, Vol. 48, 1974, pp. 371-427.

24. Chalres Lindblom, The Intelligence of
Democracy (New York: The Free Press, 1965),
pp. 139, 145, 177-178.

25. Dorothy Nelkin, Technological Decisions
and Democracy: European Experiments in Political
Participation (Beverly Hills: Sage Publications,
1977).

26. Crenson, op cit.

4

Environmental Mediation:
Defining the Process Through Experience

Gerald W. Cormick and Leota K. Patton

INTRODUCTION

The Office of Environmental Mediation at the University of Washington in Seattle, Washington, was established to assist disputing individuals, groups, organizations and agencies to reconcile their differences. Supported by the Ford Foundation and the Rockefeller Foundation, the Office is part of a continuing attempt to apply third party dispute resolution techniques to non-labor social conflicts in the United States. The effort began in 1973 when Office Director Gerald W. Cormick and colleague and former Co-director Jane E. McCarthy began an assessment of the possibilities of applying the negotiation/mediation process to environmental disputes. An extensive series of discussions with representatives of parties to major environmental conflicts indicated an eagerness to explore new avenues for resolving their differences. These discussions and an independent review of the elements of a variety of disputes suggested that at some point in the development of many environmental disputes, the negotiation process facilitated by mediation might be an appropriate means of resolving conflict.

As a result of this assessment, it was decided that an experimental effort should be made to mediate an on-going environmental conflict. That first mediation effort was in a dispute (described below) concerning flood control, river basin planning, recreation and urban growth.

During that formative period the effort, then known as the Environmental Mediation Project, was based at Washington University in St. Louis, Missouri. In June, 1975, the Project relocated as

the Office of Environmental Mediation in the
Institute for Environmental Studies, an
interdisciplinary research and teaching program at
the University of Washington.

ENVIRONMENTAL MEDIATION: AN OPERATIONAL
DEFINITION

Environmental disputes are those social
conflicts emerging over issues of resource use and
allocation. Such issues include concerns over land
use, facilities siting, pollution control, the
depletion of non-renewable resources and the
management of renewable resources.
Environmental disputes differ substantially
from the classic two-party labor-management
dispute model from which most definitions of the
mediation process--and the role of the mediator in
that process--are drawn. For example, in contrast
to the two well-defined and balanced adversaries in
labor-management disputes, environmental conflicts
typically involve a number of parties of varying
status and power, ranging from citizen groups and
private corporations to public agencies and
elected officials. Whereas in labor-management
relations legislation and experience have evolved
into a clearly defined framework for the
negotiation process, the framework for
negotiations and third party intervention in
environmental disputes must be created as an
integral part of a specific dispute resolution
process. Moreover, while in the labor-management
relationship such issues as wages, management
rights and due process are amenable to review and
renegotiation on a continuing basis, environmental
disputes often concern issues of a relatively
irreversible nature.
As a result, while the essential definition of
the mediation process may remain constant whether
applied in international diplomacy, in labor-
management relations or in environmental
conflicts, the situational variables which impact
on its implementation vary substantially from one
area to another. The purpose of creating an
operational definition for a process such as
mediation is to identify that set of situational
variables which will determine whether or not the
process will actually function in a given instance.
This paper, therefore, offers the following
operational definition of the "mediation process"

as it applies to environmental disputes. It has served and continues to serve as the operating definition of mediation as implemented by the Office of Environmental Mediation and should serve as the point of departure whenever reference is made to the mediation efforts of the Office.

A definition of mediation offered by a variety of labor relations oriented authors serves as an adequate general definition of the basic process. Paraphrased from several sources, the Office provides the following broad definition in its literature and brochures:

> Mediation is a voluntary process in which those involved in a dispute jointly explore and reconcile their differences. The mediator has no authority to impose a settlement. His or her strength lies in the ability to assist the parties in resolving their own differences. The mediated dispute is settled when the parties themselves reach what they consider to be a workable solution.

There are a series of important considerations in this brief definition: 1) The involvement of the parties in the mediation process is voluntary. 2) There will be a joint or face-to-face exploration of the issues, albeit supported by caucuses of one or more individual parties with the mediator. 3) The mediator does not have the authority to impose settlement. The Office makes a further commitment that should joint agreement not be achieved, neither it nor the mediators it appoints will make public recommendations or report on areas of agreement or disagreement. 4) The mediator facilitates the negotiation process by assisting the parties to reach a resolution acceptable to them. Unlike labor mediation where the mediator usually enters a dispute subsequent to a breakdown in the negotiation process, in environmental disputes the mediator may be required to initiate the negotiation process, facilitate the negotiations themselves, and assist in devising a process for joint implementation of any agreement which may be reached where no institutional relationship between the parties previously existed. 5) The mediator shares the responsibility of ensuring that any agreement reached represents a workable solution--one which is politically, physically, and financially feasible. This responsibility on the part of the

mediator increases in an inverse relationship to
the experience and sophistication of the least
skilled party to the dispute.

The above discussion presents the broad
definition of the mediation process which the
Office of Environmental Mediation explores with
parties considering the possible application of
mediation in disputes in which they are involved.
However, additional considerations are essential
in applying this general definition to specific
environmental disputes. In order to ensure that
our Office offers its services only in situations
in which mediation is both ethically and
practically appropriate, we have developed the
following additional criteria.

It is through the application of this set of
criteria that the general definition of mediation
is made appropriate to the settlement of environmental conflicts. Together these criteria
describe the situations within which the process
may be effectively applied. These criteria are
explicitly discussed with the parties to a dispute
in order that they themselves can better assess the
desirability of participating in a mediation
process.

1. Mediation involves the use of "third party
   intervenor(s)" who work from an impartial
   base.
   Mediation techniques are used in some
   degree by most people in our society.
   Parents attempting to help children settle
   their own arguments, lawyers negotiating
   to achieve an out-of-court settlement, and
   elected officials working to create
   consensus among constituents on
   legislative action all use the techniques
   of mediation to decrease conflict.
   However, the formal use of the mediation
   process implies the intervention of a
   third party whose primary role is to
   promote agreement among conflicting
   parties. This third party intervenor, or
   mediator, has no power to impose
   solutions, as does the parent or elected
   official. Neither can the mediator be an
   advocate for any of the conflicting
   parties, as is the lawyer. It is essential
   that the mediator work from an impartial
   base. A perception by any of the partries
   to a dispute that the mediator is directly

79

supported by or beholden to any interest group which is a party to that dispute not only destroys the credibility of the mediator, but also creates broad distrust of the legitimacy of the mediation process. A mediator supported primarily by industrial groups may create the impression that mediation is another mechanism to grease the wheels for development. Likewise, a mediator supported primarily by environmental groups may be perceived as offering another means for delay.

2. Mediation is a decisionmaking process.

This stipuation has become of critical concern as the mediation of environmental disputes has become an increasingly popular concept. There have been attempts to redefine and revive the planning and citizen involvement processes by calling them "mediation." Unfortunately, masquerading an otherwise legitimate citizen participation process under an assumed name only misleads the participants and generates suspicions regarding the efficacy of employing any mediation process.

The use of the mediation process requires that adversaries move beyond their publicly held positions. Unless there is a commitment by the appropriate agencies or other implementing bodies that the mediation process will result in decisionmaking, the parties may unwittingly prejudice their future stands before the real decisionmakers. The mediators must therefore be satisfied and able to make a commitment to the parties that, if they are willing to make accommodations in order to achieve agreement, that agreement will be implemented by the appropriate agencies.

3. Mediation requires some relative balance of power between the several parties.

The parties to a dispute will be willing to enter with "good faith" into the negoti- ation-mediation process to the extent that they are unable to act unilaterally in what they perceive to be their own best interest. Therefore, unless the parties directly involved in a dispute have some relative ability to exercise sanctions over one another, there is slim possibility that good faith mediation will occur.

Legislation and case law in the U.S. have served to create a relative power situation in the environmental arena, often through the ability of the parties to use a variety of processes to delay implementation. On the one hand, corporate and other groups wishing to do something can delay imposition of limiting standards or policies through appeals and variances, often while carrying on business as usual. Such delay can bring irreversible consequences (such as in timber harvesting or land development). On the other hand, environmental groups can delay implementation of projects through strategic use of public hearings, the permit process and the courts. Such delay can cause costs to escalate (as in new plant construction), perhaps to the point where a particular project is no longer financially feasible.

There are also a variety of other sanctions. Environmental groups often find themselves in the position of "always being against everything." Unfavorable publicity can have broad implications for a corporation. Public agencies who are often caught in the middle of such disputes may reap negative appraisals from all sides.

It is where such a relative power balance occurs that it is in the best interest of the parties to seek some natural accommodation of their differences. Where such a balance does not exist one or another party may merely use the process to their own advantage by further delaying action on decisions.

4. <u>Mediation is appropriate when an impasse has been reached</u>.

Mediation is a tool for resolving impasse. In the labor relations context such impasses are usually the result of a breakdown in the negotiation process. In environmental and other social disputes

81

where no established bargaining relationship exists, the impasse may occur before negotiations have begun, since there is no legitimate arena for an exploration of issues in a shared decisionmaking format.

We have found it necessary to operationally define mediation as occurring at a point _after_ an impasse has been reached. This is directly related to our concern outlined above that, unless the parties have developed and displayed a relative capacity to exercise sanctions, one on the other, they are unlikely to enter good faith bargaining directed toward accommodations of their differences.

Pre-impasse mediation is also more likely to fall into the citizen involvement format in which agreement does not necessarily lead to decisions and implementation.

There are a number of other felicitous (for meaningful bargaining) circumstances which typically occur at the point of impasse. These include:

a) the issues are defined;
b) the parties are visible and highly involved;
c) there is some sense of urgency; and
d) there is at least a dawning realization that none of those concerned can unilaterally achieve their objectives at reasonable cost.

5. <u>Mediation will result in compromises being made</u>.

The word "compromise" has strong negative connotations. It may often be tempting for the mediator to suggest that all of the parties will "win." In fact, relative to present realistic expectations, all parties may only be relatively "better off" if an accommodation can be achieved than they would have been if the conflict had followed its present course. If this ability to be "better off" did not exist, there would be no reason to enter into the mediation process. However, the parties are not likely to gain all that they would desire through mediation.

At times, however, we may misapply the concept of compromise.

The decisionmaking process, as it relates to environmental disputes, has two distinct phases: (1) establishing priorities and (2) developing programs to accomplish those priorities. There will always be legitimate differences in priorities among persons with varying perspectives and divergent aspirations. These might include, on an international scale, questions of agricultural production and human settlements vs. wildlife and wilderness protection, and on a local level, questions of urban and industrial growth vs. farmland and open space. But differences in priorities cannot be dealt with in terms of "right" and "wrong"--all are "right" or legitimate. To accommodate these differences, therefore, is not a "compromise" in the sense of doing something less than what is "best." It is determining what is best.

Only after determining priorities is it possible to legitimately proceed to develop solutions and programs. It is here that there may well be determinable "best" decisions. If there is a consensus as to what the priorities should be, there is much less danger that disagreements will be translated into unfortunate compromises and second-best solutions.

Saul Alinsky, a man believed by many to be an "uncompromising" advocate for civil rights, observed:

"Compromise is another word that carries shades of weakness, vacillation, betrayal of ideals, surrender of morals principles. In the old culture, when virginity was a virtue, one referred to a woman's being compromised." The word is generally regarded as ethically unsavory and ugly.

But to the organizer, compromise is a key and beautiful word. It is always present in the pragmatics of operation.

It is making the deal, getting the vital breather, usually the victory.

If you start with nothing, demand 100 percent, then compromise for 30 percent, you're 30 percent ahead."(1)

To summarize the following is the general definition of mediation, as employed by the Office of Environmental Mediation:

Mediation is a voluntary process in which those involved in a dispute jointly explore and reconcile their differences. The mediator has no authority to impose a settlement. His or her strength lies in the ability to assist the parties in resolving their own differences. The mediated dispute is settled when the parties themselves reach what they consider to be a workable solution.

This general definition of mediation is made applicable to environmental disputes by the following additional criteria:

1. Mediation involves the use of "third-party intervenor(s)" who work from an impartial base;

2. Mediation is a decisionmaking process;

3. Mediation requires some relative balance of power between the parties;

4. Mediation is appropriate when an impasse has been reached; and

5. Mediation will result in compromises being made.

MEDIATION EXPERIENCE OF THE OFFICE
OF ENVIRONMENTAL MEDIATION

The operational definition presented above does not constrain the mediated process to a single doctrinaire approach. The Snoqualmie and I-90 disputes described below meet the criteria of that definition. However, that common basic orientation nevertheless resulted in different formats which met the needs of those specific

84

situations. Mediators must avoid the temptation of
forcing dispute situations to fit some format which
they have developed rather than recognizing the
specific realities attending a conflict.

The Snoqualmie Dispute

The Snoqualmie-Snohomish River basin (see
Figure 4-1) forms a green bracket around the
eastern edge of the Seattle metropolitan area. The
river basin can be divided into three distinct
sectors: (1) the upper valleys of the North, South
and Middle Forks of the Snoqualmie which flow
through steep alpine valleys; (2) the middle valley
which stretches from the confluence of the three
forks of the river and includes two towns of about
12,000 population each; and (3) the lower valley
from the base of the Falls to Puget Sound, where
the river meanders through rich farmlands.

Following a serious flood in 1959, the local
county sponsored a U.S. Army Corps of Engineers
study which eventually resulted in a proposal to
build a flood control dam on the Middle Fork. The
residents of the middle valley supported the
proposed dam as it would give "100 year" flood protection to their homes and businesses. The farmers
in the lower valley endorsed the proposal because
it promised "30-year" flood protection from crop-
damaging spring floods. A coalition of environmental and citizen groups opposed the dam on the
grounds that it would open the flood plain to urban
sprawl, interrupt a free-flowing river and was
unjustified on a benefit-cost basis.

Under existing Corps practice, the Governor
of a State must approve any major Corps project
before federal funding will be sought. In late
1972 Washington Governor Evans opposed the dam, as
proposed, on the grounds that it would be
"environmentally disruptive." However, the
Governor expressed his continuing concern over the
flooding problem. The 1972 action led to a joint
Corps of Engineers-State study of alternatives
which in late 1973 again found the proposed Middle
Fork Dam to be the best flood control proposal.
The Governor stated in his continuing opposition to
that alternative but indicated that some step had
to be taken to resolve what many felt to be a
worsening flood problem.

Those opposed to the proposed dam, meanwhile,
were in the posture of waging delaying actions
against each new proposal without being able to

Figure 4-1. The Snoqualmie-Snohomish River Basin

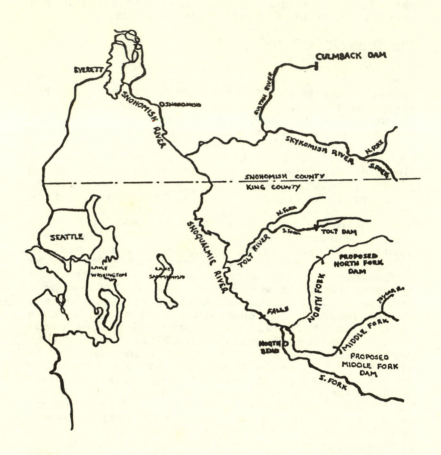

confront their primary concern, which was land-use
planning for the basin. Those seeking flood
control, on the other hand, were faced with
continuing economic hardship in terms of damage to
crops, homes, businesses and public works. There
was a growing realization that each of the several
groups had a form of "veto power." For the
foreseeable future, through mobilizing political
and legal opposition, the environmentalists could
effectively halt flood control efforts.
Conversely, those who were seeking flood control
could prevent, through the same legal and political
processes, any coordinated planning effort in the
valley, inevitably leading to unplanned growth and
sprawl. Without the Governor's support, the Corps
would not undertake any project. And, without the
support of the Corps, necessary federal funds would
not be available.

The Environmental Mediation Project (EMP)
became involved in the dispute in late 1973.
Preliminary discussions were held with the State
and the Corps, the primary decisionmaking bodies,
to determine whether or not they would support
mediation of the dispute. Based on initial
contacts with the various "parties" (environmentalists, farmers, residents and public
officials) and a first assessment of the issues, it
was determined that mediation could be a useful
tool in resolving the impasse and that there was a
reasonable expectation that a consensus could lead
directly to the implementation of any agreement.

The EMP then discussed with the Governor the
possibility of his formally appointing the Project
Director and Assistant Director (Gerald W.
Cormick and Jane E. McCarthy) as mediators.
Following the voluntary commitment from the
parties involved to participate and an assessment
by the prospective mediators that a good faith
effort was possible, the Governor formally
appointed Cormick and McCarthy on May 7, 1974. The
Governor requested a report on their progress by
June 30, 1974.

An immediate task, already under way, was to
define the parties to the mediation effort. Public
hearings records and other sources indicated
leading spokesmen for various positions. The
mediators conferred with these and many others,
describing the process, discussing the dispute and
asking, "Who are the ten or twelve persons who, if
they could agree on something, have the kind of
influence and stature such that the various

groups--farmers, environmentalists, etc.--could reasonably be expected to support them and any agreement they might reach?" About ten names of persons who represented all important positions and shades of opinion in the conflict emerged from this lengthy process, and these ten became the "core group" for the mediation effort.

The core group participated on the understanding that, while they were not <u>formal</u> representatives of any organization, they were responsible for representing the concerns of their "natural" constituencies and for ensuring that those constituencies would support them in any positions taken or decisions reached.

The mediators provided a link to the key parties not "at the table." These parties included the Governor, the Corps of Engineers, and county and state officials. These linkages were dessential in order to ensure that the emerging recommendations would be translated into public policy at the local, state and federal levels of government. The mediaton team had made a commitment to both the citizens directly involved and to the decisionmaking agencies that, unless such support was assured, the process would be aborted.

Several initial points were established which proved an important impetus to the discussions. The environmentalists discovered that the farmers did not wish to sell their land to subdividers and would, in fact, support stringent controls to prevent such development. The residents of the towns and surrounding areas began to listen to and understand the development concerns of the environmentalists and recognized that uncontrolled development would make the valley less desirable to them as well. The environmentalists discovered that sprawl was occurring legally and illegally despite the floodilng, and that continued flooding was not, in itself, an adequate tool for growth control. The environmentalists also began to perceive that any "win" predicated only on delay was temporary and that a future serious flood--as was to occur in December, 1975--could not only lead to a dam being built but to the environmentalists being blamed for damages and injuries. The focus became, "How do we provide some level of flood control, ensure the continued economic viability of the farmers and the towns, and build the kind of land use plans and controls that maintain the valley as a greenbelt with broad recreational value?"

At the end of June, the mediators reported to the Governor that meaningful progress was being made and their mandate was extended to September 30. By the end of September a tentative agreement had begun to take shape.

On December 6th, after two months of painstaking effort to formalize the tentative agreement in specific provisions and final language, all of the participants in the mediation effort signed a set of joint recommendations to be forwarded to the Governor.

The recommendations begin with a preamble that states:

"These jointly agreed upon recommendations stipulate a specific course of action that will lead to the development of a comprehensive land use plan which provides needed flood protection and at the same time preserves and maintains the hydrologic, ecologic and economic character of the Snohomish river basin. It emphasizes the need for coordinated planning for land use and flood protection in an area containing forty separate and often overlapping governmental jurisdictions.

The specific items included in these joint-recommendations are acceptable only as a total package" (emphasis added).(2)

The joint commitment on a total package basis has served to maintain the level of effort and support of all those involved--either all of the parties will achieve what they have agreed to or the entire agreement is void.

The agreement provides for (1) a multipurpose flood control, hydroelectric, recreation and water supply dam on the North Fork (rather than the Middle Fork) of the Snoqualmie; (2) a system of setback levees in the middle valley in natural flood storage and recreational use; (3) controlling patterns of development through the purchase of floodway easements and development rights; and (4) the establishment of a basin planning council to coordinate planning for the entire river basin. The agreement also provided for appointment by the Governor of an "interim committee" to oversee the implementation of the agreement. This interim committee is composed of participants in the mediation process along with a number of other citizens and receives technical assistance from various federal, state and local agencies.

In summary, the agreement resulted in the support of environmental groups for a major flood control structure, the commitment by farmers and urban dwellers in the basin to support substantial limitations on the use of their land, and the formation of an implementation group to ensure that flood control and land use planning proceeded simultaneously. All of the parties to the mediation process realize that without the continued support of all involved for the particular concerns of each, none of the agreement will be implemented. This "package" concept has served well as a means of binding the parties to the agreement.

On December 17, 1974, in a press conference called to announce the agreement, Governor Evans stated that he "thoroughly endorse(d)" the recommendations, forwarded those recommendations to the Corps of Engineers, and announced the formation of the interim committee to oversee implementation of the agreement. Prior to the press conference, the Governor had received letters of formal support for the agreement from the Washington Environmental Council, the League of Women Voters, the Sierra Club, the Alpine Lakes Protection Society, and the Valley Greenbelt Association (the farmers' organization), as well as from officials of the towns in the valley. Feature coverage from both the print and electronic media emphasized the broad endorsement received for the agreement, thereby publicizing and strengthening those commitments.

Since that time the implementation has proceeded on schedule. Both the planning for flood control structures and the design and implementation of the land use standards and mechanisms are under way and partially achieved.

THE INTERSTATE 90 DISPUTE

The original plan to extend Interstate 90 (I-90) westward from the east side of Lake Washington into downtown Seattle was approved nearly 20 years ago (see Figure 4-2). That plan envisioned 26 lanes crossing the lake on various bridges, but over the years the project had been scaled down. The 1975 Washington State Department of Highways design called for 10 lanes: 4 automobile lanes in

90

Figure 4-2. Interstate 90 and the Seattle Area
Transportation Network

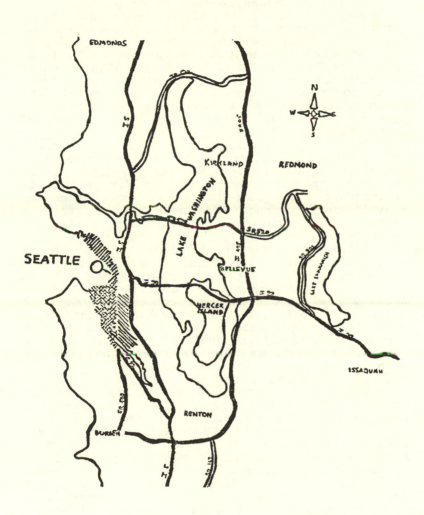

each direction and 2 transit lanes (commonly referred to as 4-2T-4).

Actively opposed to the 4-2T-4 proposal were various environmental and transit-oriented citizen groups and appointed and elected officials from the City of Seattle. The Department of Highways design was supported by the commuter cities of Bellevue and Mercer Island. The local county (King County) was generally in favor of the proposal, while Metro (the county-wide transit agency) needed the transit capacity and was willing to support any reasonable design which included designated transit lanes.

The City of Seattle had most recently expressed its opposition to the 4-2T-4 design in a resolution in January, 1976. The principal reason for their opposition was that the City wished to accommodate the increasing peak-hour commuter travel demand through development of the transit system rather than through additional automobile capacity.

Citizen opposition to I-90 was based on opposition to the development of any major transportation corridor serving commuters on the basis that such transportation facilities encourage urban sprawl. Others were concerned about the noise, air pollution and aesthetic blight which could result from such a facility. Finally, over the years of conflict some citizens had come to completely distrust the Highway Department's methods and procedures, and wished to "teach the Highway Department a lesson."

The citizens opposed to I-90 construction had successfully delayed the project through the Seattle City Council and the courts. The City Council had been fairly responsive to their concerns and opposed the 4-2T-4 design. The State Department of Highways had been delayed by legal action on the adequacy of the environmental impact statement and other, largely procedural, issues. Estimates of how much longer the project could be tied up in court varied from one to five years. The $500 million plus project was escalating in cost at an estimated $140,000 per day.

Citizens and elected officials in Bellevue and Mercer Island fully supported the 4-2T-4 design. These communities house the commuters who endure the traffic snarls and admittedly unsafe conditions on the present facility. Recognizing the enormous cost of any construction across the lake and into the city, Mercer Island and Bellevue

92

residents wished to assure that, at the end of the 6 to 8 year construction period, the facility would be large enough to accommodate peak-hour travel demand. Given that the existing facility operating with 3 lanes in the peak direction was usually congested and slow-moving, they believed 4-2T-4 to be the minimum design which could satisfy their needs.

The King County Council had expressed a compromise position. They supported constructing a facility which in the first state would have 3 automobile lanes in each direction plus 2 transit lanes (3-2T-3), but which would be expandable at a later date to 4-2T-4. They were anxious to find some acceptable compromise to avoid the large amount of federal funds available for the I-90 project being lost to the region. However, the compromise which they suggested was acceptable to neither side.

Officials in Metro were also anxious that the funds for building the bridge across Lake Washington not be lost to the region. Presently, Metro's buses become tied up in automobile traffic congestion and thus are not able to provide fast and efficient service from the east side into downtown Seattle. Dedicated transit lanes across Lake Washington and into the City would solve that problem. Metro did not have funds available for construction of such a transit facility and, consequently, had supported any highway design which provided transit lanes.

Events had reached an impasse by the beginning of 1976. The Department of Highways had issued a new draft environmental impact statement, which had been required by the courts as a result of a citizens group lawsuit. The State Highway Commission, which has ultimate decisionmaking authority, was reviewing hearing records and the response to the draft impact statement in order to decide whether the 4-2T-4 design would be the basis for the final environmental impact statement. The Commission realized that in order to receive state and federal funding for this project, they needed the full support of all the local jurisdictions. The Commission, as well as the other supporters of the 4-2T-4 design, recognized that it was highly unlikely that federal funding would be forthcoming in the face of Seattle's active opposition. However, other attempts at accommodation among the local jurisdictions (such as King County's combined 3-2T-3/4-2T-4 suggestion) had failed.

93

The Office of Environmental Mediation first began to consider involvement in the I-90 controversy in mid-February 1976, after being approached by various parties to the dispute. Extensive discussion with all of the major parties and individuals involved made it clear to the mediators, Gerald W. Cormick and Leota K. Patton, that the I-90 dispute had reached a stage where use of the mediation process was appropriate. An impasse clearly had developed. The issues were defined and the parties were highly visible. None of the parties were achieving their objectives. Additional automobile capacity was not being constructed; neither was transit being improved across Lake Washington. All parties to the dispute felt an increasing sense of urgency as the prospect heightened that all federal funds for the I-90 project would be lost to the region.

After extensive discussions with all of the parties and with the informal concurrence of Seattle, Bellevue, Mercer Island, Metro and the Highway Commission, the Governor apointed Cormick and Patton of the Office of Environmental Mediation at a press conference on March 16, 1976.

The Office had established its reputation as an appropriate and impartial base for mediators through its work in the Snoqualmie dispute in Washington state. However, impartiality is a fragile attribute. One local reporter initially questioned whether mediators based at the University of Washington could be impartial because a leading citizen opponent of the I-90 plan is the wife of the former Dean of the University of Washington law school. However, after checking with supporters of the I-90 plan, the reporter was reassured of the mediators' credibility.

In this case the participants in the mediation process were elected officials formally representing the four jurisdictions and representatives of the Department of Highways and Metro. The State Highway Commission, which has the legal decisionmaking authority over interstate highway design, was represented through the Director of the Department of Highways. The Commission had endorsed the mediation process and was prepared to implement the results of such a process, insofar as it was legally and financially possible. Because the Commission was represented at the negotiating table, they were protected from the possibility that an agreement might be reached which was not possible for them to implement.

During the many months of mediation, the formal negotiating sessions were open to the public and attended by the various advocates and covered by the media. Several were televised in part. The mediators maintained a communications link with the various citizen groups to enable them to work effectively through their elected representatives. Outside of the formal meetings the mediators carried messages, researched points of concern and initiated discussions among those directly involved in order to clarify positions and perspectives.

After failure by one or another of the parties to ratify a series of preliminary agreements, agreement in principle was achieved in early November. After some language clarification and formal ratification by the several bodies, that "Memorandum Agreement" was signed on December 21, 1976, in a public ceremony presided over by Governor Evans. Signatories to the agreement were the mayors of Seattle, Bellevue, and Mercer Island; The King County Executive, the Chairman of the State Highway Commission and the Chairman of the Metro Executive Board.

The agreement calls for a 3-2T-3 configuration with special provisions for access to the transit lanes for carpools and general traffic originating on Mercer Island. The improvements in the I-90 facility are to be accomplished in conjunction with major transit improvements in other urban corridors and transit inter-connections to the central cities of Seattle and Bellevue. Provision is made for determining means for limiting automobile access to I-90 during peak hours east of presently developed suburban areas. The facility will be lidded-over through portions of Seattle and Mercer Island in order to minimize the environmental impacts and to encourage urban redevelopment. Finally, provision is made for joint committees, composed of citizens and elected officials, to assist in planning and oversee implementation.

Once again, the agreement was developed as a package and the language specifies that the various aspects, such as highway construction in the I-90 corridor and transit improvements elsewhere, should proceed in concert. Funding must be approved for the entire I-90 project, including amenities, before construction may begin. Thus, while no elected body may bind its successors, the agreement is designed in such a manner as to require the continued cooperation of the parties since the support of each is predicated upon the implementation of the entire agreement.

CONCLUSIONS

We wish to reemphasize that, while there are certain inviolable criteria which provide an operational definition of the mediation process, that process is capable of a variety of configurations. For example, one variation apparent from the above discussion is that in the Snoqualmie dispute the central mediation effort was carried out between private citizens, while the mediation provided a link to elected officials and the responsible agencies. In contrast, the I-90 mediation process was primarily between elected officials and agencies, whlie the mediators provided a link to concerned and powerful citizen groups.

A dispute in which the Office of Environmental Mediation is presently formally involved centers around questions relating to future development of a major port. The issues which have been raised include the use of dredging, dredge spoils disposal, protection of wildlife habitat, recreational opportunities and jobs. The format for that mediation process is a citizen group constructed in a similar fashion to that devised in the Snoqualmie Dispute, but working constantly with a technical advisory group selected from affected federal, state and local agencies.

Our greatest concern for the future continues to be the development of a definable process known as "mediation" in order that prospective users of the process have some reasonable expectation of what their involvement will entail and of what outcomes might be expected to result.

We have no quarrel with other processes-- indeed a multiplicity of processes is required for the wide variety of situations which are faced. However, those of us who are purporting to practice mediation have an ethical responsibility to those who seek our mediation services to ensure that mediation has certain broadly established charac- teristics upon which they may make an informed decision.

REFERENCES

1. Saul Alinsky, Rules for Radicals (New York: Random House, 1971), p. 59.

2. Recommendations for Land Use Planning and Flood Control for the Snohomish River Basin (Seattle, Washington: December 17, 1974). (Mimeographed.)

5
Environmental Conciliation

Paul Wehr

INTRODUCTION

Rural communities in Western Colorado are under increasing pressure to permit exploitation of valuable energy, recreation and water resources. The conflict generated as local governments and their constituents are pressed to approve or disapprove such projects is often severe. This chapter describes a university-based effort at applying conciliation techniques to a dispute over a proposed ski resort in one Western Slope Colorado county. The conciliation effort tests the proposition that citizens of local political units can, through a citizen costing (evaluation) process, resolve disagreement over an environmental issue by approximating consensus on the positive or negative value of a specific proposal.

The objective of this conciliation effort is to facilitate the articulation of the underlying values of citizens which collide over this site-specific dispute, and to develop a consensus regarding the project so that political officials can determine if it should be approved, modified or vetoed.

THE SETTING

There is something for everyone and every occasion in Lewis Carroll and I begin my remarks with what seems an appropriate lead-in passage of his because it aptly suggests the nature of environmental politics in Colorado(1):

'I don't think they play at all fairly,' Alice
began, in a rather complaining tone, 'and they
quarrel so dreadfully one can't hear oneself
speak--and they don't seem to have any rules
in particular:

at least, if there are, nobody attends to
them--and you've no idea how confusing it
is. . . .

We like to think that our research is helping
to establish some rules and procedures for
producing local environmental decisions out of
current conflict and confusion.

Colorado is a state with special potential for
environmental and resource-related conflict.
There are two major reasons for this.

Environmental and resource decisions most
often involve a number of governmental agencies and
levels since nearly 50 percent of the state's land
area is federally-owned. The resources thereon are
managed by federal agencies including the U.S.
Forest Service, the Bureau of Land Management, the
National Park Service, the Bureau of Reclamation,
the U.S. Fish and Wildlife Service and the Energy
Research and Development Agency. Certain federal
mineral resources--for example, 73 percent of the
federal coal in Moffat and Routt counties--
underlie private land, a factor further
complicating resource decisionmaking. Federal and
private surface ownership in a coal-rich section of
Northwest Colorado is arranged in checkerboard
fashion. Local and state government agencies are
increasingly outlining decisional responsibility
for themselves in these areas, as well. Thus,
viewed both vertically and horizontally, the
number of governmental units participating in
environmental/resource decisions is substantial,
as is the corresponding need for coordination and
conflict management among and within these units.

A second condition stimulating environmental
and resource conflict within the state is the great
quantity and variety of resources here. An energy
map of a section of northwestern Colorado indicates
how abundant fossil and synthetic fuel potential is
in one of several energy areas in the state
(oil/gas, coal, oil shale--to the South uranium).
Plans to exploit this potential are reflected in
Figure 5-1, and still further in energy facilities
projected for the state (Table 5-1).

Figure 5-1. Historical and Projected Coal Production from Study Region

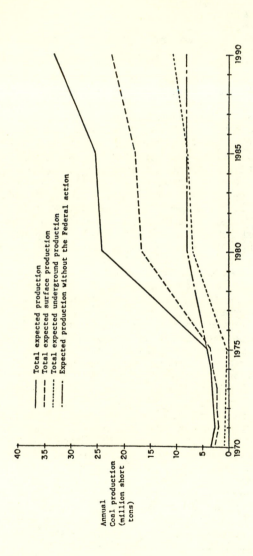

Total expected production
Total expected surface production
Total expected underground production
Expected production without the Federal action

Annual
Coal production
(million short
tons)

Table 5-1. Projected Facilities for Colorado

1)	Coal Mines (underground and strip)	35	(total production ca. 51 million tons/year by 1980)
2)	Oil Shale (mine/retort complexes)	7	(total production ca. 355,000 bls/day)
3)	Coal Gasification	1	
4)	Coal Liquefaction (slurry pipe lines)	2	(water requirements from 8-15,000 AF/Y)
5)	Electricity Generating Plants		
	a. Coal-fired	16	(6280 megawatts)
	b. Nuclear-powered	1	(1100 megawatts)
	c. Hydro-electric	4	(297 megawatts)
			(7677 megawatts) Total

A winter sports and outdoor recreation map would show a similar abundance of skiable peaks, wild rivers and wilderness areas throughout what is called out here in "high country."

A water map of Colorado would show a number of major rivers such as the Colorado, Platte, Arkansas and Rio Grande originating in the state and feeding the most arid regions of the nation. Coal and oil shale development, to the degree that it takes place, will claim much of this water.

By way of illustration, of the proposed water impoundment storage in the Yampa River Basin alone, which will store ca 1,902,000 AF/Y, 1,562,800 or 82 percent is committed principally to energy development, and the general assumption among responsible development, and the general assumption among responsible officials is that a larger portion than that will be diverted from agricultural and other uses as needed for energy development (Table 5-2).

As demands for energy, water and outdoor recreational space have increased sharply in the past decade, we have seen a notable upsurge in resource utilization with a corresponding upswing in environmental and social impacts associated with resource exploitation.

The Alpine ski boom, for example, excepting a slight deceleration in the 1973-74 recession has become a kingpin of the state's economic growth. Similar growth to that noted here at Vail has taken place and is expected by most to continue at other ski centers in the state, although opponents of specific new areas may reject such straight-line projections (see Figure 5-2).

The rise in Colorado urban water use is suggested by figures from the Denver Water Board that reflect increasing pressure on Western Slope water (see Figure 5-3).

Here we see the existing expansive water collection, storage and transmission systems feeding Metropolitan Denver with water from both sides of Continental Divide (see Figure 5-4).

Table 5-3 illustrates the Board's projection of water demands for the metropolitan area for the next quarter-century—a near doubling of current consumption. I should add once again that such projections are hotly disputed by opponents of transmountain diversions.

As one would expect, building and operating ski resorts, strip-mining and mine-mouth power generation, and impoundment and transmountain

102

Table 5-2. Proposed Reservoirs in Yampa River Basin

Reservoir	Stream	Capacity Acre-Feet	Principal Use	Decree Held By	Date of Decree
Yamcola	Bear River	6,500	Irrigation	CRWCD(1)	2/26/63
Bear	Yampa River	11,600	Irrigation	CRWCD	9/30/61
Blacktail	Yampa River	229,000	Power	RMPC(2)	1/16/66
Woodchuck(3)	Yampa River	40,000	Multiple Use	CRWCD	6/29/59
Pleasant Valley	Yampa River	43,200	Irrigation	CRWCD	6/29/59
Wren	Fish Creek (Yampa)	2,200	Irrigation	---	9/15/69
Hinman Park	Elk River	44,000	Power	PSC(4)	8/4/64
Trout Creek	Trout Creek	23,300	Power	RMP	4/28/67
Dunckley	Fish Creek (Trout)	57,100	Irrigation	CRWCD	7/20/63
Twenty Mile	Fish Creek (Trout)	15,300	Irrigation	J.E. Lutrell	7/22/61
California Park	Elkhead Creek	36,000	Irrigation	CRWCD	8/7/62
Rampart	Fortification Creek	12,100	Irrigation	CRWCD	8/7/62
Craig	Yampa River	44,500	Power	UC & MC(5)	---
Thornburgh	Milk Creek	31,800	Irrigation	YJCD(6)	8/7/62
Juniper	Yampa River	1,080,000	Power	CRWCD	6/8/54
Cross Mountain	Yampa River	142,000	Power	CRWCD	12/--/74
Pot Hook	Slater Fork	65,000	Irrigation	CRWCD	---
Savery	Savery Creek	18,600	Irrigation	CRWCD	---

(1) Colorado River Water Conservation District; (2) Rocky Mountain Power Company
(3) Woodchuck Reservoir may be an alternate to Pleasant Valley; (4) Public Service
Company; (5) Utah Construction and Mining Company; (6) Yellow Jacket Conservancy
District. Note: Information contained in these tables was obtained from the
Colorado River Water Conservation District.

Figure 5-2.　Eagle County Skier Visits, 1969-1970 to
1974-1975, with Projections to the
1985-1986 Ski Season

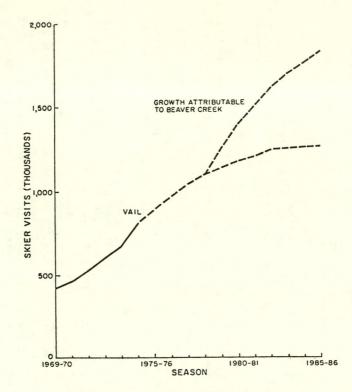

Source:　Colorado Ski Country, USA; BBC estimates.

Figure 5-3.   Attendance at the Vail Ski Area,
1962-1963 to 1974-1975

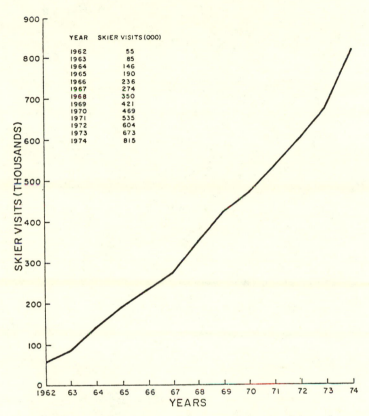

YEAR	SKIER VISITS (000)
1962	55
1963	85
1964	146
1965	190
1966	236
1967	274
1968	350
1969	421
1970	469
1971	535
1972	604
1973	673
1974	815

Note: The years shown reflect skier
visits for the season.   For example,
the figure for 1962 represents the
1962-1963 season.

Source: U.S. Forest Service, Colorado
Ski Country, U.S.A.

Figure 5-4.   Denver Water Supply System

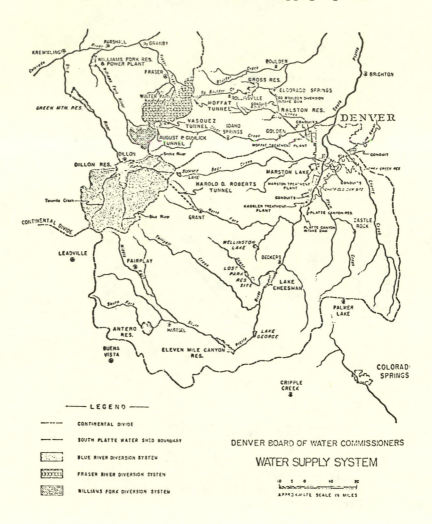

DENVER BOARD OF WATER COMMISSIONERS

WATER SUPPLY SYSTEM

Table 5-3. Water Consumption for Facility Planning
Denver Population and Water Demand Forecasts

YEAR	Population Served	Maximum Year Annual Demand[1] Ac. Ft.	Max Day[2] Demand MGD	Max Hour[2] Demand MGD
1973	904,000	209,000	499	761
Present System Capabilities	---	298,000	620	830
1980	1,130,000	269,000	662	1,011
1990	1,406,000	339,000	888	1,341
2000	1,680,000	413,000	1,144	1,711

[1]Includes raw and treated water customers and system loss.
[2]For treated water customers only.
[3]Figures provided to the BLM via the Denver Water Department April 1974.
"Foothills Project - Environmental Impact Assessment."

diversion of water create substantial environmental and social impacts in the predominantly rural areas where these resources are located. The social conflict often produced by and in the impacting process may disrupt and weaken rather fragile political communities.

Community controversy is not necessarily dysfunctional for a locality's political health. To the contrary, as James Coleman notes, "community disagreements are also a measure of community life"(2), and may well be an indicator of political vitality and citizen participation. Boom towns, however, tend to be exceedingly vulnerable as regards their political capabilities, and unregulated controversy may produce severe and long-term political disabilities for them. Our interdisciplinary research team, then, sought a way, as an agent of a state university, to serve these impacted communities in resolving conflict in such a way that local government would be strengthened to survive subsequent disputes. The Environmental Conciliation Project is resolving particular disputes while developing a general procedure by which local governments might increase their ability to manage impact and the conflict it generates.

Three aspects of environmental conciliation were of particular interest to me and my colleagues: First, the mapping and structuring of a dispute(3), an initial step in settlement strategy; second, the role that perceived and real differences in social judgment play in both the generation and resolution of a conflict(4). Third, methods of influencing communication patterns and styles toward tension reduction in conflict situations.

After consultation with state and regional government officials in the winter of 1976, we in the Environmental Conciliation Project began work with two county governments confronted with serious environmental disputes. I have described in a preliminary report(5)--a few copies of which I have with me today--the larger problem of environmental impacts and disputes in Western Colorado. A survey of that problem led us to Eagle County, where in response to a request from its Board of County Commissioners, (and Government offices) we agreed to assist in resolving the conflict over Adam's Rib.

108

THE PROBLEM

Eagle County is about 60 miles wide, with its
county seat, Eagle, about 130 miles to the west of
Denver (see Figure 5-5), and until the early 1960's
was a rural county of ranching, mining, and
timbering activity. The creation of Vail brough a
recreational boom and a population influx to the
eastern part of the county that has substantially
changed its character. In the late 1960's the
valley was selected as the route for highway
Interstate 70--an event of great impact
significant the the county. A second major winter
sports complex, at Beaver Creek, was given final
approval in 1976 and a third, Adam's Rib, is now
proposed for the western part of the county--a
proposal that is very controversial. Figure 5-6
shows the western half of the country with the
shaded areas indicating the proposed Adam's Rib
development.

CONFLICT PATH

The Adam's Rib dispute began with the
designation of Adam and Eve mountains as being of
good skiable quality by the USFS, in a statewide
inventory. Between 1972-74, the HBE Corporation of
St. Louis quietly purchased 5600 acres in proximity
to those mountains and subsequently opened a design
team office in Eagle the county seat. 1976 was a
significant year during which the proponent
submitted preliminary plans for a 13-village,
4-season resort, served by monorail, with an
18-hole golf course; and commissioned and financed
a socio-economic impact study of the proposal.
That year also saw the Callaway Affair come to a
head in Crested Butte and Washington and a major
policy shift by the U.S. Forest Service to give
local communities veto power over ski area
proposals. Simultaneously, the state was
completing its Winter Resources Management Program
that would determine the siting of new ski areas
through a Joint Review Process. Adam's Rib would
be the proposal to test the JRP.

During the summer of 1976, citizen's groups
supporting and opposing Adam's Rib coalesced, and
the state sought postponement of a county decision.
County officials were delighted to oblige since the
issue was as clear as mud at that point and still
is. A public hearing in mid-summer at which the
socio-economic study was discussed added fuel to
the fire, so to speak.

Figure 5-5. State Planning and Management Regions and Councils of Governments

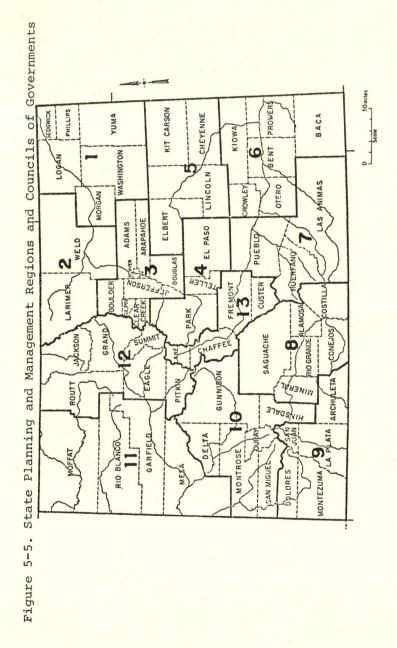

Figure 5-6.   Western Eagle County, Colorado

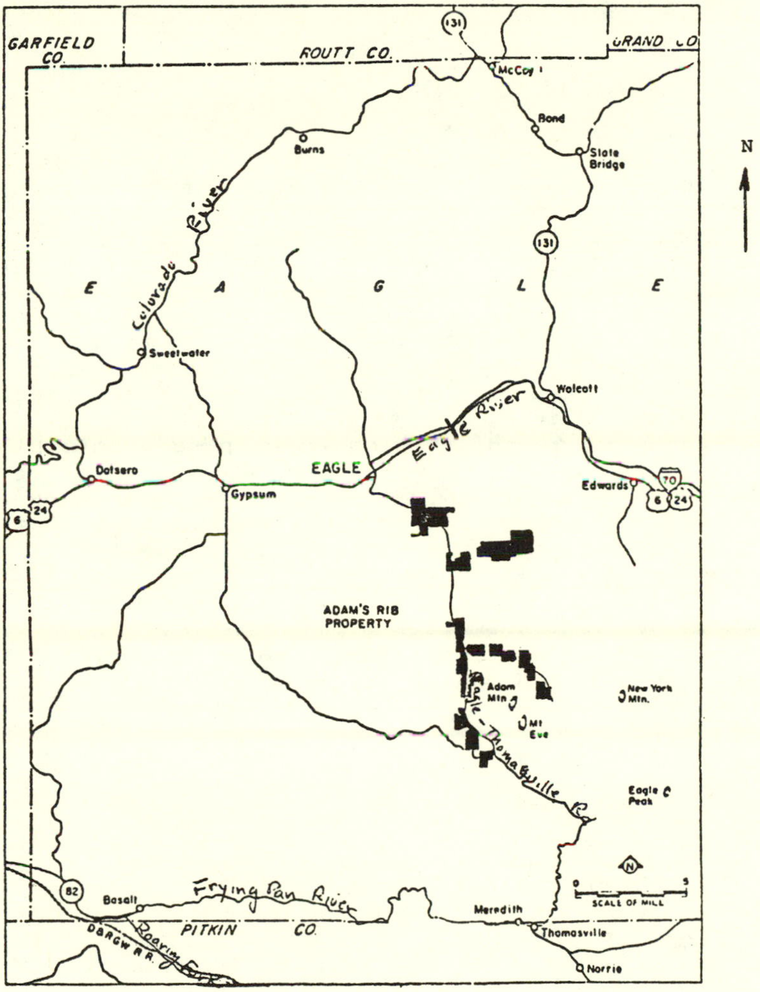

Source: Adam's Rib Recreational Area.

It might help at this point to look at three important dimensions of the conflict (see Table 5-4).

CONCILIATION PROCEDURES

The conciliation procedure we are using in Eagle County integrates the three approaches I mentioned earlier: communication facilitation; structuring the situation for consensus; and judgment analysis. Tension over Adam's Rib has been heightened by the absence of sufficient information about the project and possible alternatives to it. Rumor fills the information void and suspicion of opponents that approval has already been decided is great. Our team, with the help of the county planning office and the local community college, is forming a citizens study panel--by which information concerning Adam's Rib costs and benefits will be maximized. The citizen's study group will also provide a channel for communication citizen preferences to local officials who now get such information sketchily through petitions, letters and the like.

The success of such a group as both a citizens forum and a transmitter of public sentiment to local officials depends largely on how representative of the total population it is. If it is seen as merely another pressure group it will have limited usefulness. Selection of its members, then, is critical.

The Values Survey

A values map of the county population is an initial step toward the selection of the citizen's study group. A survey of 400 residents randomly sampled is now underway to determine value judgments about possible futures for the county. We developed an interview technique on the basis of citizen meetings, during which we found that peoples' concerns about Eagle County's present and future direction could be organized in five dimensions, each described by a number of cues. From these dimensions are created 30 possible futures which are shown to respondents, 30 combinations of different amounts of the five value dimensions, and by way of linear regression analysis we can produce a sort of values map showing respondents clustering by way of the weights they give the five dimensions, and some

112

Table 5-4. Decisional Structure, Parties, Issues

1   Decisional Structure -- Joint Review Process
- a.   Two agreements
- b.   U.S. Forest Service
  - 1.   Eagle-Aspen Planning Unit
  - 2.   Leasing Adam and Eve Mountains
- c.   State of Colorado--WRMP siting decision
- d.   Eagle County
  - 1.   Rezoning area concerned
  - 2.   Revising county master plan
- e.   Proponent--

2   Parties
- a.   Primary
  - 1.   Proponent and "Ski Adam's Rib group
  - 2.   Concerned Citizens for Eagle and Other Opponents
- b.   Secondary
  - 1.   Eagle County Commissioners and Planning Commission
  - 2.   Governors Office, State of Colorado
  - 3.   U.S. Forest Service, White River National Forest
  - 4.   U.S. Fish and Wildlife Service
  - 5.   Northwest Regional Council of Governments

3   Issues
- a.   Uncertainty about Beaver Creek impact
- b.   Public costs and benefits of AR project
- c.   Distance of project from major transportation routes
- d.   Environmental and social impacts
- e.   Need and demand for more ski areas
- f.   Economic diversity--snow drought
- g.   Water consumption implications

113

Table 5-5. The Value Dimension Sheet

PUBLIC SERVICES

Low	High
Schools have basic facilities and few teachers	Schools have modern facilities and many teachers
Volunteer firemen and one or two policemen	Professional fire and police departments
A few buses cover just the main roads	Frequent bus service all over
Little nearby medical care	Lots of nearby medical care
Little TV, radio and press service	Plenty of TV, radio and press service
Small public library	Large public library
Amateur music and dramatics	Plenty of professional concerts and plays

ECONOMIC CONDITIONS

Low	High
Only one or two major sources of employment	Many major sources of employment
Few jobs available	Many jobs available
Low family incomes	High family incomes
Low property values and taxes	High property values and taxes
Few investment opportunities	Many investment opportunities
Nearby stores carry basic items	Nearby stores carry wide variety of goods
Little new housing available	Much new housing available

114

Table 5-5. Continued

LOCAL SELF-DETERMINATION

Low	High
Many state and federal regulations	Few state and federal regulations
Little citizen involvement in local government	Much citizen involvement in local government
Outside groups can override local interests	Local groups can control outside groups
Local needs often not considered in government decisions	Local needs usually considered in government decisions

ENVIRONMENTAL CONDITIONS

Low	High
Polluted air and water	Pure air and water
Little protection of wildlife	Much protection of wildlife
No natural scenery nearby and little open land	A lot of natural scenery nearby and plenty of open land
Lots of noise from traffic, industry and people	Little noise from traffic, industry and people
Public places and roads are crowded	Public places and roads are uncrowded

Table 5-5. Continued

SENSE OF COMMUNITY

Low	High
City atmosphere	Small town atmosphere
Fast pace of life	Slow pace of life
Many people moving in and out of community	Few people moving in and out of community
Neighbors seldom know each other	Neighbors usually know each other
People feel isolated	People feel they belong
Citizens do not know public officials personally	Citizens know public officials personally
High crime rate	Low crime rate

Figure 5-7.   Values Questionnaire Examples

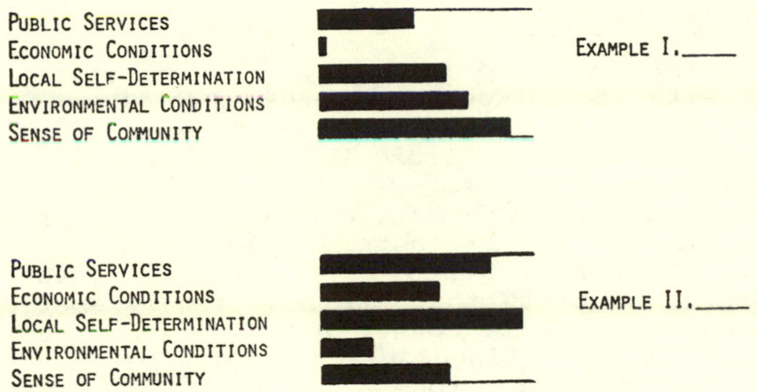

PUBLIC SERVICES
ECONOMIC CONDITIONS
LOCAL SELF-DETERMINATION
ENVIRONMENTAL CONDITIONS
SENSE OF COMMUNITY

EXAMPLE I.____

PUBLIC SERVICES
ECONOMIC CONDITIONS
LOCAL SELF-DETERMINATION
ENVIRONMENTAL CONDITIONS
SENSE OF COMMUNITY

EXAMPLE II.____

117

relationships between those weights. On the basis of earlier results with a similar instrument, we expect from Table 5-4 different clusters and will then select the membership of the citizen's study group to reflect those clusters, and in corresponding proportions. This procedure permits us to claim for the group a fair degree of values representativeness and thereby some credibility for it with regard to the Adam's Rib issue or any other controversial policy question it might address. To insure this credibility, persons selected as "good fits" in one or another of the value clusters will be screened, as would jury candidates, for prejudgment on the issue.

The Costing Process

Once the group is formed, project staff will work with it and other interested citizens in a costing process. We assume--and this has yet to be tested--that aside from individuals with clear economic or other vested interests in approval or disapproval of Adam's Rib, citizens can approximate consensus on likely costs and benefits and feed value judgments into the local decisional process--judgments that are now largely emotional and that bombard the county officials in confusing, conflictful, and singularly unhelpful ways.

The costing process will combine expert judgments and citizen values in several areas. It may be possible to produce a combined judgment of the study group with judgment analysis techniques. A final product of this costing process might be a report to the county to include recommendations on the Adam's Rib proposal, and a description of the procedures by which the problem was studied and judgments arrived at.

The value of this approach--if it works-- would be substantial both within and beyond Colorado. Citizens increasingly demand involvement in decisions that will alter their natural and social environments, yet effective methods of such involvement remain for the most part undeveloped.

Encumberances

Certain factors make this research particularly difficult. First, Eagle County is remote from our research base--2 to 5 hours drive depending on one's destination.

Table 5-6. Costing Process

1 Expected impacts on natural environments and populations

      (e.g., elk and deer herds, eagles, fishlife, air

      and water quality)

2 Expected impacts on public Finances

      (e.g., services required, taxes generated, cash

      flow increase)

3 Expected impacts on life quality, pace, enjoyment

4 Distributional economic impacts

    a   Capital growth remaining in county

    b   Individuals, economic and demographic sectors

5 Anticipated impacts from other growth projects

    a   Beaver Creek

    b   I-70 completion

6 Alternatives

    a   Other economic growth possibilities

    b   Alternative uses for land and other resources now

        committed to proposal

    c   Project reduced in size--spare vs. prime rib

119

Political change has hindered us. Last November, two of the three incumbent county commissioners were voted out. The new board, anxious about possible lawsuits, withdrew the request for our assistance, greatly diminishing our legitimacy. The county planning staff and the local community college have fortunately filled the void, as has an ad hoc group of citizens concerned with the issue.

Eagle County's demographic instability has posed major problems. Explosive growth in the Vail and Basalt areas produces survey problems, such as large numbers of transients, vacation homeowners, empty lots, homes under construction, mobile homes there one day and gone the next.

Resistance to our intervention from the proponent corporation and its supporters has been stiff. Despite our impartiality as concerns county approval or disapproval of Adam's Rib, our efforts at building citizen consensus are seen as a "spoiling" technique, by the proponents. Given their perspective and their intention to win a favorable and fast decision we are irritant--for the moment at least.

The corporation seems to have a sophisticated strategy for winning a favorable decision. It has made every effort to become "local"--a tasteful set of offices with a local payroll, top-level staff living in Eagle and participating in local governance. The head of the AR design team has become chairman of the Eagle town planning commission. He excuses himself whenever decisions concerning Adam's Rib are called for.

The proponent has sought to ease county officials into an affirmative decision in several ways. Last year it financed a socio-economic impact study of Adam's Rib. While the county government declined to lend its auspices to the study, the regional council of governments agreed to do so--thereby giving a subtle if unintentional aura of probability to the project. The major conclusion of the study was that western Eagle County folks were "by and large favorable toward Adam's Rib."

Another step in what I will call, for want of a more precise term, incremental adhocracy, is the Town of Eagle's consideration of a proposal--origin unclear--to link badly needed water system improvements to Adam's Rib own planned system. Add constant pressure on local officials--"why don't you go ahead and approve the

120

sketch plans, it isn't the final decision"; the subtle threat of undesirable alternative uses of AR land--"Subdividing the land into 30-acre ranchettes"; and the spectre of lawsuits against local officials hovering in the background--and it is not difficult to imagine the tension and confusion surrounding the issue.

The proponent is in a difficult position--with construction schedules waiting to be met, capital responsibilities and the like. One would not expect an intelligent and responsible corporation to act in a different fashion. Yet each incremental step drives a new wedge between groups of citizens and it is this dimension of the conflict that is most damaging for the county.

A final impediment to successful conciliation is the nature of the dispute itself. There is great financial and emotional investment on all sides. If and when completed, Adam's Rib in itself will represent a $55 million (1974 dollars) investment and related land and business profits would also be considerable. Opponents of AR see themselves fighting to retain a way of life and a natural environment they feel will be severely damaged if Adam's Rib is built. High levels of hostility (and even the possibility of physical violence) could also shape the dispute in the future and make conciliation even more difficult.

CONCLUSIONS

Our intervention, in both the short and long range, is designed to reduce tension and conflict among citizens, and to facilitate the formation of a consensus that will be useful to local, state and federal officials responsible for decisions on Adam's Rib. I believe we have made progress toward that end. It is of no small significance, I think, that diametrically opposed proponents and opponents of AR are now meeting regularly under our auspices and are communicating with one another in reasonable ways.

If this approach to environmental conciliation succeeds, regardless of the approval or disapproval of AR, Eagle County should be better able to wisely and peacefully make the growth decisions that promise to confront it in the future.

REFERENCES

1. Lewis Carroll, The Annotated Alice, (New York: Clarkson Potter, 1960), p. 113.

2. James Coleman, Community Conflict, (New York: Free Press, 1951), p. 3.

3. Paul Wehr, Conflict Regulation, (Washington, D.C.: American Association for the Advancement of Science, 1976).

4. K. Hammond and L. Adelman, "Science, Values, and Human Judgment," Science, 194 (1976).

5. Paul Wehr, "Environmental Peacemaking," Report to the Ford and Rockefeller Foundations, (Boulder, Colorado: Institute of Behavioral Science, 1976).

6
Mediating Environmental, Energy, and Economic Tradeoffs:
A Search for Improved Tools for Coastal Zone Planning

Donald B. Straus

INTRODUCTION

This paper tells of an ongoing search for new techniques for settling disputes involving many parties and a large number of complex and interrelated variables. The focus of the paper is on research being conducted in association with the Coastal Zone Management Program of the New Jersey Department of Environmental Protection (DEP) under a grant by the Rockefeller Foundation. As a consequence of our association with the DEP, our search was broadened to find ways to avoid, as well as to settle, disputes.

The search began in 1972 with the establishment of the Research Institute of the American Arbitration Association. Large disputes were proving increasingly resistant to the traditional intervention of mediation or other dispute-settlement techniques, and the consequences of these disputes appeared to have increasingly adverse impacts on both the short and long-run interests of an ever-widening segment of our citizenry. This new breed of unresolved and damaging disputes was to be found not only in the

---

*Editor's Note: Since this case study was completed, Mr. Straus has pursued environmental mediation techniques which are not as computer-oriented. Thus he wishes the readers to view this case study as an example of testing a technique, and not as a recommendation for others to repeat, as the tone of the case study suggests.

more familiar arenas of collective bargaining (particularly involving municipal employees), but in the newer arenas of environmental management.

As we dug deeper into our task, we found that one cause for the intransigency of these disputes was the difficulty for humans, using the ordinary means of verbal communication, to assimilate and consider all of the data and variables necessary for productive negotiation or mediation. The game of "what if," so integral a part of both problem-solving and dispute resolution, was being smothered under an information overload each time an effort was made to develop a new proposal. We needed to find some way to break the available information and data into human-sized chunks to consider at the front, or information gathering end of the cycle; and to retrieve the information in human-sized chunks for developing new proposals and for evaluating their consequences.

We also found it helpful to think of disputes as an incident in the problem-solving cycle. Disputes can occur at any time during the cycle, not only at the very end when positions are hardened, when new alternatives are difficult both to develop and to get considered, and when all alternatives tend to be drawn in sharp dichotomies of win-lose, fight or surrender.

From this analysis, we developed the theory that in a complicated problem-solving cycle, consensus should be sought first on the data that are needed to reach a solution before any attempt is made to reach a consensus on substantive solutions. This process we have called "data mediation" and "data validation." We also have sought to identify and resolve disputes as early as possible in the problem-solving cycle rather than waiting for the whole process to move toward a deadlock involving a whole bundle of unresolved disputes.

While this notion, once stated, may seem obvious, it is nevertheless a new way of thinking about dispute-resolution. Typically, mediation and other third party interventions are withheld until an impasse arises at the bitter end of the process. In small disputes, this is often advisable in order not to interfere with the creative interplay of direct negotiations between the participants. But where disputes involve more than two parties and where the process may last over many years, the tradition of withholding dispute resolution intervention by third parties until an impasse develops loses much of its validity.

In summary, this new way of thinking about disputes is:

1. That they are incidents in the problem-solving cycle to be cleared away as soon as possible.
2. That it is necessary to find and to apply new dispute resolution techniques because of the increased complexity of the issues which must be considered.
3. That these techniques must be applied flexibly and as soon as a dispute arises at different points in the problem-solving cycle.

Finally, we have attempted to develop improved procedures of man-computer interaction seeking to combine the exclusively human attributes of wisdom and judgment with the superior computer attributes of a large memory storage and the capacity to consider multiple variables simultaneously.

THE STRENGTHS AND WEAKNESSES OF MEDIATION

Mediation is an old art that began to evolve in the middle years of this century into a skilled profession. William E. Simkin, former Director of the Federal Mediation and Conciliation Service, said in 1967: "In the last year we have talked at length about mediation as a profession and the professionalization of the mediator"(1). Although most often applied to labor-management disputes, it has been employed in the resolution of disputes of all kinds--from marital relations to those that have erupted over racial tensions in communities, in prisons, in Indian reservations, etc. There are a number of definitions of mediation, but perhaps the simplest and most authentic is the following: "An advisory intervention by a third party in dispute negotiations with the purpose of helping the parties concerned find a resolution"(2).

Simkin provides a more ambitious definition, and distinguishes between "conciliation" and "mediation," as follows:

Conciliation is conceived of as a mild form of intervention limited primarily to scheduling conferences, trying to keep the disputants talking, facilitating other procedural niceties, carrying messages back and forth between the parties, and generally being a 'good fellow' who tries to keep things calm and forward-looking in a tense situation.

Mediation is frequently thought of as a slightly more affirmative function. The mediator may make suggestions. He may even make a procedural, or on rare occasions, substantive recommendation. But since he has no power and authority, these somewhat more agressive tactics are considered to be without significant potency(3).

There is another term which is beginning to appear in the literature of third-party involvement in disupte-settlement: "the facilitator." One definition of this activity is:

The facilitator is a meeting chauffeur, a servant of the group. Neutral and nonevaluating, the facilitator is responsible for making sure the participants are using the most effective methods for accomplishing their task in the shortest time . . . . The facilitator offers a menu of possible ways of attacking the problem, and waits until there is agreement on one particular process. Then the facilitator keeps the group on track until it has accomplished what it set out to do or wants to change direction. By getting all the group members to use the same tool at the same time on the same problem, the facilitator can transform a group from a multi-headed animal to a creative, coordinated organism(4).

Mediation as used in this paper is really a combination of all three techniques described above under the terms facilitator, conciliator, and mediator. It is the activity of a neutral person skilled in using the available techniques for producing consensus and in using them at the most effective time and stage in the process of solving problems.
Mediation is primarily a verbal skill. It is best and most easily applied where there are two easily identifiable parties and where the issues can be negotiated and debated across the bargaining table in face to face discussion. The great virtue

126

of this procedure is its human quality. It is the extension of verbal patterns of behavior which are common to all interpersonal communications and provides an opportunity, in a setting that is only slightly more formal than ordinary conversation, for individual representatives to seek a mutually acceptable zone of agreement through verbal threats, promises, and persuasion. Oral presentations, written briefs, and audio-visual aid can all be utilized by the negotiating parties and the mediatiors to play a dynamic game of "what if"--developing new bundles of proposed actions, impacts, benefits, and costs in the effort to discover one or more that will be acceptable. It is a very human, people-centered process which permits the interplay of many subtle, political, emotional and aesthetic arguments.

The weakness of this procedure is that verbal communications (whether written, oral, or visual) can handle only a small number of variables at a time. Although human understanding can encompass the notion that a single action, for example damming up a river, will have an impact on an almost infinite number of identifiable concerns, the verbal means of communicating these concerns is capable of describing them in bundles of only a few at a time. As the number of parties increase and as the number of variables multiply, the inadequacies of the verbal negotiating model become more apparent and so does the need for better methods of seeking a solution. We must find ways to increase the human capacity to consider an exponentially larger number of variables than are possible under traditional negotiating techniques, and at the same time retain the human qualities of interpersonal interaction that are essential.

MAN-COMPUTER INTERACTIONS -- A PROMISING ASSIST

Foundation and government research funds are already being spent in generous amounts to seek improved methods for man-machine interaction. At least one well endowed international research organization, the International Institute for Applied Systems Analysis in Laxenburg, Austria, has a team of over 80 scientists who are working almost exclusively on the application of computers and systems analysis to problem-solving in the environmental field. The Institute receives its major support under a joint agreement of the U.S. and U.S.S.R., a recognition at the "summit" not

127

only of the importance of these problems, but of
the promise these new technologies hold for helping
in their solutions. Many university research
centers and think-tanks within the U.S. also have
similar programs under way.

The computer is still a relatively new device.
It is usually employed in such nonhuman activities
as billing, airline reservations, military gaming,
engineering design, and other mechanical
operations which do not involve the human
attributes of compassion, judgment, aesthetic
values, intuition, diplomacy, self-interest
altruism, or inventiveness. In the laboratories
and research centers referred to above,
interactive models capable of some human
interaction can be found. There has, however, been
surprisingly little opportunity to test these
techniques under live situations. It is
exceedingly difficult to persuade opposing parties
with a live and current set of problems to
experiment with new techniques which could have an
unpredictable effect on their relative bargaining
power. There is a great need for the opportunity
to bring these models out of the laboratory and to
test them under live conditions--not only for the
purpose of perfecting the models themselves, but
also to get decisionmakers accustomed to, and
skillful in, the use of these new tools.

If computers are to be used as an aid to
negotiations and joint decisionmaking, there are a
number of requirements that must first be met:

1) All concerned parties must have access to
   the same computer.
2) The data in the memory bank must be deemed
   valid and acceptable by all parties.
3) The way the computer "computes" the data
   must also be understood and accepted.

For example, to answer the question of the
impact of a high-rise apartment dwelling for 100 or
more families, a large number of items must be
considered and computed such as: the demand for
water, the output of sewage and solid waste, energy
demand, vehicular traffic generation, contribution
to noise and air pollution, and many more. The
mathematical formulas for developing these impacts
must have previously been "programmed" into the
computer (these are called "algorithms"). Each
formula in an algorithm can be discussed in
understandable terms by those actively concerned

128

with solving a particular kind of problem. But once programmed, the computer can compute a bewildering amount of impacts in a fraction of a second. If these impacts have been understood and accepted by prior agreement, the computer can be a powerful tool for searching and finding acceptable solution to a highly complex problem. But this requires a long advance period of joint effort to "build" the computer model. Without such joint effort the computer can become a barrier to consensus rather than a road to agreement.

If the computer has been previously programmed by agreement of the participants, each party can introduce proposals which will activate the computer to predict the multiple impacts on all pre-programmed features of the environment. These impacts can then be assessed not only by the party that introduced the proposal, but all other parties who are interacting with the computer and who are participating in the decisionmaking process. This interactive use of the computer duplicates in a somewhat mechanical way the kind of verbal interaction that takes place across the bargaining table, but permits the simultaneous consideration of many more variables and by many more paties. What still is in the future is the capability of making this interaction response to plain language proposals and interrogations, capable of quick responses to counter proposals, and flexible enough to accommodate quickly and economically to changing conditions as new data are introduced, or old data corrected.

For the above reasons, our search for new tools has been concentrated on ways of handling the overload of data, and of making possible human interaction with the mechanical hardware used to store, analyze, integrate, and retrieve the data.

By no means is a computer useful for handling all aspects of an environmental decision. But where, in a complex case, computers are employed, we believe that all participants should use, and therefore have easy access to, the same computer. We recognize, of course, that both the ultimate locus of decision and the existing computer hardware typically reside in the same government agency and that any sharing of the computer must therefore be acceptable to and made possible by, that same agency. In spite of the obvious difficulty inherent in this procedure, we believe that any government agency responsible for environmental management will find this a more effective procedure for accomplishing its mission than if it were to restrict the development and use of the computer to its own staff.

Data Mediation(5)

Important early decisions must therefore be made with regard to the common data base and the weights and impacts assigned to the various factors chosen for the model. It is at this point that early differences of opinion and incipient disputes can be identified. We decided to employ the normal methods of mediation at this front-end of the problem-solving cycle, seeking to obtain as much agreement as possible, and where failing to get complete agreement, to at least narrow the differences, before the data are put into the computer.

The process of data mediation and validation requires a disaggregation of the large universe of available factors and data into bundles that do not overtax the capabilities of human verbal interaction. Ordinary discussion, debate and mediation, can then be utilized during the process of storing into the data bank items and of developing "algorithms" which can later be retrieved for seeking a solution.

The computer model must provide the user with access to its stored data in an easily comprehensible form. Ideally, it should permit the user to test different alternatives, providing him with predicted impacts. It should also allow him to assess the impacts and to change proposals in order to achieve results which appear more compatible with the emerging zones of acceptable solutions. The outputs of the computer, while serving this game of "what if," must be accepted as valid by all participants in the process. In practice, this will probably mean that data mediation and validation must be a continuing procedure and should be employed whenever a party indicates distrust in what comes out of the computer.

The Intuitive Interactive Model

The computer must not be viewed as a decisonmaker. It is simply a tool to help facilitate the very complex human activity of decisionmaking. For this reason, the products of the computer must be in a form that will permit a return to verbal forums of communication, negotiation and debate. The bundles of aggregated data and impacts that emerge must be easily understandable. There must be an agreed methodology for reducing the number of bundles to not more than seven to ten at a time so that the human process of decisionmaking can be resumed. As a preliminary step toward this ambitious objective, we have developed the Intuitive Interactive Model which will be described in greater detail below.

Since many decisions to protect the environment require sacrifices today to avoid catastrophes or to enhance the quality of living tomorrow, part of the art of environmental management is the skill of making the future consequences of an action seem as real as if it had been experienced. If the decision is to be acceptable, all concerned citizens, or at least those who lead and influence the opinions of others, must be persuaded that these difficult trade-offs are valid, equitable and wise. We have therefore built early citizen involvement into our procedures, with all disputes resolved as soon as perceived.

Citizen involvement is not only necessary as a practical matter, it is also becoming a standard feature in our legal structure of environmental management. For example, under the grant given by the National Oceanic and Atmospheric Administration to the New Jersey Department of Environmental Protection, it is stated that the New Jersey DEP must "show evidence that the State has notified and provided an opportunity for full participation in the development of its management program to all public and private agencies and organizations which are liable to be affected by, or may have a direct interest in, the management program." If computers are to be used in the process, it is necessary that the barriers to human interaction with the computer be reduced to an absolute minimum.

The attempt to use computers in democratic decisionmaking is not new. There is, however, a gap between theory and practice which is very difficult to span. There are a number of reasons for this, among which are the following:

1) Researchers in this field, particularly those working with computers, think and speak in mathematical terms. On the other hand, most

131

politicians, managers, and other persons in leadership positions typically have little acquaintanceship with mathematics and most have received their formal education before the advent of computers. For this reason, it is difficult for the researchers to communicate their ideas to the practitioners, and the practitioners feel insecure and tend to be skeptical of the uses of computers in areas of negotiations and human interactions.

2) In the real world, the decisions with which we are concerned have consequence which are long-term and often involve millions of dollars. There is a natural conservatism about experimenting with procedures, the outcomes of which are unpredictable. Interest in these procedures is easily generated. Acceptance to experiment with new procedures under live conditions is most difficult to achieve.

3) Partly because of the above reasons, and also because the technology itself is quite new and quite limited in its applications, use of these new procedures even under the best of conditions carries with it certain risks such as: causing a delay in the proceedings, heightening rather than diminishing the controversy, or altering bargaining power. Tests under live conditions are necessary before their reliability and effectiveness can be increased, but their reliability and effectiveness must be improved before any large-scale use of them under live conditions can be expected. This chicken-and-egg dilemma is a difficult one to break through.

The New Jersey Department of Environmental Protection Project (6)

We were therefore most fortunate to find in David J. Bardin, Commissioner of the Department of Environmental Protection of the State of New Jersey, a person who had both the courage and the imagination necessary to encourage the use of new procedures in connection with his coastal zone responsibilities. David N. Kinsey, Chief, Office of Coastal Zone Management, Division of Marine Services, New Jersey Department of Environmental Protection, has had the direct responsibility for integrating our program into the complex functions for which he is responsible.

The first three years of the New Jersey Coastal Zone Management Program were divided as follows: 1) the first year, ending September 1975,

132

was to be devoted to the compilation of an environmental inventory; 2) the second year, 1976, to the analysis of the data and to the development of guidelines for planning for the coastal zone; and 3) in the final year, 1977, to the development of a coastal zone management policy.

The American Arbitration Association proposed that during the first year of research it would develop procedures for obtaining consensus from the various concerned participants with regard to the inventory that was being collected. This proposal was submitted jointly by the American Arbitration Association and the N.J. Department of Environmental Protection to the Rockefeller Foundation and a grant was received from the Foundation on February 21, 1975. Basic to the first year's program was the concept of data mediation and data validation.

Over 100 different organizations, both private groups and local governments, were identified as having an interest in the Coastal Zone. These organizations include county and municipal governments, local planning boards, and various public authorities on the governmental side; and everything from the Audubon Society to the Petroleum Institute on the private side. They were invited to participate, under AAA auspices, in the validation process as the inventory was collected by the DEP.

The validation process consists of:

a) Identifying data which should be gathered.
b) Identifying data which are uncertain and therefore unreliable for prediction.
c) Identifying disputed data and mediating out the disputes if possible.
d) Where agreement is impossible, seeking through mediation to narrow the differences.
e) Clearly labeling and making specific the disputes over data which cannot be entered into the inventory by agreement; or eliminating the data which are too controversial to be useful.
f) Identifying additional data which should be collected.

As the second year of the DEP Coastal Zone Management Program approached, it became apparent that the volume of data and its method of storage was still not convenient for decisionmaking. Even

133

if the data could be easily retrieved, the number of variables and interrelationships were too complex to be used effectively in the traditional verbal processes of problem-solving and dispute resolution. We had to find some way to return the data to people so they could use it in human interaction.

We also decided to confine our geographic area of research to one township and to work with those groups concerned with the decision affecting that township.

Intuitive Interactive Model Applied

Accordingly, in our second year proposal to the Rockefeller Foundation, we requested assistance in developing computer technology for storing and retrieving the data and for making possible interaction with the data in a program that could be used by the ordinary citizen. We called this the Intuitive Interactive Model.

The proposal was approved, and, from April 1976 - April 1977 a Rockefeller Research Fellow was assigned full time to the New Jersey Department of Environmental Protection, one of whose primary functions was to help develop a computer progarm for this purpose.

Early in the summer of 1976, a computer package was discovered that had already been developed by Professor Yehonathan Hazony of the Computer Gaphics Laboratory of Princeton University and which could be adapted to our purposes. A contract was made with the Princeton Compuer Graphics Laboratory to put on its computer all of the available environmental data pertaining to Dover Township in Ocean County. This project is now nearly completed and will be ready for testing under "live" conditions in the spring of 1977.

This computer program has the capacity to display on a TV-like screen a map of the area and can, on command, put on the map: political boundaries, man-made physical features such as marinas, roads, buildings, power lines, sewage facilities, etc.; air quality at various monitoring stations; water quality at various monitoring points on streams; land fill and other important features of the flood plains; the slope contours; and a number of other physical features.

In addition, on command, the computer will "zoom in" on a smaller section of the map thus giving much greater resolution and detail.

The computer will also print out maps for distribution in four colors.

In addition to its mapping capabilities, the computer will print out in tabular form a large number of other physical characteristics of the region.

By using a special "electric pencil," the user can also add or subtract physical features, redraw roads, and do a number of other alterations which will then be incorporated into the program and will subsequently display the physical consequences of these changes.

This model is designed to assist both in the planning process for coastal zone environmental management, and also in the specific decisions regarding building license applications. For example, a builder with a new project will be able to ask the computer to display the specific site in which he is interested, will then be able to ask the computer questions concerning the existing environmental impacts, and will be able to test his proposed plans in the light of the existing environmental conditions and the environmental restrictions that have been administratively established. The builder could further play "what if" with his proposal, trying to modify it to fit into the environmental requirements.

So much for what the IIM is designed to do. Now to describe briefly how it accomplishes these tasks.

The IIM consists of four interrelated decisionmaking aids. One is a series of information packages which address the impact of development on such indicators of environmental quality and economic benefits as air emissions and quality, water demand, solid waste management and property taxes.

The second decisionmaking aid is a computerized data bank, which is keyed to information required on the proposed CAFRA Procedural Rules and Regulations of the OCZM for the permit program. There is also a capability for reproducing maps, zooming in on designated sections of the maps, and accepting changes drawn on the maps with an electric pencil.

The third decision aid is a programmed text which informs the lay participant how to use the information packages and computerized data bank.

The fourth aid is a computerized simplification of the important information from the information packages. This last step uses

135

mathematical algorithms to compute the impact of proposed invasions into the environment, and allows the user to play a rapid game of "what if" with various alternative modifications of his original proposal. For example, the key information from the air emissions information package has been stored in the computer in such a way that it will instantly calculate the emissions which will result from different programs. If a developer tells the computer the number and type of dwelling units and the type of heating systems being planned, the computer will correlate these with air pollution resulting from home heating, electric generating station emissions, and transportation emissions.

An information base has been collected for Dover Township and has been digitized in the form of maps and tabular data. Our next steps will be to update the existing information packages and add new packages in a "data mediation and validation" procedure involving Dover Township participants. We will then be ready to use the IIM in live planning programs and dispute settlement activities.

The role of the AAA when this program is in operation will evolve with experience. Whatever this role may be, it must be compatible with the statutory authority and responsibility of the various local, state and federal government bodies that may be concerned. Chief among these is the New Jersey Department of Environmental Protection which is charged by law both to develop coastal zone management plans and to grant permits for new construction(7). Whatever tasks the AAA may perform must be at the request, or at lesat with the consent, of the DEP. Participation by other government agencies or private citizens must also be voluntary. The AAA has no legal responsibility or authority to intervene, nor does it seek any. It should also be noted that the CAFRA Act provides various review and appeals procedures in the event of disputes(8). Of course there is always the possiblity of resort to the courts.

DATA MEDIATION AND VALIDATION PROCEDURES

Data mediation and data validation procedures were first tested under the AAA's New Jersey DEP Program during the winter and spring of 1975.

Examples of the kind of data then being collected by the DEP, and the potential for disputes in each category, are given below:

o Flood Areas: There are various approaches to the delineation of flood-prone areas. Each of these approaches may be perfectly valid for the purposes for which they were intended. But different approaches will result in favorable impacts to some, and unfavorable to others. A process of data validation need not determine which is the "most correct" approach, but rather should determine which data should be put into the inventory and clearly label the data so that all who later seek to evaluate the program will know on what assumptions the flood-prone areas have been determined.

o Extent of Oil and Gas Reserves: Estimates of oil and gas reserves, before extensive exploration, can vary widely. A management program should clearly label which estimate is used, and for what reasons. It would seem critical to allow "concerned citizen" involvement in choosing which forecast is to be used if the resulting program is to be accepted. Barring consensus, at least full understanding of the estimate or estimates chosen should prove to be helpful in the ensuing discussions.

o Ownership Patterns: Some of the mapping in an inventory will refer to boundaries of private property. These can easily and quickly get out of date. A clear and obvious example of "data validation" would be to display such maps in the affected localities in order to pick up errors or changes which have occurred since the map was drawn.

o Accident Probabilities: Probabilities of accidents, including oil spills, atomic plant accidents, explosions, etc., are always a potential source of controversy. While it is clear that no precise predictions can be made, the basis for various estimates is subject to rational debate.

137

The first data validation meeting was held in Trenton, New Jersey on May 2, 1975.

The meeting was well attended by approxmately 70 representatives from a wide variety of public and private organizations.

In the invitation to the participants, they were advised that nine inventory factors would be considered at the meeting. These included: Bathymetry, flood areas, geology, ground water, land use, slope, soils, tidal wetlands, and vegetation. Summary sheets of these factors were attached to the invitation and the participants were asked to review them prior to coming to the conference.

To aid in preparing for the meeting, the following guidelines were suggested: (1)

1. Before coming to the meeting, become acquainted with those inventory factors which apply to coastal zone problems of greatest interest to you and the agency or organization you represent.
2. Be prepared to comment as specifically as possible. Do not merely say that you do not like the data. Be sure to tell us in what specific ways you feel the data are in error or are inadequate.
3. Be prepared to say whether you think the suggested data should be and can be revised, or whether you would like to suggest totally different kinds of data or data available somewhere else.
4. Whenever possible, it would be helpful to come prepared to accept the data now available, even though you may wish to criticize and have corrected certain specific items. In such cases, again please try to be as specific as possible.

_____

[1]Memorandum of Dr. Edward P. Feinberg, Assistant Chief, Office of Environmental Analysis; New Jersey Department of Environmental Protection, mailed to participants of the New Jersey Coast Zone Management Conference with a letter of April 16, 1975.

5. We recognize that in many cases there simply do not exist, and cannot be developed, data which are totally adequate to the task. In such cases, you may wish to suggest certain cautions in using the inventory data.
6. There may be data which you feel are necessary for the proposed inventory factors and which have not been suggested. In such cases, please come prepared to tell us whether, in your knowledge, such data are available. If they are not available, please be prepared to tell us how you propose that they be collected or developed and what would be approximate cost and time involved.

Everyone at the meeting was given a validation form on which was listed all of the inventory items to be considered. Every participant was asked to check on the form either "yes" to indicate validation without reservation, "yes with comments," indicating approval of the data but with reservation as amplified on a supplementary sheet, or "no," indicating that the respondent had no opinion.

Various members of the DEP staff presented the data with the aid of slides and mimeographed materials. After each item was presnted, I, as the AAA data validator, took the chair and opened the meeting for discussion.

As we had anticipated, most of the early comments focused on the procedure. It was necessary for me to repeat several times that a vote for "validation" at this pint merely indicated that it should be put into the inventory as the "best available" and did not commit the individual or his organization to accept it without further review. It was explained by me, and acknowledged by representatives of the DEP, that we were seeking the cooperation of those present, that we were not asking to coopt them. It was only after full discussion of the procedure and purposes of the meeting that we were able to make more rapid progress with the data validation process.

It will be recalled that most of the data presented at this meeting were of a general nature and, for the most part, came from recognized and well established governmental sources. From impressions gained during the discussions, and from the forms handed in by the recipients either at the meeting or by mail following the meeting, most of the data presented were either totally acceptable, or acceptable with reservations and cautionary warnings with regard to their use. A number of suggestions were also received for additional data that existed but were not presented by the DEP staff. Most of these data were known to the staff, but were not considered useful or sufficiently accurate for inclusion in the inventory data. All of these additional items were reviewed again by the DEP staff, and later validated as acceptable.

In the May 2, 1975, meeting, one inventory category, namely that on flood plains, was recognized as still in dispute. The report of this meeting stated:

> The next step in the data validation process will be a small meeting conducted by DEP staff in coperation with AAA, on the category of Flood Areas. The purpose of this meeting will be to review the various methods of Flood Area delineation and assist the Coastal Zone Planning staff in specifying publicly the constraints, limitations, and advantages of each method. This meeting will serve the purpose of identifying specific disputes in areas of controversy, if any, so that AAA can use its mediation techniques to achieve consensus on the Flood Area's data. The small meeting format will also give participants an opportunity to inspect directly the data being reviewed.

The Flood Area's data validation meeting was scheduled for August 15, 1975 in Trenton. It had to be postponed until September 18, 1975. At the meeting, six different methods of delineating Flood Areas were described by resource people selected by the DEP. These methods were:

- Soils - Marco Markley, U. S. Department of Agriculture

- Vegetation - George Pierson, N. J. DEP

- Occasional flood - Dirk Hofman, N. J. DEP

- Remote sensing - Gary Peterson, Pennsylvania State University

140

- Regional flood of selected frequency - Steven Stankowsky, U. S. Geological Survey

- Flood Profile and backwater curve - Dirk Hofman, N. J. DEP

Mr. Straus retained Dr. Leonard Zobler, Professor of Geology at Barnard College, as his technical advisor and assistant mediator.

There were 11 participants at this mediation session in addition to the technical advisors. Among them were representatives of the Sierra Club, various county planning boards, The Petroleum Institute, the American Littoral Society, and representatives of the construction industry.

At the meeting a consensus was reached on a workable mix of methods of delineating flood areas for coastal zone planning. Following the meeting a report was issued by the DEP containing the recommended methods and seeking from the participants on the larger mailing list any comments before the results of the meeting would be considered "validated."

The AAA's role during the discussions was to define as accurately as possible the areas of difference that arose. This Mr. Straus was able to do with considerable success with the assistance of his technical advisor, Professor Zobler, and Mr. David Kinsey, who chaired the meting. During the meeting it was developed that data on flood plains were spotty and wholly accurate in only a few places which had been thoroughly surveyed. This awareness alone, the group concluded, was useful and should be recorded to be used to deflate statements in future disputes which, based on the findings of this meeting, were patently false. It was also agreed that in the future the DEP would use the best available data for planning, drawing upon the guidelines developed during the course of the meeting. The DEP will further emphasize "caution" with regard to any data which, at the present time, cannot be considered scientifically accurate. It was recognized that if a dispute arose in the future with sufficient public interest, the DEP would consider developing additional data for site-specific decisions.

The majority of participants at the May 2 meeting either felt unqualified to register their opinions on the data or were, for other reasons, reluctant to do so. Some of this reluctance, in my opinion, was caused by the difficulty to relate the

141

data to the particular concerns of the individuals who were present.

This early experience raised the question of when wider involvement, beyond the DEP staff, with data input should begin. It soon became clear that without a narrower definition of the uses for the data, a data inventory could become hopelessly large and much time and money spent in its compilation could be wasted. The wider the public participation, the more true this statement becomes. The uses to which data are to be put should therefore determine at what stage in the compilation process public participation should be invoked, and who from the "public" should be involved.

General data, such as bathymetry, flood plains, census data, etc., usually come from recognized sources and it can be assumed that most of them will be accepted with little controversy. But other data of a more specialized kind should probably be gathered and put into the inventory with as much consensus as possible from those who are concerned with the decisions to be made.

In reviewing this early experience form the perspective of the DEP, David N. Kinsey has this to say:(1)

Data Validation

The initial data validation experiment lasted from February 1975, with the first introduction of the concept at the Toms River series of Public Agency and Private Organization meetings, through the report that documented results of the September 1975 data validation meeting on Flood Plains data. The data validation experiment unfortunately coincided with the beginning of the DEP general public participation efforts to involve various publics in coastal zone management program development. Data validation became synonymous with public participation in coasting planning in the eyes of some, a confusion which did not

---

[1]Letter of December 21, 1976 from Kinsey to Straus commenting on the first draft of this paper.

contribute to the success of either project in
its early months. The initial problem with
the data validation concept was that it was
abstract and had little meaning for the
participants in the process. The publics
were, and continue to be, concerned with the
outcomes of the process: decisions on
individual permit applications, and the
policies contained in the management program.
Until the general tenor of those decisions
became clear, and until the general
objectives of the coastal zone management
program became clear, the data validation
concept was simply too abstract for many
people.

In July 1975, DEP began a short-term
planning effort, the preparation of Interim
Land Use and Density Guidelines for the
Coastal Area. The aim of this document was to
establish an interim framework for making
decisions as to location and density of
individual CAFRA permit applications. The
second aim of this project was to establish a
framework for vigorous public debate on the
evolving coastal zone management policies for
CAFRA and other portions of the State's
coastal zone. Preparation of this coastal
management document benefited from selective
public input, beginning with meetings held in
the fall of 1975 with builders, coastal county
planning directors, and environmental groups.
To avoid further confusion, the data
validation experiment was not pursued at that
time. Rather, DEP/OCZM efforts at involving
various publics concentrated on the substance
of preparing the Interim Guidelines.

At the same time, DEP/OCZM staff
continued in-house long-term coastal planning
efforts. Extensive analysis began of
approximately twenty coastal resource and
coastal land and water use issues. The
DEP/OCZM staff had completed the required
inventory in September 1975. Extensive use of
that inventory and other accumulated
information was the next logical step.

At the same time, DEP/OCZM staff
continued various efforts to improve the
CAFRA permit application process. It became
increasingly clear that sharing the

information used in making project design and permit application review decisions would benefit the building community, local planning agencies, and concerned citizens, as well as DEP/OCZM staff.

By December 1975, we clearly recognized the need for data to make two kinds of decisions: first, very short-term, site-specific, project design and permit review decisions, and second, long-term regional planning decisions, incorporated in the Interim Guidelines and more particularly in the final coastal zone management program. A recognition of the vast data needs and data manipulation requirements led to decision to continue the computerized information system research efforts already begun to design and develop an information system to serve both the short-term and long-term needs. This decision coincided nicely with the evolution in the AAA/DEP research effort, which recognized by fall 1975 that more effort should be devoted to the uses of data, prior to emphasis on the validity of the data. This recognition coincided and complemented the DEP/OCZM decision to emphasize preparation of the Interim Guidelines and analysis of the coastal resource and coastal land and water use issues and policy alternatives, with a recognition that a computerized information system would assist both of these efforts in the long term.

CONCLUSIONS

Earlier in this paper we pointed to various limitations inherent in verbal communications. The limitations were the inability of humans engaged in ordinary discourse and negotiations to keep track of the large number of variables required in making a logical decision. For this reason, we suggested that the participants should put the variables into the computer so that it could provide mechanical leverage to the human frailties of memory and the ability to consider more than a dozen or so variables at the same time.

We have developed easily understandable, effective, and practical ways for achieving the input stage of this procedure. Technically speaking, both the hardware and the software are

144

more than capable of accomplishing this task. We have not, however, wholly solved the problem of retrieving the data in acceptable aggregated bundles which will permit a return to verbal communication, although we believe the Intuitive Interactive Model is an important first step. This problem must, however, be solved before we can expect totally satisfactory results form the Intuitive Interactive Model or its successor models. It bears repeating that the computer is no substitute for human judgment in making decisions. All the computer can do is to aggregate an inhuman volume of interrelated data into human-sized chunks. Even if our project is eventually totally successful, the process of solving environmental problems and settling environmental disputes will appear on the surface to be very much as it is today. The only (and important) difference will be that the negotiators will have the best available facts and predictions at their disposal as they exert their bargaining power, wisdom, prejudices, self-interests, altruism, and greed. If the result is not a better world, at least it will not be because of ignorance. The disputes may be as difficult and as bitter as today, but the decisions reached should be of a better quality. This would be no small achievement.

REFERENCES

1. Dunlop and Chamberlain, editors, <u>Frontiers of Collective Bargaining</u> (New York: Harper & Row, 1967).
2. Katherine Seide, editor, <u>A Dictionary of Arbitration and Its Terms</u> (New York: Oceana Publications, Inc. for the American Arbitration Association, 1970), p. 146.
3. William E. Simkin, <u>Mediation and the Dynamics of Collective Bargaining</u> (Washington, D. C.: Bureau of National Affairs, 1971), pp. 25-26.
4. Michael Doyle and David Straus, <u>How to Make Meetings Work</u> (New York: Wyden Books, 1976), p. 35.
5. For a detailed description of data mediation see p. 177 ff.
6. Professor Michael Greenberg of Rutgers University has been my close collaborator in the design and implementation of the New Jersey DEP Project. He conceived and designed the Institute Interactive Model. He is now writing a more

detailed and technical description of this model
which will be available, when completed, at the
Research Institute of the American Arbitration
Association.

7. New Jersey Coastal Area Facilities' Review
Act of 1973 (NJ S A 13:19-1 et seq.).

8. Ibid.

7
Participatory Evaluations of Energy Options for California:
A Case Study in Conflict Avoidance

Laura M. Lake

INTRODUCTION

The experiment described in this chapter differs from the site-specific studies detailed in Chapters 4 and 5, and from the regional data validation experiment described in Chapter 6. Thus it is important to define here the process which was tested. "Participatory evaluations" are not public participation exercises(1). Rather, the process analyzed here is a form of third party intervention in the planning process for the purpose of more effectively involving the public in programmatic decisionmaking. Effective involvement entails providing a sense of political efficacy for the participants and obtaining constructive advice from interest group leaders on their goals and objectives so that planning activities can anticipate public concerns well in advance of final project design controversies.

There are many publics to be included in this process, and it is particularly helpful to political officials if a consensus among competing interest groups can be obtained regarding minimum parameters for planning. For example, it will be shown in this chapter that many community groups want to have electricity demand projections justified before they will even consider evaluating power plant technologies or prospective power plant sites. They also want to know whether the power plants will be constructed to serve the needs of the local community or to export electricity to urban centers far away.

Conflict reduction processes can be employed to reduce second-guessing for administrators by identifying mitigating measures early in the planning process so that litigation is not necessary for environmental groups and community leaders to utilize in order to influence decisions. Thus the approach utilized in this chapter differs markedly from the site-specific, post-impasse "mediation" technique employed by Gerald Cormick and Leah Patton in Chapter 2.

It is important to note again that third party intervention in the planning process is not public participation. Public participation processes can be characterized as follows: they are voluntary, involve self-selected individuals who provide statements (which are advisory and often post-decisional) at public hearings. These hearings are pro forma methods for involving the public in frequently frustrating, one-way communications. They are usually presided over by public relations or legal counsel of the agency rather than by an official with substantive knowledge in the program. Often these proceedings leave the participants more frustrated than before the hearings.

Unlike public participation, third party intervention in the planning process, as described here, involves a neutral intervenor who serves as convener, selector of participants and consensus facilitator with access to experts with substantive knowledge of elements of the program. But unlike hearing officers, the intervenor has no agency mission to defend, and has been authorized by the agency to seek a consensus. Thus the process is not unsolicitated advice, and leaves the participants with feelings of political efficacy and restores the collegial atmosphere to environmental decisionmaking which was initially destroyed by the advent of mandatory public involvement in environmental review procedures (see Chapter 1). Finally, third party intervention in the planning process restores interest group leaders to their traditional roles as spokesmen and representatives of their constituents, and permits them to address the substantive concerns of their memberships.

The role of third party intervenors in the planning process involves three elements:

1. Information collection to help environmental decisionmakers determine the values, priorities and substantive concerns of competing interest groups.

2. <u>Education</u> of political officials by providing them with information regarding interest group objectives and concerns; and education of disputants regarding the economic, social and technical issues in dispute, thereby equalizing the level of information available to all disputants.
3. <u>Consensus information</u> through negotiations between disputants regarding their primary objectives and their willingness to make concessions on secondary issues.

The intervenor also selects the participants to maintain balance among competing interest groups, while keeping the number of participants directly involved in the negotiations small.(2) Thus it is very important to note again that third party intervention in dispute avoidance is not a mass participation process and is instead an auxiliary process to administrative decisionmaking, and should not be an alternative to public hearings, despite the defects of hearings already noted. Since third party intervention sessions are by invitation only, it is important to preserve public access for the general public through public hearings, as a hedge against unrepresentative consensus.

UCLA PROJECT

A dispute avoidance experiment was designed by a group of UCLA faculty for the California Energy Resources Conservation and Development Commission (henceforth, the Energy Commission). The Commission was established in 1974 by the California Legislature (Warren-Alquist Act) to oversee energy planning, research and development (R & D), conservation and power plant siting regulatory decisions. Its diverse activities revolve around the Biennial Energy Plan to the Legislature which proposes a twenty year estimate of options for energy conservation, fuel availability, technology development and environmental protection, and suggests measures to avoid an energy shortfall. This planning document is the basis for future decisions to approve or to reject the Notice of Intention to construct a power plant in one of three sites suggested by electric utilities.

The first biennial energy plan was prepared in the summer of 1976, when the UCLA research group

149

was awarded a one-year contract by the Energy Commission to criticize the plan's electric supply forecast scenarios and to evaluate innovative electric generating technologies and siting options(3). By seeking a neutral evaluation of energy options, the Commission was changing the electric utilities' former hegemony over the determination of which technologies should be developed and constructed. The UCLA project report was to advise the staff of the probable impacts of both conventional and innovative technologies and to suggest R & D priorities for the Commission's budget decisions(4).

Our role as third party intervenors was to convene an evaluation process to ask interest groups to discuss power plants outside the context of immediate site-specific decisions. We were not asking the participants to decide which options were best from a technical point of view, but rather, to share with us what they were concerned about then they selected a particular technology. An additional role was to facilitate interest group tradeoffs in order to develop an accurate image of which options these groups might find acceptable and what would make those options acceptable, for example, low water consumption. This information could then help to guide the Commission's R & D decisions to develop power plant cooling technologies which consume less water.

The "sanction" available to the project team was the influence its report would have on the Commission's decisions, and the fact that the Commission was funding the study. The case study presented here describes the evaluation procedure developed and tested to involve major disputants in energy policy early in deliberations. The work was completed June 1977.

The major elements in this one-year conract from the Energy Commission were a technology assessment of promising new technologies such as solar thermal, wind and geothermal, and the development of a methodology to evaluate each of these technologies' comparative attribute for three different regions of the state: desert, inland, and coast. The Commission's staff was particularly concerned with grandiose statements made by various technology advocates in pursuit of additional R & D funds, and with the unknown environmental impacts of new innovative technologies, their costs, feasibility and reliability. The objective of the project was to

150

inform the Commission about the probable
consequences of promoting particular technologies,
and to anticipate the socio-economic and
environmental objections groups might raise
against various technologies being sited in their
regions. We therefore looked for potential
tradeoffs between technologies and between
interest groups which would be affected by the
decision to site a facility in their community.

The power plant project involved a faculty of
eight natural and social scientists and twenty
doctoral and masters students. They chose the
following ten technology options after carefully
reviewing the state-of-the-art of almost every
conceivable technology to generate electricity
during the summer of 1976(5):

-- Solar Thermal   -- "Clean Oil"
-- Geothermal   -- Nuclear (LWR)
-- Biomass Conversion   -- Nuclear Parks
-- "Clean Coal"   -- Wind
-- Coal Gasification   -- Fuel Cells

Other options, such as photovoltaic solar power and
ocean thermal gradient plants were not treated as
thoroughly in the final report after the summer
study because they were considered unlikely to be
commercially competitive with the other
technologies by 1995. The "clean" coal and oil
options referred to the use of processes to make
them comply with federal environmental standards.
Hydroelectric plants were not investigated because
the Energy Commission staff felt that the
environmental impacts of such facilities made them
unacceptable. (In addition, the Public Utilities
Commission, and not the Energy Commission,
regulates hydroelectric development.)

A similar review of siting options was
conducted during the summer and a report was made
to the Commission staff regarding the advantages
and disadvantages of innovative siting options
including: offshore, underground, floating,
undersea and in a lagoon.

RATIONALE FOR EVALUATING TECHNOLOGY/SITE OPTIONS

Until the Energy Commission was established
in 1974 power plant siting decisions were
supervised by the Public Utilities Commission of
California. Siting was not the result of an
independent assessment of the electricity

151

supply/demand forecast. Rather, it was an ad hoc process which involved the selection of a particular technology for a specific location, thereby provoking the wrath of a community which only learned about the project after there was considerable commitment to both the technology and the site. The usual recourse was to testify at public hearings and to file an environmental lawsuit against the plant proposal, to block its construction.

While these local siting disputes will remain an obvious testing ground for environmental mediation, it seems desirable to avoid such disputes if possible through third party intervention in the planning process. Such intervention involves learning about regional and local priorities and educating the public about the options available within the next twenty years. Only then can community priorities take into account the probable impacts of siting a power plant of a particular design. Our case study is thus an attempt to respond to the usual community lament, "why didn't you ask us in advance what we wanted so that this power plant would not have been so objectionable."

The project involved business, civic, environmental, labor, public health groups and public officials (county planners and county supervisors) in the evaluation of power plant technology/site options. For these are the groups which frequently clash when a Notice of Intention to construct a power plant is filed. When one project is blocked successfully in the courts, (even assuming zero energy growth through stringent conservation, the old plants will need to be replaced), the Commission and the utilities will still be left with the question, if not here, where?

The raw data regarding the "care and feeding" of ten power plant technology options was presented to the evaluation group in September 1976. They were faced with the problem of assessing the magnitude of impacts of very different technologies, i.e., pounds of pollutants per hour and acre feet of water consumed were difficult indices of impacts for the group to use for direct comparisons. We therefore requested the technology review group to rate the magnitude of each technology's impacts according to nine evaluation criteria:

152

1. Air Quality
2. Alternative Land Uses
3. Comparative Construction and Operating Costs
4. Impacts of Fuel Extraction Processes
5. Growth Inducement (Local and End-Use)
6. Health and Safety
7. Solid and Liquid Waste Management
8. Water Quantity and Availability
9. Wildlife and Vegetation Impacts.

The rating scheme utilized a logarithmic graph to indicate levels of impact for each activity, with five intervals of impact:

1 = Negligible Impact
2 = Slight Impact
3 = Substantial Impact
4 = Major Impact
5 = Saturation Impact (Irreversible)

This rating scheme is illustrated in Figure 7-1. Each respondent was requested to indicate his/her level of confidence (A, B, C, in decreasing order of confidence) for each criterion of evaluation.

The results of this modified Delphi experiment (i.e., face-to-face discussions were permitted) were analyzed to obtain the distributions of ratings. If the rating team agreed on a particular interval for an impact, we accepted this as a rough index of impact.

However, if there was a wide range of ratings for a particular impact, we requested during the next week's meeting that the "A" level of confidence respondents discuss their reasons for different ratings and develop a consensus on the rating. The results of this experiment were then used to develop an abbreviated information package for interest groups to read before they indicated their technology preferences.

Obviously these nine evaluation criteria include subsets of criteria, and are very general. It is important to note, however, that the technology group found it difficult to assign a one-to-five rating to these impacts and felt that this was a subjective judgment for which they were unqualified, i.e., it was not their role. The evaluation group explained that if they (the technology group) were not qualified to assess the impacts of the technologies they had just been studying, nonscientists would certainly find it difficult to make these judgments.

Figure 7-1.   Impact Magnitude Rating Scheme

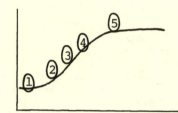

IMPACT
(Log Scale)

ACTIVITY PARAMETER

The information packages were designed to provide impact ratings and definitions for the options which were appropriate for a particular region. A short technical glossary was also provided. Each of the evaluation criteria were carefully defined, and most assumptions were made explicit.

APPLICATION OF THE EVALUATION METHODOLOGY

In order to use our knowledge of the impacts of the ten technologies in the three regions, we developed a methodology which would permit us to compare the overall technical evaluation criteria, assuming the Best Available Technology by 1995. We were interested in obtaining the interest groups' uncompromised preferences and their ideas regarding tradeoffs and mitigating measures which might make particular technologies or sites acceptable.

The experiment was designed on a regional basis to keep it from deteriorating into an environmental impact hearing for a particular community, with the ensuing rigidity, polarization and paranoia which accompany power plant siting disputes. Other factors supported the regional approach: the twenty year framework for a regional evaluation study permitted consideration of cumulative impacts on resources, lifestyles and the quality of life which a site-specific evaluation would not facilitate; and in addition, a community will often object to a plant and suggest that the plant would be far less damaging in another region. For example, coastal communities suggest that desert land is wasteland which would be far less valuable and should be used for future power plants. Desert communities, on the other hand, would suggest that the coast's ocean water is far less valuable than inland water, and power plants should therefore be sited on the coast. Regional analysis can also identify differences in information, perception of problems and levels of sophistication between coastal, inland and desert populations which might influence plans for siting a power plant in any one of these regions.

All of the known evaluation techniques were reviewed, including cost-benefit analysis, the balance sheet method, the judgmental impact matrix, the environmental evaluation system, map overlay, the ordinal method, the goals achievement matrix, Delphi, and participatory evaluation(6).

155

This review prompted the suggestion to meld the goals achievement matrix with participatory evaluation, to obtain both group goal maximization perceptions and their perceptions of possible tradeoffs between groups. This evauation methodology is termed the "Priority-Tradeoffs-Scanning Approach" (PTS)(7).

The purpose of the priority-tradeoffs-scanning approach is to obtain the goal achievement evaluation for each technology/site option for a region, alternative rankings of technology/site options of interest groups according to their uncompromised priorities, their rankings when certain criteria become paramount, for example, if air quality or water consumption were critical in selecting an option, and finally, their perceptions of the demands of other interest groups. This methodology thus moves priority articulation away from nonnegotiable statements made a public hearings toward an open assessment of how various interests can be accommodated. It starts out with the recognition that all of the interests involved in energy planning are legitimate, and that future power plant siting plans should acknowledge their concerns from the beginning.

The implementation of the methodology involved three activities:

1. A questionnaire to obtain uncompromised option preferences according to each of the nine evaluation criteria when considered to be of overriding importance as selection factors.
2. Three regional and one statewide workshops to validate the questionnaires and to discuss potential tradeoffs and mitigating strategies among interest group leaders.
3. A second questionnaire to obtain interest group tradeoffs to identify options around which a consensus existed.

Typology for Community and Group Selection

A typology for participant selection involving representative communities and a cross-section of interest groups involved with power plant siting was developed. The categories for our sample communities were those which already had power plants; those which had received a legal Notice of Intention to construct a power plant; and those for which there were no plans to construct a power plant. It was anticipated that different levels of polarization over power plant construction would be overserved by inviting interest group representatives from these three types of communities, and that the most polarized communities would be those which were currently embroiled in a siting dispute. It was also expected that the first and second categories of communities would be more informed about the technologies involved than the communities with no plans for power plants. Communities were then selected on the basis of their proximity to a meeting place for a regional workshop.

Organizations with an interest in energy issues were identified by consulting environmental impact reports for proposed power plants in California, directories of environmental, civic, labor and health organizations and public agencies involved with power plant siting (air and water quality agencies). Candidate groups were then reviewed by the project team and the Energy Commission staff to determine the breadth of their interests, membership size, positions on energy issues and their motivations for participation. These criteria were intended to eliminate groups which were extremist regarding energy issues or which were "letterhead only" organizations. Extremism in the participatory evaluation process was assumed to be dysfunctional because it would inhibit the discussion of tradeoffs between disparate groups.

Our final list of groups for each region totalled between fifteen and twenty organizations from the various sectors involved in energy siting issues. Our objective was to involve ten to fifteen representatives from these initial rosters for in-depth discussions at workshops in their regions. We purposely kept the number of participants small to facilitate discussion.

Letters of invitation to participate in the evaluation experiment were sent in December 1976 to heads of the organizations and to public officials (county planners and county supervisors).

First Questionnaire

We explained in our cover letter for the questionnaire that the results of the questionnaire would be used during our workshop and would serve as an indicator of the amount of

157

consensus, if any, within the region regarding power plant preferences, and also the groups' willingness-to-compromise, regarding the importance of various criteria. These questionnaires were mailed during January in time to hold three regional workshops in February, and the statewide workshop in March.

The first questionnaire was developed to solicit uncompromised option preferences, as well as compromised choices when particular criteria became paramount. The respondents were asked to indicate not only their preferences, but also to indicate their willingness-to-compromise (exchange priorities) between their first and second choices, second and third, and so on. A five-point willingness-to-compromise scale was indicated next to each option. Approximately twenty questionnaires were mailed to interest groups within each region.

One of the important features of this questionnaire and workshop was the role our team could play in selecting participants: a public agency like the Energy Commission is not in the position to exclude any organization from a meeting, while we, as an independent group, could control participation in order to maximize the productivity of the workshop (to keep it small).

Workshops: Desert, Inland, Coastal, and Statewide

Desert Workshop

The first workshop was held in Palm Springs on February 5, 1977 for desert interest groups. Before this workshop the participants had only met at public hearings regarding the siting of the Sundesert Nuclear Power Plant proposed by the San Diego Gas and Electric Company during the summer of 1976, to be located in Blythe, California, near the Arizona border. We took particular efforts to keep the workshop from becoming a Sundesert hearing. Yet Sundesert helped the participants to conceptualize the kinds of tradeoffs we were interested in identifying.

The twelve interest groups represented at the workshop were:

Blythe Chamber of Commerce
Colorado River Board of California
Colorado River Association (and Metropolitan
    Water District)

158

Colorado River Regional Water Quality Control
    Board
Desert Watch (an archeological preservation
    organization)
League of Women Voters, Palm Springs Chapter
Lower Colorado Advisory Committee on Power
    Plants
San Bernardino County Planning Commission
Palm Springs Chamber of Commerce (and Solar
    Energy Institute)
Riverside Lung Association
Sierra Club, Riverside Chapter

This cross-section of interest groups was selected
according to the typology described earlier. As
with any other collection of interest group
representatives, some were more articulate than
others and attempted to dominate the conversation.
As moderators, we attempted to equalize the input
from the quieter groups. This remains a sensitive
factor in any group discussion.

A chart displaying the impacts of each of the
technology options within the desert region was
placed in front of the group. The overlay chart
was used, for example, when we spoke of solar
energy, by placing a transparent overlay over the
chart which showed that while solar energy had very
little impact on air quality, it required a large
amount of water and land area, and would probably
require a large work force which would in turn
result in growth-inducement for rural communities.

The workshop resulted in the following
findings:

-- The Energy Commission's mandate to us to
   consider central power plants of about
   1000 Megawatts (electric) was considered
   to be wrong by the participants, who
   instead preferred small decentralized
   power plants of about 50 MG(e).
-- Most of the participants felt that until
   stringent conservation measures were taken
   the need for any new power plants was not
   sufficiently demonstrated.
-- They favored individual home solar
   heating/cooling systems to reduce the need
   for new electric power plants (this was not
   an option the Energy Commission had
   contracted the group to evaluate,
   however).

159

-- They experienced great difficulty thinking
about power plants which might be built
after the next ten years (the lead time to
construct plants is usually eight to ten
years, and those designs are already under
review for siting purposes--our project
was also looking at new technologies
beyond the current design period).
-- Finally, there was a general inability to
evaluate power plants on a generic,
non-site-specific basis. Participants
were accustomed to thinking about a
particular plant and its environmental
impacts, such as the Sundesert plant, and
they regularly utilized this proposed
project as a reference point to explain
their evaluations of other options.

This difficulty dealing with generic siting
was expected to be a major problem, since people
generally do not think in the abstract, and when
they do consider a problem, they think through
analogies--thus the constant reference to
Sundesert. The irony of this dilemma is that as
anyone who has ever sat through a public hearing to
review environmental impacts of projects knows,
public interest groups usually are outraged that
alternatives were not considered during the early
planning process. Yet when presented with the
opportunity to identify such alternatives, they
were stymied.
In addition to the above general findings, we
also learned that:

1. There was considerable concern about the
status of water allocation to the desert region.
Several participants (environmental interest group
representatives) felt that the region was faced
with an either/or situation: either energy or
agriculture and domestic water consumption would
be possible.
2. Participant's perceptions of technology
feasibility were based on the information they had
obtained from the mass media and from technology
advocates with vested interests in the promotion of
particular technologies. For example, statements
made in behalf of geothermal power were based on
the claim made by a former University of California
professor who is now in the business of developing
geothermal power. Another example from this
workshop was the belief that a technical

breakthrough had just occurred in Glasgow, Scotland, which would make photovoltaic power economically competitive with other technologies. Since photovoltaic power plants would not use cooling water, they were the preferred option for the desert.

3. There appeared to be two subregions within the desert: the western desert which included Palm Springs, which is affluent, and pro-conservation (in general), and the eastern desert, which is economically depressed and seeking to attract new construction to the communities there, hoping to create jobs for the local residents. However, even the eastern desert community representatives were leary of the local impacts of growth inducement, and were concerned that the additional public services required by a large power plant construction project and its subsequent operation might create a boom/bust episode in the community, and even worse, that the additional revenue generated by the presence of a power plant in a municipality would go to the county which might choose not to allocate these funds to the impacted community.

4. A general sentiment surfaced during the workshop which can be characterized as energy independence for the desert: participants felt that fuel should not be imported to the desert, and that energy should not be exported. There was a positive feeling that energy resources which are locally available ought to be utilized when necessary (wind, geothermal, solar). Some participants went so far as to sarcastically say, "we'd rather have the coast's power plants than its people." This view was echoed at subsequent regional workshops, and a year later was demonstrated in the Kern County referendum which rejected a power plant for the people of Los Angeles.(8)

5. We learned that our typology for community selection was useful and that representatives from communities with existing power plants expressed their concerns by making comparisons with the problems their communities had encountered with local power plants. Communities (Blythe) which were in the throes of a Notice of Intention to construct a power plant were the most up-to-date regarding power plant impacts, and wanted to eliminate or minimize these impacts by learning from other communities' experiences.

161

6. Several participants insisted that there was no one option which would be acceptable everywhere, and that the Energy Commission should advocate the use of a mix of technologies to achieve its supply requirements. They proposed a new power park concept to combine solar, wind and geothermal facilities in one site, and suggested that the requirements for peaking power could be reduced through a coordinated grid system with other regions and by using wind power for pumped hydroelectric storage at existing hydroelectric power plants.

7. Nuclear power was supported by several public officials from water agencies because they viewed it as the only reliable source of energy. Most of the other groups opposed nuclear power because of its large consumption of water and its solid waste disposal problems. However, even nuclear advocates preferred the innovative options for the ten years plus period, when they were given the opportunity to change their option preferences to fit this time horizon.

8. There was some concern over speculation in the purchase of water rights for future power plants requiring cool water. This is a Western United States problem which involves purchasing water rights through land acquisition, especially agricultural land.

9. Many participants recommended that the Energy Commission promote individual home solar heating/cooling units to reduce electric demand requirements so that new power plants would not be needed. Nonelectric options had not been part of our contract, and yet this was a logical response on the part of the public, which does not "box" energy policy into bureaucratic pigeonholes (another division of the Energy Commission was responsible for energy conservation studies). The participants objected to this division of labor and insisted that individual units be included in the technology option list.

10. Proponents of power plants frequently advocate them on the basis of the jobs and revenue they are predicted to generate. Several participants were concerned about the adverse impacts on communities which growth would create, and questioned whether or not the jobs would go to local residents. They suggested that a guarantee regarding employment of local residents be part of a siting package.

11. All of the participants expressed concern for national security problems associated with reliance on imported oil for electric power generation. They therefore preferred local power resources such as wind and geothermal power.

12. Participants were concerned about managing growth induced by large construction projects more effectively, e.g., inclusion of mass transit systems to reduce auto-related air pollution from an increased local population. Wind power was particularly favored because it involves a small workforce and is therefore least likely to disrupt or impact a community.

Like the Coastal Zone Development groups which Donald Straus worked with in Chapter 4, the desert group initially had great difficulty playing "what if." We think that this was in part because they did not grasp the futuristic mode of the planning process experiment and because there was still the suspicion that they might inadvertently become committed to a particular technology. Yet they did eventually contribute the information we were seeking, i.e., they evaluated the criteria they utilized in selecting energy alternatives.

Inland Workshop

The Inland Regional Workshop was held on Saturday, February 12, 1977 in the Hearing Room of the Energy Commission in Sacramento. The inland region refers to the Central Valley of California, a richly endowed agricultural region which was then suffering from a severe drought.

Nine interest groups were represented at this workshop:

    Sacramento County Board of Supervisors
    Sierra Club, Mother Lode Chapter
    California Manufacturers' Association
    San Jose Lung Association
    San Joaquin Air Pollution Control District
    Golden Empire State Health Systems Agency
    California Regional Water Quality Control
        Board, Central Valley Region
    League of Women Voter, Modesto Chapter
    California Farm Bureau

Although their five seats on the dais were empty, the Commissioners' presence was felt during the workshop: it was the most troublesome of the

163

four workshops for several reasons. The participants did not seem to understand that the inland workshop was to evaluate only inland options, despite the instructions in our cover letter. But most important, the mood was inquisitorial, and reflected a fear tha some sort of game was being played by the Commission, and they would not make any commitments to the evaluation team. Thus our neutrality and independence was not accepted immediately, and most of the first half of the meeting was taken defending the dispute avoidance planning experiment. During the lunch break one particularly critical participant requested that he be permitted fifteen minutes to poll the participants about the usefulness of the experiment. We suggested that he wait for this inquiry until the end of the workshop, and he agreed. He continued to be argumentative until it was explained that the Commission did not require public input into our study of technology/site options, that it was our idea, and that as far as the Commission was concerned, an evaluation could be conducted without their workshop participation. Resistance dried up and interestingly enough, when he was given the floor to poll the participants at the end of the workshop, he said that it would not be necessary to vote on the experiment because we had made it clear that the participants' objections to the Commission's constraints on our project would be noted "up front" in our public report to the Commission.

Thus despite this difficulty, we managed to salvage enough of the discussion to have a give-and-take on the criteria and on the options. By the end of the workshop, one of the "ringleaders" told me how much he had enjoyed the workshop and thought that it was a much "looser" forum and that he appreciated being invited.

We found that the criteria priority ranking sheet effectively kept participants from mounting their option soapboxes. However, they had difficulty discriminating between the criteria and felt that most of the evaluation criteria were public health and safety impacts and that this was the most important factor in selecting power plant technologies. It was particularly interesting to learn that the groups did not consider growth management to be an important problem; however, like the desert group, they favored decentralized power plants, stringent energy conservation

164

measures and home solar heating/cooling devices. They also advocated a mix of options and suggested that hydroelectric plants be retrofitted with wind power.

Several participants changed their option preferences after the initial discussions, and of the nine groups participating, only one remained supportive of nuclear power (as a second choice option) and advocated as his first choice, additional hydroelectric facilities on the North Coast of California, an option which would violate a moratorium on such facilities and conflict with a state law designating several major rivers in the North as wild and scenic. By and large, the group favored solar thermal, fuel cells and biomass conversion. Thus despite the initial animosity among the participants, there was actually a great deal of consensus when they got down to substantive discussion, and stopped worrying about the research project's approach. This discussion was facilitated by the use of the chart overlays which helped the participants to ask questions about the impacts of various options.

Coastal Workshop

The coastal workshop was held on February 19, 1977 at Centennial House on the campus of the University of California Santa Barbara. This facility was a large informal living room overlooking a semi-tropical lagoon on the Pacific Ocean. A much smaller group attended this workshop (no environmental interest group representatives participated, despite our invitations, although several had said that they would attend):

The League of Women Voters, Santa Barbara
    Chapter
County Supervisor from San Luis Obispo County
    (also a member of the State Coastal
    Commission)
Planning Commissioner from Santa Barbara
    County
Regional Water Quality Control Board
Building and Trade Association of Santa
    Barbara

This was the first workshop which involved elected public officials and perhaps this helped to offset the lack of environmental interest group leaders--several participants were actually involved with such groups and wore several hats during the workshop to compensate for the absence of official environmental representatives.

It is unclear whether it was the relaxed, informal setting, the smaller number of persons, or our experience in workshops acquired by that time, but the atmosphere at this workshop was very positive, despite strong differences over nuclear power. All the participants were well-disposed to the experiment and wanted to learn more about innovative power plant technologies.

Like the inland workshop, there was some confusion about restricting option preferences to the coastal region; and similarly, the group felt that most criteria were associated with public health and safety, and there was little concern about growth inducement and the need to attract a power plant to generate new jobs. In fact, the tradeoff regarding new jobs versus growth induced impacts for a community was put directly to the representative of the Building and Construction and Trade Council, who said that his organization's membership did not want jobs at the expense of the environment. He emphasized this by explaining that he had worked to build the Kepone plant in Virginia and felt that "it just wasn't worth it" to build such a plant which eventually ruined lives.

It was also the group's consensus that no coastal community would want to become industrialized and want a power plant. Rather, they perceived the economic future of the coast to be tourism, recreation, agriculture and retirement, and they wanted to keep it that way, unlike certain desert groups which desired the jobs which power plants would offer. Yet like the desert, they resented the thought of having a power plant in their communities in order to provide Los Angeles or San Francisco with electricity.

Statewide Workshop

The fourth and final workshop was held in Sacramento on March 5, 1977 in the Energy Commission's hearing room. This workshop was intended to provide an assessment of technology/site options on a statewide basis, rather than regional preferences. It was anticipated that these statewide organizations, unlike local interest groups, would be better informed on energy alternatives and less prone to accolades in praise of particular technologies.

166

Seven statewide organizations participated in this workshop:

    Air Resources Board
    Department of Water Resources
    League of Women Voters
    Pacific Gas and Electric Company
    Sierra Club
    State Farm Bureau

It is interesting to note that this workshop included for the first time a representative from an electric utility; and that it was observed by Energy Commission staff members. The absence of utility representatives at the "grassroots" regional workshops had been based on the desire to avoid the distraction of a series of harangues aimed at the utilities, rather than a discussion among local leaders of their preferences. It was therefore decided that technical expertise regarding technologies would be provided by team members and not by utility staff members. It was also anticipated that at the state level participants would be used to interacting with public officials and utility personnel and thus their presence would not be dysfunctional. The validity of this assumption was confirmed during the statewide workshop.

The statewide meeting was also distinguished from the other regional workshops by the larger number of public agency participants. However, unlike the earlier nonparticipation by public agency representatives who feared taking positions, these officials provided letters from their superiors explaining that they could not officially take positions for the agencies but that the purpose of the experiment was considered to be important to their agencies and that they were encouraged to participate as individuals expressing their private views. Thus the group of public officials did not "sit-out" the session in order to avoid taking positions.

The workshop opened with inquiries about the results of the regional workshops; the atmosphere was cordial, and the participants appeared to be prepared for discussion. Their first concern was the project's emphasis on central power plants. We welcomed their suggestion of decentralized power plants as an alternative. They then wanted to know more about the time frame for the study and several participants stressed the familiar theme of home

solar heating and cooling devices and the need to
reduce energy consumption before considering new
power plants.

Discussions of criteria ranking immediately
focused on the sources of cooling water for power
plants. This was perceived to be a central factor
in technology/site option evaluations. The group
also consistently shared a concern for
technological feasibility, dependability, and fuel
flexibility/availability. After some of these
issues were discussed and clarified, it was
observed that the statewide workshop group
frequently differentiated between their top one or
two evaluation priorities and the rest of the
criteria. Often they included "health and safety"
in their top choice category, and explained that if
the first two or three criteria were satisfied
(usually air and water quality) then the other
impacts would be eliminated or become greatly
reduced. Thus the statewide group, like the
regional workshops, tended to combine evaluation
criteria.

Although the statewide group was better
informed on technologies than the regional groups,
there were still several innovative options about
which they were unfamiliar (coal gasification,
biomass conversion and fuel cells).

Second Questionnaire and Tradeoffs

The second questionnaires were mailed to
workshop participants to ask them to rank their
compromised option choices after having had the
opportunity to learn about the priorities and
rationales of other groups. During each workshop
participants had been provided with sample second
questionnaires which permitted them to indicate
each organization's top three choices. The second
questionnaire which was mailed asked them to
indicate their choice of acceptable options next to
each group's choices. They were to write next to
the other group's choices whether they were
acceptable. If none were acceptable, they were to
leave the space blank. This process would indicate
which options might generate a consensus and
suggest which technologies might deserve
additional R & D investments.

The result of this evaluation procedure was
that we observed regional differences regarding
option preferences and on the importance of
evaluation criteria. That is, statewide

168

preferences did not mesh with regional preferences, and thus statewide energy planning, without local input, is likely to generate substantial conflict.

CONCLUSIONS

It was apparent from the workshops that participants were unfamiliar with several innovative electric generating technologies such as biomass conversion, fuel cells and coal gasification. If this evaluation procedure were to be repeated, information packets containing the state of the art technologies should be developed and provided in advance of discussions. However, it should be noted that technical information does not necessarily change attitudes and generate consensus, as a study of nuclear power plant decisionmaking in Wisconsin indicates(9).

We can only speculate that technical information can develop a consensus only if there is already agreement regarding socio-economic evaluation criteria. For example, if a group opposes a plant because it is water-consumptive, then a review of cooling water technologies might help them to develop an acceptable plan. However, if they oppose the plant because they do not accept the assumption that demand has been justified, then the review of cooling technologies is a diversionary tactic and the project must return to square A and pay greater attention to the opportunities for energy conservation and demand reduction in the service district. Conflict avoidance procedures are likely to confront this issue frequently, and it is therefore important that before environmental impact assessments commence and NOI's are filed, the issues of demand requirements, conservation, and demand reduction must be resolved. Technology/site evaluation should only start after this point has been reached.

We found that participants consistently experienced great difficulty in thinking about the future, rather than immediate option selection. In addition, generic siting appears to be an extremely difficult concept for citizen activists to accept, probably because of their fears of committing their organizations to plans which might surface shortly after the conflict reduction exercise. In addition, a period of socialization is required before the participants are willing to take the

169

plunge and candidly discuss their views. This period took approximately three hours (the morning portion of the daylong workshops). For actual commitments, i.e., site-specific consensus, regularized workshops would be required.

The socialization which did occur would not have been likely under the direct auspices of the Energy Commission or any other party to power plant decisionmaking. However, the degree of socialization achieved during the workshops was limited by the one-time-only nature of the meetings. The participants suggested that they found the meetings worthwhile and desired continued meetings to get to know each other and the subject better, and to develop a regional network to convene on energy policy matters. We found the participants were hungry for new information on energy, and appreciated learning even defects of technologies they had favored.

In conclusion, the combination of face-to-face discussions about energy policy, when coupled with tradeoff questionnaires, provided a promising conflict reduction technique for the planning process. The information collected through these meetings represents an advance over public hearings and opinion survey research which do not educate the respondents, do not permit them to socialize and interact to develop shared definitions of problems and priorities. These meetings were able to indicate potential strategies for power plant siting in the future.

The acceptance of the report's findings, including the conflict reduction experiment was facilitated by regular briefings of the project monitor, who found the project's approach useful for not only the assigned topic, but also for other agency problems such as the development of interest group consensus on regulations to implement a new statute(10):

Public agencies usually operate on a project by project basis. When overall planning (e.g., and program planning, comprehensive planning) occurs and public hearings are held, the decisionmaker is seldom provided thorough information about the rankings of a comprehensive set of alternatives by different interest groups. When information about alternatives is provided by different interest groups, the framework for their analysis is different and noncomparable,

170

resulting in an almost impossible task for a decisionmaker or staff person to rationally utilize this information. The methodology used by faculty and students at UCLA . . . provides a parallel framework of analysis for all interest groups and also directly provides useable data for decisionmaking.

We thus conclude that third party intervention in the planning process is feasible and productive and helps administrators convert environmental policy implementation from a technical exercise into a socio-economic and political process. In addition, the conflict reduction process provides a socializing experience which is valued by the participants and provides constructive advice to administrators. While it is obvious that there will still be a need for site-specific conciliation, mediation and litigation, the socialization process initiated in conflict reduction activities may provide an important element in avoiding future litigation, though this is not demonstrated by this case study.

REFERENCES

1. For example, see the Natural Resources Journal (January 1976) which is devoted entirely to public participation in the environmental field.
2. Laura M. Lake, "Mediating Environmental Disputes," Ekistics (September 1977), pp. 164-170.
3. Environmental Science and Engineering, An Assessment of Electric Power Generating Options for the State of California (Los Angeles: Environmental Science and Engineering, UCLA, August 1977).
4. Ibid.
5. Ibid.
6. For example, see: Norman Dalkey, et al., Studies in the Quality of Life: Delphi and Decision (New York: Heath & Company, 1972); N. Dee, et al., "An Environmental Evaluation System for Water Resources Planning," Water Resources Research, Vol. 9, 1973, pp. 523-535; M. Hill, "A Goals Achievement Matrix for Evaluating Alternative Plans," A.I.P. Journal, Vol. 34, 1968, pp. 19-29; J.C. Holmes, "An Ordinal Method of Evaluation," Urban Studies, Vol. 9, 1973,

pp. 179-191; G.L. Peterson, et al., "Assessment of Environmental Impacts," Ekistics, Vol. 218, 1974, pp. 23-30; W.R.D. Sewell, "Broadening the Approach to Evaluation in Resources Management Decision-Making," Journal of Environmental Management, Vol. 1, 1973, pp. 33-60; and Environment and Behavior, Vol. 7 (September 1975), devoted to social impact assessment.

7. Climis Davos, "Priority-Tradeoffs-Scanning Approach," Journal of Environmental Management (1977), pp. 259-273.

8. "Kern County Voters Oppose A-Plant: Referendum Fails 2 to 1," Los Angeles Times, March 9, 1978, Part II, p. 9.

9. John Ross, Nuclear Power Decisionmaking in the Lake Michigan Region (Madison, Wisconsin: Institute for Environmental Studies, University of Wisconsin, 1976).

10. Michael De Angelis, Project Monitor, California Energy Commission, Letter, August 1977.

8
Mediating Energy, Environmental, and Economic Conflict over Fuel Policy for Power Generation in New England

Peter B. Clark

INTRODUCTION

As I understand it, the purpose of the AAAS Symposium is to identify differences in approach and process techniques used by social scientists who, responding to environmental conflict, find themselves drawn more and more into the role of third party intervenors. I will attempt to illustrate from the experience of the Center for Energy Policy (Center) the need for an independent intermediary to facilitate multiparty (sector, agency or interest group) processes in order to develop regional public policy. To evaluate the merits of this proposition, I will refer to the role which the Center staff played(1) during different phases of the on-going evaluation of oil-to-coal conversion policies. In this case the multiparties are the region's power industry, federal and state regulatory agencies, the economic interests (fuel suppliers, transport industry, electricity consumers, etc.) and the communities most likely to be environmentally impacted by the switch to coal.

Coal conversion is an issue which has not received widespread discussion in the press. It is an issue which is about to break in the next few weeks as the Federal Energy Administration (FEA) orders a large number of New England electric generating plants to substitute coal for imported oil. The Center and its policy arm, the New England Energy Policy Council, have used the last year to work behind the scenes with the region's decisionmakers in order to clarify the inherent issues and to face the situation as early as

possible.   It is impossible to assess the
effectiveness of our efforts but it is appropriate
to take stock as this difficult issue becomes a
matter of widespread public concern

New England must make major structural
changes due to over-reliance on imported oil. When
this became apparent, there was not existing
mechanism to resolve regional energy issues or to
build consensus behind new strategies. To respond
to this need, the Center for Energy Policy was
organized as a nonprofit, publicly supported group
of professionals addressing problems of energy
usage and supply in a multidisciplinary program of
research, evaluation, policy deliberation, and
public education.

The Center staff was formed in 1974 to support
the deliberations of 40 environmentalists,
businessmen, researchers, energy specialists and
laymen who meet periodically as the New England
Energy Policy Council, a division of the Center for
Energy Policy, Inc. Created expressly to deal with
conflicts arising from differing interests and
points of view, the Council has provided a forum
where issues may be discussed, differences
narrowed, and action proposals developed.

Unlike the energy policy planning efforts on
the federal and state level, the Council has
developed a process to integrate a multi-interest
approach for the rational management of the
region's resources--whether natural, energy, or
economic. It is the desire of the Council to see
information from all sides of an issue brought to
bear on the planning process well before final
decisions are made. The Council's strengths have
been its stress on regional solutions to problems,
and its attitude of cooperation within its own
membership and towards other agencies and interest
groups.

In the two and one-half years since its
inauguration, the Center staff has helped the
Council reach policy consensus on such
controversial issues as variable emission policy
for air quality control, leasing policies for
petroleum exploration on the outer continental
shelf, policies influencing regional energy
demands and economic growth, program incentives
for residential and commercial energy
conservation, conditions for testing the
feasibility of coal utilization as a fuel for
electric generation, and the development of a
demonstration program for winterization of New

England homes which will both create jobs and reduce energy costs. The work of the Center staff is supported at the present time by two contracts: the Nuclear Regulatory Commission has commissioned an evaluation of third party participation in environmental decisions for licensing nuclear power plant sites for New England and the Energy Research and Development Administration has asked the Center to experiment with incentives to speed the market penetration of solar technology.

Consensus formation is a dynamic process involving the interaction of the Center staff as neutral facilitators and mediators with the special interests polarized around a particular policy issue in the context of third parties representing the primary economic, environmental, energy, and public interests of New England. A working policy consensus, one which can be sustained, is difficult to realize when it must be fabricated among groups normally perceived to be in open conflict. A basis for consensus is created by working together to solve problems which are mutually agreed to be fundamental to the solution of the region's energy, environmental, and economic problems.

The Center staff has developed a process of conflict resolution which utilizes formal working groups having special knowledge of each facet of the complex problem under study. As our work has focused more and more on process, it has become evident that we are playing a role as mediator among special interest groups. At first this applied only to the interests represented in the Council. More recently, this has also been applied among the region's regulatory and technical specialists responsible for evaluating issues for New England's decisionmakers.

In February 1976, the Center for Energy Policy was contracted by the FEA to help identify the obstacles to coal conversion in New England. This was a four month contract which resulted in a background report(2) clarifying the underlying environmental, economic and energy issues and a plan of action(3) prepared for the FEA by the four specialist task forces to identify the obstacles which have to be overcome before New England's power plants could switch to coal.

The FEA funding provided the staff with its first training and consultation on conflict resolution. A group from the Harvard Business School(4) with a special interest in inter-

175

institutional conflict monitored the activities of the Center staff and provided some specialized training in process techniques.

THE COAL CONVERSION ISSUE IN NEW ENGLAND

Greater coal utilization has been a national policy since the 1973 Arab oil embargo revealed the vulnerabilty of United States oil supply and OPEC sent oil import prices soaring. The U. S. has enormous coal reserves sufficient to meet energy needs long into the future but requiring major investments and technological changes in order to reduce the environmental deterioration entailed in a rapid return to a coal-based economy.

In 1974, as a first step towards reducing dependence on imported oil, Congress passed the Energy Supply and Environmental Coordination act (ESECA). Basically, ESECA provides the Federal Energy Administration (FEA) with the authority to increase the use of coal in major oil and natural gas burning installations, including power plants, while at the same time giving the Environmental Protection Agency (EPA) the authority to apply environmental requirements to such installations as are deemed necessary to protect the public.

Although about 75 plants have been selected to date, implementation of the coal conversion orders have been difficult to enforce for economic and political reasons. Coal is a dirty fuel which requires expensive technology to reduce toxic emissions to levels consistent with National Ambient Air Quality Standards (NAAQS).

In New England, resistance to ESECA conversion orders is expected to be especially strong. For example, most utilities prefer to reduce oil dependence by investing in new nuclear plants rather than retrofitting oil-fired plants to burn coal. Environmentalists fear that return to coal in New England would signal abandonment of hard-won improvements in air quality. The public is afraid it will ultimately have to pay the price of coal conversion as increased electricity rates and environmental damage. Business and industry view the ESECA strategy as an interim solution at best, requiring risky capital investments and endless regulatory hassles.

The Center for Energy Policy wanted to be involved in clarifying this issue before enforcement orders were issued by FEA because the region has not yet taken a fair look at coal as a

major fuel option. Given the controversial nature
of the economic and environmental impacts of
increased coal utilization, an objective of the
Center was to determine by working with the
region's policymakers whether a consensus could be
formed about the ESECA project's acceptability

The ESECA legislation calls for a
complicated, multistep procedure for determining
which plants should be forced to convert back to
coal. Complexity is created by two problems:
federal multiagency involvement in issues
requiring a compromise between their specialized
regulatory missions; and overlapping
responsibilities between federal and state
environmental decisionmaking processes.

The question of whether a project is
acceptable to the community of interests found
within the states of New England will not be
decided by the environmental-economic
practicability determinations required by the FEA
office. Therefore, the Center set out to determine
whether the basis for acceptability of the ESECA
conversion orders exists among the principal
actors involved in formulating the region's
energy, environmental and economics policies.

THE CASE FOR THIRD PARTY INTERVENTION

Third party intervention in environmental
policy implementation involves entering a
multidimensional conflict in order to help resolve
policy issues requiring acceptance by public
officials and private interests of complex tradeoffs between energy, environmental, and economic
objectives. The intervenor's function is not to
play the traditional conciliatory role between two
disputants. In this case the role is more that of
ombudsman, acting to keep the parties
communicating, and facilitating all sorts of
communications processes.

Conflicts arise because of the
multidimensional and multiparticipant character of
the problems. Misunderstandings are caused by
characteristic asymmetries underlying the
composition of the groups required to reach
agreement. There is asymmetry between access to
information and the distribution of funds to
investigate the consequences of a given decision.
For example, there is a quantitative difference
between the data and technical services available
to power companies analyzing the impact of coal

177

conversion. Also, the risks associated with making a wrong decision are quite different with respect to the company that must finance conversion and the regulatory agencies that must guarantee no adverse impacts on public health and the environment. Finally, there is asymmetry among the values placed by different participants on the resources being allocated such as invested capital, labor, fuel costs, natural resources, environmental conditions.

In order to characterize these asymmetries, the facilitator may use the skills of the economic planner, helping the participants to evaluate where public costs and benefits are not reflected in private costs and benefits. At other times, the facilitator's skills must be those of a lawyer, political scientist, technical expert, or labor negotiator. If and when the intervention calls for these skills and they are found wanting, there is an erosion of credibility with one or more of the participants tht has the potential of undermining the effectiveness of the consensus-building process.

In order to establish the capability to meet multiskill requirements, the Rockefeller Foundation has funded Professor Lawrence Susskind(5) and a multidisciplinary team of MIT professors to build capacity for complex environmental planning and conflict resolution processes into the state and federal agencies responsible for preparing environmental impact statements (EIS). In contrast to that experiment, the Ford Foundation has funded the Center for Energy Policy in order to provide third party involvement for conflict resolution on regional energy and environmental issues. By means of the former grant, third party intervention skills are being built into staffs of agencies responsible for regulating the environment. In the latter project, independent, third-party services have been created on an experimental basis.

Third party intervention processes can be applied in a variety of circumstances where reform of established procedures would yield more efficient environmental decisionmaking and a socially more acceptable solution. The conflict may include all parties represented in a regulatory process, for example, a licensing proceeding, the review of an environmental impact statement, or in our case the application of the Energy Supply and Environmental Coordination Act.

The interests in conflict may also include
public agencies with different constituencies and
missions. For example, a public utility commission
views its mission to assure that the power needs of
the area within its jurisdiction are met with as
good a balance as possible between the interests of
the utilities and their consumers. However, the
state and federal environmental protection
agencies may subordinate power needs to policies
designed to maintain water and air quality. The
state water rights agency may have yet another set
of goals and statutory mandates.

Conflicts naturally arise when the law
prescribes checks and balances by requiring two or
more agencies with conflicting responsibilities to
share in a decision. Environmental watchdogs have
been created by laws frequently designed to
regulate and enforce standards, seldom to plan
trade-offs with other public policies. Marc
Messing of the Environmental Policy Institute
explains the conflicting missions of
environmentalists and planners as follows(6):

> The interests of the public in general,
> and investors as private interests, are not
> necessarily incompatible, but they may be
> fundamentally different. The environmental
> interests of the public involve a basic,
> cautionary protection; the protection against
> possibly immeasurable, or undetectable, but
> genuine damages either to the public health,
> or to the systemic equilibrium of the natural
> environment. Beyond the general range of
> public environmental concerns ranging from
> billboards to bottle bans, agencies of
> environmental review must utilize the best
> available technologies and knowledge to
> determine safe, or acceptable, levels of
> environmental change.
>
> In an epistemological framework which
> suggests that our understanding of the
> thresholds of environmental impacts are
> bounded by the limits of our monitoring
> equipment, agencies responsible for
> environmental review must assume that both
> the public and the environment suffer from
> exposures to families of potentially
> hazardous materials, even where there is a
> lack of supporting empirical evidence. The
> public interest is protected by the
> affirmative demonstration of environmental

compatibility, rather than the assumption of environmental compatibility.

Private interests, on the other hand, must assume environmental compatibility in the absence of contrary evidence, and must make long-term plans, or plans with long-term impacts, on that basis. Reconciling these differences is not impossible, but it is necessarily expensive

Finally, I would draw a distinction between planning agencies and agencies for environmental review. It seems to me that the function of environmental review is environmental protection, and that a review agency must be responsible for amassing empirical information about the boundaries and the functions of environmental systems, and be empowered to protect the natural environment against uncertain, but likely dangers. These dangers include man-made pollutants. A planning agency, on the other hand, must try to plan systems consistent with available information about environmental dynamics and expectations of social growth.

The thrust of this paper is predicated on the hypothesis that environmental regulators can also act as resource planners with respect to future options. Compromise in policy formation requires an appreciation of the alternative uses of resources and a world where the restrictions can vary. Marc Messing has pointed out that if you make people responsible and accountable for their decisions, you do not have to work to get compromise or consistency among their overlapping responsibilities. I feel that if an environmental regulator's and energy planner's perspective and functional mission are fundamentally different, then the execution of their unique responsibilities may lead from incompatibility, to conflict, and to a stand-off.

Resolving Conflicts of Public Utility Policy and the Environment

The inability of nonpublic agencies to resolve conflicts is demonstrated by the difficulty one has of finding, or for that matter constructing, a private agency with competence and motivation to enter into the substance of the fields in dispute unless compensated by one of the

180

conflicting interests. Because the utility industry is regulated in the public interest, a private organization could not exercise the regulatory powers needed to make binding determinations related to energy use of environmental controls. Exercise of regulatory and enforcement authority is an essential part of the reconciliation of conflicting interests. While most instances are handled on a negotiated basis without need for formal enforcement proceedings, knowledge on the part of the several interests that there is an applicable body of law and that some relevant public entity can compel a resolution is a necessary part of a viable accommodation mechanism.

In the environmental field the usual institutional method for representing the public interest is to construct a multimembered commission, giving the board a representative character. Whether a public utility commission, an energy facility siting council, or an environmental advisory board, there will be two or three agency heads and several lay members representing special constituencies such as labor, industry, conservation, health, and the consuming public. Wherever interests needing reconciliation or entry into the decision forum are identifiable. Then public participation involving permanent representation on a policy commission that votes decisions has been the commonly accepted solution.

Normally a commission must deal with environmental and consumer policy as an adversary proceeding. This troubles those who argue that government decisions should not reflect the voting power of the stake holders. Instead, they recommend that public policy be determined in an impartial and objective manner. Therefore, it is often felt that a regulatory requirement, a licensing decision, or setting environmental standards is the job of impartial government officials rather than a contest for votes among vocal and powerful stake holders. Decisions by decibels often reflect the biases of the political choices made when deciding upon the composition of the board. Government should implement policies that balance the interests of all, including those in a majority of the population as well as those directly impacted as citizens and consumers. For this reason, the forces which compose the public interest may change from issue to issue.

181

Given need to determine the changing public interest with respect to energy and environmental issues, perhaps a new form of public participation, a temporary working commission, could be an effective counterpart to existing institutions. A permanent staff of facilitators with a range of critical skills would be an effective agent for resolving policy disputes if the deliberative body could be changed from issue to issue. Rather than freeqing the distribution of power among those represented in a permanent commission, a method should be found to provided flexibility for bringing together the critical interests which vary from case to case.

An example of when public participation would be valuable in the energy, economic and environmental fields is during the preparation and evaluation of an environmental impact statement. Institutionally, if those responsible for the preparation of impact statements had a method for involving constructive public participation at an early stage in the investigation, many of the criticisms that are reinforced by intervenors, public petitions and editorial comment in the media could be avoided. Preparation of an environmental impact assessment is an event signalling the beginning of a decision process where trade-offs involving conflicting interests could be incorporated in a consensus building process orchestrated by independently supported environmental mediators.

THIRD PARTY INTERVENTION PROCESS

Factors Influencing the Choice of Process Techniques

As the last section explained, the responsibilities of regulator and planner are not the same. Recognition of this fact is of central importance when attempting to design a process which will permit them to cooperate with other public interests in order to identify and jointly sign off on the economic and environmental conditions which will make coal conversion of New England power plants practicable.

Regulatory agencies view their role and responsibility as maintaining restrictions and implementing the law. Converting a large number of power plants to coal involves the perspective of planners not enforcers. The dilemma is how to get regulators into a problem solving mode rather than defenders of the status quo.

A constraint which has permeated many of the deliberations of the four task forces working on coal conversions has been the perspective of the regulator. The regulator's attitude can easily disillusion other members of the work group. Everyday enforcement responsibilities causes the regulator's behavior to be interpreted by other participants as lacking in imagination and initiative. As participants it is necessary to break up the problem into its component parts. We have found it very challenging to have regulators think as planners; it has been difficult to develop a creative, open-minded approach which looks at alternative solutions. Therefore, a process must be designed to permit the regulator to consider compromise, the opportunity costs of different resource allocations and a trade-off among stated goals.

A primary goal of the Center for Energy Policy has been to identify policies which are in the best interests of the region. Many of the issues have come to New England because of national priorities and initiatives. Another constraint we have encountered is that federal agencies represented in the region are often unable to set regionally sensitive policies. Instead, their officials feel a conflict of interest when evaluating a regional program because they interpret their primary responsibility as enforcing federal policy and maintaining consistency with national standards. It would be unusual for them to volunteer to recommend that Washington make a special case of a regional policy reflecting the best interests of New England.

Another factor influencing the process design is that most participants start with static assumptions. Because of their overspecialized technical backgrounds, they hold deterministic views. Engineers working in the energy and environmental field seldom envision policy changes or suggest creating new incentives. We have encountered specialists who are not able to identify with the overall issue; they have no vision of the content. Therefore, the Center staff spends many hours orienting the participants to the background situation. We attempt to relate the macro aspects of the policy to the familiar micro situation.

The integration of laymen and technical specialists can be problematic. Public participation may threaten the security of public officials responsible for environmental decisionmaking. Larry Susskind has found that the more the agency staff attempts to involve the decisionmaker or the public as participants in the process of preparing and assessing an environmental impact statement, the less secure (the less indispensible) he or she will become. A task of the MIT project is to teach EIS technicians to build citizen capability and organizational capacity without jeopardizing their own feelings of self-esteem.

Finally, we have observed a great reluctance among all participants to distribute controversial documents for discussion. This is especially true if the draft contains normative statements or judgments attributable to one or another group. Progress is very slow if value judgments are recorded. Similar behavior has been observed with respect to data that is not validated by all participants. Including information in a document gives it legitimacy, a life of its own. Recording one faction's information may challenge others to get out their own data or state their assumptions more clearly. We have frequently been forced to follow procedures (without the aid of computers) that closely resemble the approach taken by Donald Straus(7).

Propositions About Third Party Intervention

In this section I will outline a number of propositions which I think will improve third party intervention. The propositions were all suggested by the experience of mediating the coal conversion issue. In this case, the three principle interests are the electric utilities with the capability of burning coal, the FEA which must select the power plants for mandatory conversion under the ESECA law, and the EPA which must judge the effectiveness of each plant's air pollution control capability. In addition, there are four or five economic interests plus a full range of environmental and public interest groups which will be taking positions with respect to coal conversion. The Center as a mediator is not entirely an impartial, disinterested party. The staff of the Center in many other projects are expected to identify the

184

best energy, environmental, and economic policies for the region. Therefore, coming from the Center the staff is seeking to identify a supportable consensus. We are not advocates for a particular interest group but work to identify an economically and politically feasible policy consensus for the region.

I have observed that many participants have more to gain by perpetuating the dispute than by reaching a compromise. This observation has led the Center staff to act as uninvolved facilitator to keep pushing for resolution of the issue because the region will have gained if an acceptable solution is identified.

The Center has tried a variety of techniques in order to change the group's motivation. Stalling or avoiding the issue may also be costly to interests not actively represented in the process. In the remainder of this section I will outline a number of propositions which we think should be part of the process of third party intervention. The balance of the paper will discuss the Center's experience in using or violating the propositions listed below.

1. Pick participants to represent constituencies in addition to their official affiliation.
2. Maintain active participation of the original stakeholders by setting up a two-level process for decisionmakers and policy people in an action planning group and for technical specialists and regulatory authorities in technical task forces.
3. Be able to cut across existing institutions by creating temporary policy planning groups that disband when the issue is resolved.
4. Hold problem solving sessions where it is necessary for each member of the group to state "what if" a change of policy were to occur.
5. Use process techniques to overcome restrictive attitudes of participants.
6. Use the professional credentials of peers on each side of the issue to help specialist participants extend their perspective.
7. Meet individually from time to time with each of the participants in order to

establish and maintain a secondary line of
trust and communication.

8. Set agenda for each session to reflect
   participants' definition of issues and
   follow group priorities, all hidden agenda
   items must be identified.

9. Keep process sessions and most meetings
   off the record.

10. Mandate the mediation process, whether by
    high-level authority or media
    reenforcement of the group's stated
    intentions.

11. Obtain financial support for the mediation
    process either from independent sources
    unrelated to the potential outcome and
    issues at stake, or from the combined
    resources of the group shared equally by
    all participants.

12. Avoid a potential source of conflict by
    preventing the group from attempts to
    reassess past events in order to establish
    the intentions or motivations of different
    parties.

13. Use the focus of an environmental impact
    statement to organize the substantive
    agenda of the group.

14. Develop a symmetrical data base as a
    precondition for reaching consensus.

15. Teach respect for the values of other
    parties in the process.

16. Document dissenting positions as part of
    any recorded policy consensus.

17. Use communications techniques to increase
    the binding nature of the solution by
    broadening the constituency with other
    interest groups and the general public.

Observation Errors and Small Sample Bias

In this section I will make a series of
somewhat unrelated observations about mediation
problems encountered in the coal project. Given
the technical complexity of the issue, I omit all
reference to the substance of the energy, economic
and environmental analysis and policy
recommendations. Instead I will attempt to
evaluate the advantages or reasons for
recommending each process proposition, drawing
lessons from the unresolved issue of coal
conversion in New England. When I agreed to write
about the Center's experiences in the

186

environmental field, I anticipated completing the
coal conversion project or resolution of other
environmental disputes. The observations that
follow are made by a practitioner involved in an
on-going and extremely complicated technical and
regulatory conflict. While the Center is actively
involved in other New England energy policy issues,
it is still too early to judge whether our
activities as environmental mediators will help
reach an acceptable trade-off between conflicting
policy objectives.

I would add one additional disclaimer. There
is little science in the process experiments
conducted by the Center. We did not develop a
prior hypotheses nor use a control group in order
to measure the effectiveness of our techniques.
Simple pragmatism and learning-by-doing, rather
than an intricate theory of conflict resolution,
have served as the basis for the initiative taken
by the Center. My inquiries to pros asking for
established techniques in the field of multiparty
conflict resolution yielded one response: there
are almost no guidelines, theory or recorded
experience. Perhaps one day a grounded theory can
be established by drawing together the common
threads of the variety of experiences stemming from
the initiative of those represented at the
symposium.

Phases of the Center's Intervention
in the Coal Conversion Issue

The task chosen by the Center was to search
out (by bringing together the principal actors
involved in the issue) a set of conditions and
policies that would permit New England power plants
to burn coal in a manner that would not caus
environmental deterioration nor economic hardship
on the end-users of the electricity. If possible,
it would be desirable if these conditions could be
realized during the implementation of the FEA's
program to implement the ESECA legislation.

The activities of the Center can be divided
into three stages. During the first stage, the
Center prepared several unsolicited proposals to
study the potential for the long-term utilization
of coal in New England. Funding was obtained after
a year of proposal writing and negotiation. Under
an FEA contract the Center convened a planning
group selected to design an action program to spur
coal conversion. However, many of the obstacles

preventing the FEA from issuing conversion orders were economic and environmental policies in conflict with FEA's goals. The Center's investigation involved four task forces asked to identify the regional barriers to coal conversion. The New England Energy Policy Council recommended against issuing coal conversion orders under existing regulatory conditions. The Center staff worked with many of the region's policymakers to identify incentives which might stimulate voluntary coal conversion. Nonetheless, Washington FEA's reaction to the task force reports was to discontinue the funding of the Center's mediation process and to discredit the findings wherever possible. The regional office of the FEA then decided to set up its own project. It asked the coal committee of the Federal Regional Council to make recommendations to stimulate increased coal utilization.

During stage two, the Center attempted to obtain a more general mandate for continued work on the issue. Letters of support were sought and received from most of the participants in the Action Planning Group formed during phase one. The community of interest established between the environmentalist and the utility management confounded the FEA's own initiative. At this point the FEA asked the Center management not to continue the Action Planning Group's deliberations of alternative policies. Instead, FEA asked the chairman of the New England Energy Policy Council to intervene, using his personal diplomacy. A series of meetings to improve the communication among the top level principals were arranged. A spirit of renewed cooperation was achieved through this personal intervention.

Before stage two came to an end the coal committees of the Federal Regional Council (FRC) proposed that a single unit of one of the power plants selected as a candidate to receive conversion orders should be converted for a one-year period to test the economics and monitor the environmental impacts that would be associated with coal conversion. At this juncture the Washington office of the FEA visited the region to assess the degree of opposition likely from utility companies, state energy advisors, and environmental regulators. Confrontations at the meeting caused the FEA to again delay the date for issuing Notices of Intent to the Spring of 1977. Furthermore, there has been no action on the

Shiller plant since the August hearings and EPA's decision to issue the Notice of Effectiveness. There remains serious doubt about the acceptability of the federal program among regional interests.

Phase three of the Center's involvement began when the New England Electric System responded to the FRC's proposal to test coal burning at a single unit. The coal committee of the FRC was asked to identify a plan of action. Being neutral, the Center was nominated to be impartial third party to chair the subcommittee designated to plan the conditions of the test. The Center staff has maintained an active role, working with many of the earlier participants in order to clarify each issue within the general policies of coal conversion. Lack of financial support has meant that the staff could only commit to a very part-time involvement.

Many man-days of personal meetings, telephone calls, coordination, and official task force deliberations have been devoted to the clarification of the hidden issues preventing rapid decisions for variance requests to convert a single unit to coal burning. The Center has just presented a report explaining and identifying the environmental regulatory conundrums(8). Initiative must be taken to resolve policy problems at the national level in order to avoid several years delay. Meanwhile the Center's staff has prepared a policy study(9) suggesting a number of initiatives which could be taken at the regional level to create incentives that would break the status quo with respect to coal conversion policies. This paper is in a discussion draft and will not be published for another few weeks.

Phase four of the Center's involvement is likely to begin on March 6 when it is rumored FEA will issue Notices of Intent to a large number of the region's electric utilities.

EVALUATION OF THE PROCESS PROPOSITIONS

The work of the Center was funded by a contract from the Office of Fuel Utilization at the Federal Energy Administration in Washington, D. C. The contract was negotiated as phase one of a longer-term inquiry into the options for coal utilization in New England. The funds made available were less than one-third of the original request and were sufficient for only a few months work. From the outset the Center staff feared that

189

there would be insufficient resources to reach a significant conclusion or arrive at a policy consensus. Proposition 2 was being violated because the only participant providing support was the FEA which had a clear objective.

The Center's contract called for the preparation of an action plan to stimulate coal conversion in New England, including the designation of those units which should be issued Notices of Intent. The Center negotiated for a looser interpretation of the terms of reference because it did not feel there was sufficient time to do the economic and environmental impact analyzes required to designate the most appropriate set of plants. Instead we agreed to identify the major obstacles preventing rapid conversion of oil-fired plants to coal. We set out to work with the principle interests involved on all sides of this issue to identify the conditions and to attempt to reach a consensus on the policy incentives which would make coal conversion economically and environmentally practicable for New England.

Proposition 10 stresses the importance attached to having a high-level mandate for the work of the neutral intervenor. All of those participating in the project were suspicious of the fact that the FEA was funding the Center's activities. There was always a significant doubt concerning the motives of the Center personnel because it was assumed that a single source of funding implied that we were paid to find answers consistent with the FEA's objectives. Only by establishing a record of fair mindedness was trust finally established to some degree.

Since it was impossible to receive formal authorization from a chief executive, we attempted to set up a self-authorizing initial meeting for the project. The Center enlisted the support and participation of the principal authorities and private sector interests that would be effected by coal conversion policies. The fact that they had a stake or a vested interest in the outcome of the proceedings drew them into the process and created a self-mandating commitment to the serious consideration of alternative policies. As Laura Lake has observed, regular briefings of the decisionmaker or a senior aid on the progress of the mediation process increases the likelihood that the decisionmaker will accept the solution and that the mediator will have the sanctioning power

necessary to make a settlement stick(10). An
important objective of our choice of participants
in the Action Planning Group was that they would
designate technical staff to work on a day-to-day
basis with the Center-organized technical task
forces. Thus the more specialized participants
regularly briefed their senior policy-level
colleagues on the progress of the talks. Normally,
the Center staff briefed the senior officials who
had agreed to serve in the Action Planning Group
from time to time with progress reports and
personal communications.

The principles of Proposition 1 were used to
select the participants asked to serve on both the
Action Planning Group level and in the technical
task forces. We began by attempting to identify
exactly what constituency had what vested interest
in the outcome. We also considered which types of
participants could be expected to sell or advocate
the results of a settlement to their constituencies
once the solution had been developed and a
consensus reached by the mediation group.

The Action Planning Group could include only a
subset of those most directly affected by coal
conversion. Thus, we selected only two utility
company presidents rather than each of the seven
companies with power plants on the candidate list
for conversion orders. The Region 1 Administrator
of the Environmental Protection Agency and the head
of the Massachusetts Department of Environmental
Quality Engineering were asked to serve, but we
felt it would be impossible to ask the senior state
environmental official of every New England state.
To compensate, we invited a public utility
commissioner of the State of Rhode Island and the
energy Advisors of the states of Connecticut and
Massachusetts to represent the positions which
their counterparts from other states might take.
Thus, the Action Planning Group included coal
suppliers, transportation officials, regulatory
agencies, utility companies, environmental
interest groups, consumer interest groups, and the
Region 1 Administrator of the FEA.

The Action Planning Group initiated the
process. At our first meeting we developed an
agenda together which incorporated the objectives
and concerns of all of the principle interest
groups. This agenda was transformed during the
meeting into a work plan that called for four task
forces to be formed to deal with the technical
issues related to coal supply and economic, coal

191

transportation, costs of conversion to the power
plants and the finance of capital investment, the
assessment of environmental impacts, and the
effect of alternative strategies on the choices
being considered by the other task forces.
Feedback loops occur between the Action Planning
Group and the technical task forces. At the
inaugural meeting the members of the Action
Planning Group were asked to designate technical
staff members to participate in the task forces.
Significant commitment of time, personal, and data
was made at that meeting which mandated the purpose
of the project.

The Center staff then filled in the missing
perspectives and representatives of omitted
constituencies by inviting other specialists to
participate in the task force deliberations. It
has always been gratifying that so many people
would willingly contribute their time, information
and technical support to voluntarily work on this
project.

Process Techniques Used in Stage One

Proposition 2 recognizes that it is difficult
to keep full participation of the original high-
level actors throughout a project extending over
several months. The tendency of agencies and
private companies to send second and third level
representatives lacking authority to take
positions was effectively overcome by the two-
level design for policy and technical
participation. If one or more of the stakeholders
does not continue to give full participation, the
value attached to participation by others is
significantly diminished.

Consensus building requires that all parties
(representing key constituencies) participate if
you are going to have a binding consensus. When
the going gets tough and compromise is called for,
some of the key actors may be unable to stay fully
involved for political and strategic reasons. The
two-level organization again helps with this
problem. The only real casualty in this process
was the FEA. Because of rivalries between the
regional office and the Washington group which
contracted the Center, we were unable to obtain a
continued involvement by either group durig the
study of coal conversion. Thus a major benefit of
learning the concerns of other participants
(Proposition 15) was lost to the FEA. Without the

learning experience the FEA found it difficult to accept the position taken by the technical task forces, they questioned the symmetry of the data base (Proposition 14), did not feel bound to implement many of the recommendations and they did not identify with the consensus reached (Proposition 2).

Finally you will note in Figure 1 the interaction between the activities of the Action Planning Group and the technical task forces and the information flows going to the Subcommittee of the New England Energy Policy Council. The planned plenary sessions of the Council created another high-level endorsement of the process. The public interest nature of the New England Energy Policy Council gave an important credibility to the activities of the Center staff as they organized the project. While the deliberations of the participants were kept off-the-record (Proposition 9), knowledge that the position taken would be communicated to the Council for input to their policy discussion created an effective feedback link to a credible third party known to all of the principle actors. Accountability in the eyes of the region's public interest leadership was an important factor contributing to the serious involvement of all participants.

I have stressed that no record is kept of the process sessions; this does not mean that the outcomes are not carefully recorded and analyses of critical points developed. All sessions were tape recorded but verbatim records with attribution were not typed. Participants received summaries of the progress of their work groups and others in the overal process. The issues were carefully drawn without reference to positions taken by each participant.

Attention is given to turning points. Assumptions made by each participant and a record of their value laden (normative) statements influences the mediator's choice of issues to be added to the agenda for further consideration. This last decision requires considerable judgment on the part of the facilitator assigned to each of the task groups.

I believe that the Center staff is relatively inept at drawing on the process techniques known to overcome the restricted attitude of participants. Proposition 5 addresses the importance of process techniques for third party intervention. Meeting organization, role-playing, bird-dogging the issue, speaking up on related issues raised on the hidden agenda of participants, knowing when to stop discussion, paper writing, the timing for the introduction of new expert testimony, efforts to promote within-group advocacy, and the art of communication outside the official meeting all contribute significantly to the effectiveness of the process.

Proposition 4 points out the function of all of these process techniques is to create a "problem-solving" approach in the sessions. Most participants start with static assumptions. One way to overcome this constraint we found was to force the participants to formulate incentives rather than new rules (restraints). Considering "what if" the constraint (cost, regulation, resource availability, tax, environmental impact, etc.) were changed or relaxed. This is equivalent to parametric variations used to test the sensitivity of a given policy solution. It has the benefit of helping the enforcers of the constraint evaluate the impact of changes on the behavior of the system. It also helps them overcome the regulatory mentality, to plan by anticipating and recommending the benefits of finding compromise solutions rather than maintaining the static enforcement-oriented reactive mode.

Proposition 6 suggests that it may be useful to capitalize on the common professional training of the participants representing all sides of the issue in order to help the specialist participants extend their perspective. We try to select technical participants for task forces who do not know each other but who have similar training and interests. Take the case of the environmental task force, the environmental officer of a utility company is probably a chemical engineer. Similar credentials are required for his counterpart from state and federal environmental agencies, the Lung Association representatives of each state, a Harvard Public Health professor, an MIT researcher, a consultant from a contract research firm such as Walden Research, Environmental Research and Technology, MITRE Corporation and an Arthur D. Little scientist. Few of this task force woud have listened to each other's preoccupations or proposed solutions. We think the process must bring education in the norms and technical ideas of other participants. In fact, much of the voluntary involvement we believe is predicated on the advantages of this aspect of the experience.

The mediation procedures outlined by Laura Lake suggested that "technical experts should not be granted participant status" and may testify only at the discretion of the mediator(11). The experiment undertaken by the Center was to try for policy consensus among technical specialists now controlling regulations that presently prevent any possible trade-off among policy objectives. We believe the regulators must become sensitive to the opportunity costs measured in terms of economic, energy, and environmental variables. The organization of our process, however, was designed to keep experts out of the direct policy negotiation by separating the technical task forces from the deliberations of the Action Planning Group. Consistency was maintained, however, between these two groups by having the technical participants brief their policy counterparts in the Action Planning Group.

Outcome of the Stage One Mediation

A principle result of the task force deliberations was the collection of a common data base. In the early meetings we discovered that each participant had his own facts often drawn from a special case or a national average which did not reflect the conditions of the region. An important objective of the technical deliberations was to validate a commonly acceptable data base.

Public interest groups may operate at different scales of concern, each pursuing a dimension of the problem most closely related to their own needs. The Center staff sought a format for organizing the investigation of the policies which determined the practicability of coal conversion. Proposition 13 suggests that the focus of an environmental impact statement is a useful construct to organize the substantive agenda for the group's deliberation. If we broke the problem into component parts distributing the work among the four task forces, the problem is a very interrelated one because choices made on one aspect of the logistic or economic system will affect the costs, emissions, operating efficiencies, and finance in other aspects of the system. We would like to have set up the analysis in a computer program so that a wide range of simulations could be explored. However, time and resources were insufficient to follow that approach.

195

Left to their own priorities, public officials would decide what interests to involve sin the preparation of an environmental impact statement (EIS) by following the prescriptions of law and regulation. The concerns of public interest groups should be incorporated in the guidelines for the preparation of an EIS. This in effect was the agenda adopted by the Center's mediation of this problem. This is partially characterized by the Center's efforts to develop a symmetrical data base from the very beginning of the negotiation process.

The concept of symmetry is used here to reflect the confidence of the different participants in the information generated by the investigation. Because they are part of the process from the start and engage actively in the validation of the data base by questioning assumptions of other members and contributing their own information and working assumptions, a commonly accepted description of the problem evolves.

We found that each of the public agencies required by the ESECA law to make findings operated from an entirely different set of facts. Pains were taken to challenge every number. We identified each person's assumptions for its use. Sometimes special experts were called in to evaluate the data and make projections. In the end, only task force-accepted data was used in the background report. We say the commonly accepted information information creates a symmetrical data base for others.

A major failing of the Center's stewardship of the process was that we did not insist that FEA officials participate at every step of the process. The final report of the working groups was rejected by the FEA because they did not trust the facts and figures included. Efforts were made to avoid identification of particular plants for fear that the data generated might be used in later legal proceedings. The Washington FEA group did not challenge the numbers during the debate by the technical specialists at the task force level. Criticism came only after the task force reports were distributed to the Action Planning Group. In the end, the contract officer was unwilling to approve the Center's final report for payment until all numerical analysis had been removed, leaving only qualitative findings. Because the results of the New England Energy Council deliberations and the work of the Center's team of environmental facilitators resulted in conclusions and policy recommendations which were not consistent with the mission of the Office of Fuel Utilization, the FEA decided to withhold the Center's report from the NTIS.

Although the staff prepared several reports for the FEA, we clearly bungled the opportunity to have all stakeholders go through the learning experience together. Once the numbers were put on the record, there was no way to restore the confidence of the contracting agency in the process.

Proposition 16 points out that a policy consensus must permit dissent. The extent of the dissent is important to the decisionmaker. Likewise, the basis for non-consenting parties to reject consensus very often is caused by a conflict of values or objectives that must be taken into consideration during the process itself. A fundamental tenet of the process techniques (Proposition 15) is to establish respect for the basic values of all parties and awareness of their basic responsibilities during the process of the mediation. We failed during stage 1 of our mediation to make explicit the points of conflict between the FEA and the EPA.

Because the Center's work on coal terminated when the FEA funds were exhausted, the Region 1 office of FEA set up its own project. It encouraged the Federal Regional Council coal committee to investigate conditions by which coal could be burned in the region. The action plan report and the background study were used extensively by the committee in reaching its findings(12). Though not widely distributed, these reports did create a set of ground rules for further deliberation on this issue.

Proposition 17 recommends that intervenors use a variety of techniques to increase the binding nature of the solution by broadening the constituency with other interest groups and the general public. This is a controversial requirement because if begun too early it might appear that the intervenor was politicizing off-the-record negotiations and deliberations of the group. Laura Lake suggests that "meetings with related interest groups may be convened by the intervenor or by participants in order to negotiate a common position and reduce the number of iterations necessary to arrive at a

settlement"(13).   If begun too early, however,
efforts to broaden the support for views of some
participants may be seen as a power play.
Maintaining universal trust in the propriety of the
third party intervenor is of primary importance.
Yet, at the right time the intervenor must have the
technical skills (of communication, public
relations and politics) to use the media, other
interest groups, and the mandating authority to
make the solution stick. Public awareness of the
coal conversion policy options, not details of the
process itself, would make it easier for
participants to sell the compromise to their
constituencies.

Stage Two of the Center's Intervention Efforts

The Center in June 1976 drafted a number of
policy changes which it thought could create
compromise conditions to keep the process going.
Unfortunately, the common stance taken by
utilities and environmental interests against the
FEA position undercut most opportunities for
compromise. The Center solicited letters of
endorsement and support for the mediation from many
of the Action Planning Group participants.
Testimonials were sent to the Washington FEA office
in order to unlock continued funding. In fact,
joint funding (Proposition 11) conditional on a new
FEA commitment was suggested by EPA and the
utilities. Instead, FEA told the Center that the
New England Energy Policy Council position, the
background data, and the identification of
barriers to coal conversion outlined in the action
plan report should not be used by the Action
Planning Group in late June.

The FEA prevailed upon the Council chairman to
abandon that strategy and to use instead personal
diplomacy to negotiate a different method to test
coal conversion feasibility. This process
involved several months of talks and resulted in a
general understanding among the participants in
the Federal Regional Commission study that a test
experiment involving a single operating plant
might be an appropriate compromise. If coal could
be burned on an experimental basis, the question of
the economics, availability of coal, operating
penalties, air emissions strategies, moanitoring
of ambient air conditions, and designation of a
waste-disposal site for sludge and ash could be
fully developed and documented.

Proposition 7 suggests the effectiveness of limited personal contact by the intervenor as a necessary counterpart to group activities. The personal intervention of the Council chairman at this stage of events was necessary to establish a second level of trust and communications. The stakeholders (in this case FEA and EPA officials and utility executives) must have trust in the fairness of the intervention process and feel that their priorities have been heard and understood. Attention to these factors, through off-the-record discussions in small groups and individually, resulted in a compromise.

Stage Three Developments

As explained earlier, stage one ended with a serious dispute prevailing over the accuracy of the numbers used to evaluate the consequences of coal conversion. FEA in Washington decided to solicit new information from New England utilities. In addition, the Office of Fuel Utilization hired several new consultants to develop yet another set of estimates of the future availability of different coal types, their long-term prices, bottlenecks in the transportation system, and capital costs for the plant conversion and the retrofitting of pollution control equipment.

At the same time, a serious debate was taking place within the region over the ability of the different plants to meet emission limitations and national ambient air quality standards after the switch to coal. All estimates were based upon plume trajectory models which lacked actual calibration by checking predictions against the monitored date collected while coal was being burned. For this reason, the utilities and EPA could see the mutual advantage to firing one of the units in the region for a test period. This would determine the adequacy of the modelling estimates which are used to set region air quality control strategies today.

You might ask why the models could not be checked against the monitoring data collected when coal was burned during the oil embargo. Several studies have been made but the operating procedures of the utilities and the monitoring capabilities of the regulatory agencies could not be duplicated if plants were converted to coal today. Proposition 12 states that a great deal of conflict can be avoided if the group does not attempt to reassess past events in order to establish the intentions or motivations of different parties. Incriminations often lead to strong emotional outbursts and a hardening of lines.

We found it is especially difficult to review the period of time when Brayton Point, Somerset, Mount Tom and other New England utility plants burned coal during the 1974 oil embargo. EPA and state environmnental agencies issued short-term variances which were prematurely terminated by the regulatory agencies. Efforts to establish the facts about operations, costs, emissions and monitored ambient concentrations during the energy oil-to-coal conversion period inevitably created tension within the group with regard to the motivation of different parties. It is far easier to plan a new demonstration period of coal burning than to sort out experience recorded a few years ago.

Analysis of policy trade-offs often involves adjusting the relative importance of the values held by different interest groups. The process must teach respect for the values of other parties. During the mediation process, special techniques of value clarification can be incorporated in the substantive agenda of technical and factual investigations. In our case, the FEA decision maker controlling the timing for issuing Notices of Intent made his first visit to New England to discuss the conditions under which ESECA orders would be made. For the first time he realized what the utility executives and regional regulators of the environment, and the energy policy advisors were concerned about. The FEA record of the six months since that visit speaks for itself. The final conversion order for the Shiller plant in New Hampshire has not been issued. The Notices of Intent for the twelve plants and twenty-two units on the candidate list has been substantially revised and further delayed pending further analyses of the ESECA program.

The Center's Role During Phase Three

This phase is characterized by efforts for burning coal outside of the ESECA program. It begins when the New England Electric System volunteered a unit at its Brayton Point plant to make an eighteen month coal conversion test. It will probably involve petitioning for a six-month variance to burn the high sulfur, high ash coal in

200

the existing coal pile, and a twelve month variance to burn a medium sulfur, low ash coal without installing a flue gas desulfurization system.

The Center for Energy Policy was asked to organize a small subcommittee to draw up plans for the test demonstration. In this new role, the Center is acting in the more traditional capacity of mediator between the utility company and the environmental regulators at the state and federal levels regarding a site-specific decision. The negotiators have gone back and forth over approximately a two and one-half month period.

The process has clarified the regulatory points at issue. A firm proposal has not been defined by the power company, however. Regulatory policy has also been carefully delineated for the first time. Unfortunately in focusing on this aspect of the issue, the process has forced the EPA to consider reclassifying the air pollution control region surrounding the power plant. If this happens it will completely change the conditions on which the plant would be able to operate if it were forced to convert to coal.

The final resolution of this issue either as part of the ESECA process which will begin in this region in the next ten days, or by the voluntary conversion of one or more of the power plants is not possible to predict. The intervention of the Center for Energy Policy has expedited the determination of many interest groups to set their own policy priorities. The center's role as a neutral third party facilitator for various members of the energy and environmental policy community has been established. Each party now checks with Center staff as they consider taking a new position with respect to coal conversion. The intervention has in part led to the Center becoming a clearinghouse for information. The problem is that we now do this on a volunteer basis and no longer have sufficient financial or staff capability to pursue the issue to bring it to a logical conclusion.

CONCLUSIONS

Only very limited conclusions can be drawn from the Center's experience. It is a matter of opinion as to the efficacy of the Center's involvement. I am sure that there is more known about coal conversion both within the Action

201

Planning Group and in the public domain than would be the case if the Center had not intervened in this issue. In some sense the region is better prepared for the policy debate which will soon begin when the ESECA orders are issued. We have also uncovered a willingness to voluntarily convert to coal under economic and environmental conditions that will not penalize the electricity customers of the plant converting to coal.

This paper has outlined a number of propositions which in combination describe a technique for intervening as an independent facilitator in multiparty disputes. The case has not been made for the independent funding of this process by the parties whose interests are at stake. The public sector or foundations are the most appropriate sources of support to test the role of the environmental intervenor. We have yet to show that the intervention has been socially productive providing a timely compromise to an energy, environmental and economic conflict over fuel policy for power generation in New England.

It should be noted that because environmental legislation continues to grow while governments are busy creating economic and energy stimulants, the probability of interests at conflict will increase disproportionately. Asn an economic I am discouraged by the almost total inattention to the cost and inefficiency caused by exclusive reliance on regulations to police the environment, administrative law to institutionalize the process, and the courts to resolve the ensuing conflicts. Policy implementation by means of economic incentives and penalties would be administratively more efficient. Instead, Congress confronts the planner with a maze of overlapping regulations which complicate environmental planning. For example, power plant licensing, non-degradation policies for air quality maintenance, thermal discharge policy in rivers or in coastal waters, and Coastal Zone Management plans for energy facility siting, offshore oil development and airport planning of multisector, multiconstraint and multiobjective policies are required.

The situation requires institutional innovation. A combination of services would help: a facilitator to see that bureaucratic rivalries do not create incentives for delayed action; an independent capability to apply intervention skills outlined in this paper could also be effectively applied to a wide range of issues likely to require conflict resolution early in the decisionmaking process. I would propose that the Council for Environmental Quality be given sufficient funds to study where and how environmental mediation services should be provided to ease the growing criticism leveled at environmental planning because of public participation, inter-institutional conflicts and NEPA-type procedures.

REFERENCES

1. The description and evaluation of the Center for Energy Policy's program set forth in this paper is the sole responsibility of the author. Policy discussion may not reflect official positions of the New England Policy Council or of institutions giving financial support to the Center. I wish to than the Center's staff (Richard Daifuku, Beverly Drake, Richard Furman, David Hearding, Lillian Morgenstern, David O'Connor and Elizabeth Wuthrich) for attempting to apply the process of policy planning by consensus building to this controversial issue. Whatever success the Center's approach may have is largely due to their skill and perseverance.
2. Center for Energy Policy, "The Impact of Power Plant Coal Conversion on New England Energy Policy," Boston, May 10, 1976.
3. Center for Energy Policy, "Action Plant Report to Stimulate the Use of Coal in Electric Utility Power Plants in New England," prepared under FEA Contract, Boston, May 1976.
4. A project directed by Professor Richard Walton is preparing a paper evaluating the Center staff's efforts to develop a consensus on policies affection coal conversion. Because of the preliminary nature of their findings, the Harvard team have felt it best not to show a draft research paper to Center staff.
5. Lawrence Susskind, "Environmental Impact Assessment: Technical and Institutional Frontiers," Preliminary Proposal to the Rockefeller Foundation, MIT, July 19, 1976.
6. Marc Messing prepared these observations in response to the question raised by the Nuclear Regulatory Commission on the efficiencies of environmental decisionmaking. I have taken the liberty of quoting his answer to the question,

"Would a combined planning and environmental review agency improve decision-making?" because of the important distinction he recognizes between two government agency's responsibilities and their respective assumptions about how each deals with unknown parameters.

7. Donald Straus, "Mediating Environmental, Energy, Economic Tradeoffs: A Case Study of the Search for Improved Tools for Coastal Zone Planning," AAAS Symposium Proceedings (Chapter 4).

8. Center for Energy Policy, "FRC Coal Committee Proposal: A Test of Coal Burning at a Power Plant in New England," February 15, 1977.

9. Center for Energy Policy, "Confronting the Problems of Converting New England's Power Plants from Oil to Coal," January 1977.

10. Laura M. Lake, "Mediating Environmental Disputes," Ekistics (September 1977), pp. 164-170.

11. Ibid.

12. FRC Coal Committee, "New England Potential for Increased Use of Coal," New England Federal Regional Council Energy Resource Development Task Force, September 1976.

13. Lake, op cit.

9
Mediating the West Side
Highway Dispute in New York City

Laura M. Lake

INTRODUCTION

In 1971 the Governor of New York, Nelson A. Rockefeller, and the Mayor of New York City, John V. Lindsay, signed a <u>Memorandum of Understanding</u> which authorized the Federal Highway Administration of finance the planning costs for a roadway to replace the dilapidated and dangerous (pavement sections were collapsing) elevated West Side Highway along the Hudson River in Manhattan. Three years and seven million dollars later, the West Side Highway Project Staff published a <u>Draft Environmental Impact Statement for Interstate 478</u>, which proposed five alternatives for replacing the highway(1):

1. The Maintenance Alternative
2. The Reconstruction Alternative
3. The Arterial Alternative
4. The Inboard Alternative
5. The Outboard Alternative

---

*This research was presented at the Annual Meeting of the American Society for Public Administration, Chicago, Illinois, April 1975. It is included in this book to provide an illustration of the inability of mediators to resolve environmental disputes in which delay is to the advantage of participants, and in which the mediator has failed to obtain political support for implementing a consensual settlement.

Replacing the highway is an extremely expensive undertaking. For example, the Outboard Alternative would involve landfill and was estimated to cost approximately $1.1 billion for about four miles of highway. The environmental impact statement for the West side Highway (WSH) was severely criticized because it did not provide an analysis of the "transportation plans for a given area, including as one required alternative the possibility of doing nothing at all"(2). (This alternative became know as the "No-Build Alternative.")

During the three years of highway planning, considerable polarization had developed between civic, business, environmental groups, the impacted communities and the highway planners, and New York City faced a transportation policy implementation dilemma(3): the old West Side Highway had been closed since 1973. Something had to be done to provide a nonlocal street route for automobile and truck traffic, and at the same time, under the 1970 <u>Federal Clean Air Act</u>, New York City had to abate air pollution, which was primarily due to automobiles.

The West Side Highway mediation experiment was designed to determine the local citizens' preferences and their concerns about transportation. It hoped that the mediation sessions would develop a consensus on transportation. It hoped that the mediation sessions would develop a consensus on transportation priorities for the city, and might be viewed as a policy implementation process for federal air quality laws and two federal transportation policies: building Interstate and Primary System Highways, and subsidizing urban mass transportation.

Organizational Fragmentation and Policy Implementation

The mediation sessions took place within a political decisionmaking system which involved a diverse set of participants and jurisdictions which are summarized in Table 9-1, below which utilizes an analytical scheme similar to one employed by Pressman and Wildausky(4) which indicates participants' objectives, perspectives and sense of urgency. There was no attempt made to involve these decisionmakers in the mediation experiment either directly or indirectly, with the

Table 9-1. Parties To The West Side Highway Dispute Who Were Not Included
In The Mediation Experiment

PARTICIPANT	CONNECTION WITH WEST SIDE HIGH- WAY	PERSPECTIVE AND MAJOR OBJECTIVES	SENSE OF URGENCY
Action for Rational Transit	Coalition of local groups which opposes I-478, favors mass transit, and filed suit to stop I-478.	Stop I-478	High (con)
State Assembly and Senate Representatives	WSH is within several Assembly and Senate Districts. Several opposed I-478 last summer and are now being joined by the rest.	Represent voter by informally advising Governor Carey to veto road	Moderate (con)
Congresswoman Bella Abzug	I-478 within her district. Influenced increase of Interstate transfer to $550 million.	Represent voters, influence House Public Works Comm. decision on I-478 funding	Moderate (con)

Table 9-1. Continued

Manhattan Borough President Percy Sutton	Member of WSHP Steering Committee. I-478 in his district.	Wanted a landuse study. Announced opposition to I-478 on March 3, 1975	Moderate (con)
Chairman, City Planning Commission, John Zuccotti	Developed own "Westway" plan for I-478; advises Mayor Beame, who endorsed "Westway."	Wants "Westway" six lane I-478 accepted.	High (pro)
Mayor Abraham Beame	Veto power by not transferring right-of-way to state.	Accepted "Westway" plan. Banned new capital works projects and stopped work on Second Avenue Subway.	High (pro)

208

Table 9-1. Continued

Governor Hugh Carey	Veto power by not providing 10 percent state matching funds for federal 90% share for Interstate.	Skeptical about the need for an Interstate. Appointed a five person trans- portation task force. Approved I-478 on March 7, 1975.	Moderate (pro)
Metropolitan Transit Authority	Member WSHP Steering Committee.	Anti-I-478, endorses Interstate transfer.	High (con)
U.S. EPA, Region II	Responsible for accepting environmental impact state- ment for I-478 and granting construction permit.	Reviewed draft e.i.s. during summer 1974, and gave low rating Claimed that NY State was in violation of Clean Air Act. Could block I-478.	Unknown

209

Table 9-1. Continued

New York-New Jersey Port Authority	Member of WSHP Steering Committee. Controls access to Hudson River, can raise tolls, end commuter discounts and help finance additional mass transit.	Anti-mass transit transfer because of competition with existing Port Authority mass transportation facilities, and revenue from automobile tolls.	High (pro)
Tri-State Regional Planning	Interstate compact organization (N.Y., N.J., Conn.) which must approve the WSHP before federal funding is possible. Approval is based on compliance with state air quality controls plans.	Prepared a regional transportation plan	Moderate (pro)
West Side Highway Steering Committee	22 member city-state policymaking body to direct planning process, including representatives of six community planning boards within the West Side corridor.	No consensus on WSHP. Community Planning Boards oppose I-478. Interested in seeing transportation policy implementation.	High (split)

exception of the Steering Committee of the West
Side Highway Project, which was represented by the
community planning boards' participants.

The federal government's influence on the
West Side Highway Project was significant because
of the Interstate and Primary Highway System
programs which provide a 90 percent and 70 percent
(respectively), subsidy to states. The Federal
Highway Administration also contributed $7 million
for I-478's planning costs. In addition, a 1973
federal ruling made it possible for a city which
already had an Interstate approved for funding to
withdraw its Interstate plan and request that a
related amount of funds from other sources be
transferred to finance specific mass transit
projects within the same urban area. The amount of
money available through the "Interstate transfer"
for I-478 is now $550 million(5).

Federal environmental statutes also
influenced the West Side Highway dispute through
the National Environmental Policy Act's
requirement that an environmental impact statement
be developed for any federally assisted project.
This provided the opportunity for environmental
groups to debate the impact of the highway on the
West Side's communities, and environmental case
law has strengthened the positions of these
citizens and provided them with the legal standing
for a suit to block the Interstate.

The Governor of New York could veto the WSHP
through his control of the state's matching funds
for the federal highway grant program. (The State
of New York annually receives approximately $57
million for the Primary Highway System, of which
about $27 million is designated for use within New
York City.) During the mediation experiment, a new
Democratic governor was elected, who, unlike his
Republican predecessor, was not predisposed to
automatically support an Interstate. He appointed
his own five person Task Force on the West Side
Highway Project, which included two mediation
participants(6). In a sense, Governor Carey
coopted the mediation experiment, and appeared to
be seeking a consensus on transportation
priorities.

Abraham Beame, the Mayor of New York City
(1973-1977) could have vetoed the West Side Highway
Project by not granting the rights of way for the
highway to the state, (which would reimburse the
city for the rights). The mayor was advised by the
Chairman of the City Planning Commission, John

Zuccotti, who proposed his own plan for a six-lane
Interstate, on November 21, 1974(7), the day after
the mediation group's press release(8).

The national and local economy suffered
substantial declines during the mediation
experiment, e.g., Mayor Beame imposed a ban on all
new capital projects and stopped the Second Avenue
Subway and Third Water Tunnel projects because of
cost overruns. The City is anxious to stimulate
the economy through a capital-intensive project
like the Interstate.

Thirty-nine local block associations and
environmental interest groups consolidated their
opposition to the WSHP by forming Action for
Rational Transit (ART) in September 1974(9). In
December these groups filed suit to block the WSHP.

Finally, at the age of 85, Robert Moses, one
of New York City's best known planners, and former
head of an agency which had planned the original
West Side Highway, presented his own plan for the
WSHP(10).

A MEDIATION PROCESS MODEL

The following nine points serve as a model for
environmental mediation and are used to evaluate
the West Side Highway mediation experiment.

1. Careful premediation leg-work is necessary
in order to identify all of the parties to a
dispute and to determine if continued delay
benefits any of the parties, or if they all desire
a settlement. The mediation participants must be
selected by the mediator. During this preliminary
stage the mediator must determine who might best
represent all of the interests to the dispute, and
take special efforts to keep the group small so as
to facilitate the speed of the deliberations. The
mediation participants need not formally represent
organizations, but rather, constituencies, and
should be expected to "sell" the settlement to
their constituencies once it is developed and
endorsed by the mediation group.

2. The mediator should have a formal
authorization from the chief executive (mayor or
governor) and regularly brief the decisionmaker or
a senior aide on the progress of the mediation
process. In this way the decisionmaker will be
most likely to accept the solution, and the
mediator will have the sanctioning power necessary

to make a settlement stick. (However, any disgruntled citizen can still initiate litigation, for the mediation process is not binding as a consent order is.)

3. The mediator should operate on a full-time basis, and may be an outsider to the community, or a resident. The essential qualifications are trust and neutrality.

4. The mediator need not be an expert on a particular environmental or resource issue, but should have an awareness of the dimensions of the dispute and recall to uninvolved (neutral) experts who may serve as consultants to the mediator. Technical experts should not be granted participant status, and may testify only at the discretion of the mediator.

5. Meetings of related interest groups may be convened by the mediator or by the participants in order to negotiate a common position and reduce the number of iterations necessary to arrive at a settlement.

GROUND RULES

The mediator, Donald Straus, former President of the American Arbitration Association, set the ground rules for the sessions(11): he would not take positions, but would attempt to facilitate discussion and compromise, with the goal of developing a unified position on the West Side Highway Project. This consensus would then be used to influence the West Side Highway Project Director, Lowell Bridwell, former U.S. Highway Commissioner. Conciliation and negotiation were to be based on altered priorities as a result of this educational process(12). The mediation experiment was encouraged by Bridwell. This interest in the experiment appeared to coopt the process in the eyes of several participants, and the relationship of the West Side Highway Project probably contributed to the inability of the mediation process to reach a settlement. Bridwell's proprietary interest in the experiment illustrates the(13):

> . . .functional concentration of authorities in bureaucracies. . . .Discretionary authority has shifted less among political officials than it has from them to bureaucratic experts and professionals . . .

in . . .environmental   planning,   and transportation.

The role of the Regional Plan Association, a professional, nongovernmental organization, also compromised the mediator's independence (Point 6). John Keith of the Regional Plan Association was both a co-convener of the mediation experiment and a participant. This was a confusing role in the eyes of several participants.

The mediator stressed that he was a volunteer, and not subject to control by anyone. However this total independence became a handicap, rather than an asset, for he was not authorized (Point 2) by either the governor or the mayor (the veto powers), and no one was obliged to implement the group's recommendations. Without a delegation of authority, the mediator lacked sanctions, and this contributed to the participants' hesitancy to make concessions for an outcome which could not be guaranteed by the mediator.

Other procedural and organizational problems also influenced the mediation experiment throughout the sessions. A full-time mediator (Point 3) was needed to do the necessary homework (Point 1) outside of the mediation sessions in order to advance the discussions who could brief the mayor and governor or the key staff members (Point 2) and talk with groups which were not necessarily represented at the table (Point 5). Another problem which impeded settlement was related to the selection of participants and their standing as members of the mediation group. Technical consultants to the community planning board participated fully in the mediation experiment and voted when their board members were absent (Point 4).

PARTICIPANTS

Participants were selected by co-conveners Christopher Wright of the Rockefeller Foundation and John Keith, President of the Regional Plan Association. (Point 1 of our model requires that the mediator select participants.) The participants represented civic, business, environmental groups and the impacted neighborhoods' community planning boards. While there were no representatives present from the federal, state and city governments, technical

214

resource persons were present, including two
members of the West Side Highway Project staff and
traffic engineering consultants to the community
planning boards. In all, about <u>thirty-eight
participants</u>, representing twenty-three groups
attended the first session. This high rate of
attendance was sustained throughout the five
sessions, but the large number of participants made
the deliberations move slowly (Point 1). A list of
the participating organizations is appended.

Table 9-2, below, indicates that the
distribution of positions was fairly even.

Participants were selected on the basis of
their constituencies and their groups' attitudes
toward the West Side Highway Project. According to
John Keith, no one was invited who was avowedly
opposed to shifting positions on the basis of
further information and concessions from other
participants(14), and thus there was the
likelihood that other groups would proceed to
litigate, and that the highway proponents were
attempting to coopt the mediation group in order to
influence the mayor and the governor on their final
decisions. Several persons were dual
representatives, e.g., Marcy Benstock of the New
York City Clean Air Campaign also represented
Action for Rational Transit, a coalition against
the Interstate; and John Keith of the Regional Plan
Association, Carolyn Konheim of the Scientists
Committee for Public Information, and Kenneth
Patton of the New York Real Estate Board, were
members of newly elected Governor Hugh Carey's
Transportation Task Force.

FIVE MEDIATION SESSIONS

The following chronological account of the
five mediation sessions presents an analysis of the
attitudinal transitions (including reversals)
which developed during and between sessions, and
provides a sense of the challenge of consensus
formation. The reader will observe that signalling
of issues, seeking information, developing
proposals, and reaching a consensus were phases of
the West Side Highway mediation experiment which
occurred out of sequence. For example, after an
initial consensus was reached at the end of the
fourth session, we found that at the beginning of
the fifth session the West Side Highway Project
staff made a presentation on traffic forecasting

Table 9-2. Participants and Perspectives in West Side Highway Dispute

PARTICIPANT	CONNECTION WITH WEST SIDE HIGHWAY	PERSPECTIVE AND MAJOR OBJECTIVES	SENSE OF URGENCY
Regional Plan Association	Co-convener, participants (professional regional planners)	Resource persons; civic concern and interest in mediation	Moderate (pro)
Community Planning Board Members*	Participants (impacted community)	Concerned with traffic congestion pollution and stability of community	High (pro/con), depending upon which community planning district
Consultants to Community Planning Boards	Resource persons and participants	Advocated specific configuration 4 or 6 lane interstate); did not vote unless board member absent	High (Board 4 pro, Boards 2, Boards 2, 7, 9, 12 con)

216

Table 9-2. Continued

Civic Groups	Participants (general concern for NYC)	Concerned with economic and environmental considerations, wanted improved highway and improved mass transportation	Moderate (pro/con)
Environmental Groups	Participants (anti-highway)	Concerned with improving air quality) auto dependence within regional and particularly within NYC	High (con)
Business Groups	Participants (real estate value changes from highway; jobs from highway contracts; reduce congestion and transportation costs; increase executives' commuting case)	Concerned with loss of jobs for NYC, loss of tax base, etc.	High (pro)

*Member of WSHP Steering Committee

217

data interpretation, an earlier point of contention, which was gratuitous. The mediator might have anticipated the need for such information earlier, and coordinated the presentation with the deliberations.

First Session: Introduction, Signals, and Questions

The West Side Highway mediation experiment's first session was convened in the Board Room of the Rockefeller Foundation on August 14, 1974, by Christopher Wright* of the Rockefeller Foundation and John Keith, President of the Regional Plan Association. They introduced the mediator, Donald Straus, of the American Arbitration Association. Straus proceeded to describe his goals for the experiment (see "Ground Rules").

The issues which were to be iterated throughout the following four sessions were revealed as participants were asked to comment on ten statements which had been prepared as a draft agenda by the Regional Plan Association. The group's ability to agree on general statements oscillated sharply with its inability to agree on how to best implement these generalities. For example, most participants agreed that the old elevated highway structure should be razed, and that it should not be replaced by another elevated structure. But they could not agree on the desirable vehicle capacity for the highway's replacement.

Five major points were articulated during this three hour session which became the parameters for possible negotiation:

1. Participants were concerned about the vehicle capacity of the replacement highway: the consultant for three combined planning boards argued for a four-lane road so that no additional vehicle capacity would be created which might induce additional traffic. Another consultant to a planning board argued that a six-lane Interstate would relieve local traffic congestion by diverting local street traffic and by accommodating

---

*Mr. Wright is now a member of the Carnegie Institution's Staff, Washington, D.C., and served as a discussant at the AAAS Symposium on Environmental Mediation.

trucks which had never been permitted on the old
West Side Highway.

2. Environmental interest group
representatives wanted to determine the economic
and social costs of highway, (15) and claimed that
a six-lane Interstate would violate the 1970 Clean
Air Act. They therefore advocated the Interstate
transfer option for mass transportation. (The
"relationship of price/or cost to number
service"(16), was a compelling argument, since the
four mile $1.1 billion highway would serve only one
percent of all entries into the Central Business
District, and over ninety percent of the people
arriving in the Central Business District come by
mass transit.)

3. The future disposition of land which might
be created as a result of landfill for the
"Outboard" configuration of I-478 (about 200
acres), was challenged by environmentalists, who
wanted guarantees that such land would not be used
for speculative purposes.

4. Participants from the local community
planning boards wanted public access to the
waterfront and the residential and commercial
integrity of their communities to be guaranteed.

5. Business leaders felt that the economic
health of New York City was vitally linked to the
West Side Highway and that businesses would leave
New York unless I-478 were immediately built.

At the end of the first session the
participants agreed that there was a potential for
consensus, and that another session was warranted.
They were confused about highway and mass transit
funding mechanisms, and requested clarification
about the laws, funding levels, deadlines, design
specifications, and the Interstate transfer. The
dispute between the two sets of traffic consultants
also puzzled the group (Point 4), and a
subcommittee was selected to prepare an agenda on
traffic issues for the next meeting.

Second Session: Recapitulation

The second session provided the consultants
with a forum to continue their technical dispute
over a four or six-lane Interstate (Point 4).
Their exchange somewhat obfuscated the other
issues which had stimulated the mediation
activity.

219

The next volley of accusations was exchanged between the environmental group representatives, who demanded aid for mass transit, and the business leaders, who pleaded that a new highway be constructed with dispatch. Somewhere between these two positions were the civic groups, which appeared to be equally concerned with air quality and a healthy city economy (see Table 1).

The participants became rigid in their positions, and a little headway was made. They concluded after an entire day of discussion that federal officials should be invited to explain the technical requirements for mass transit subsidies and highway funding. (The need for this information had already surfaced during the first season.)

Third Session: The "Inevitable" Highway

Participants listened to presentations by the Associate Administrator of the Federal Highway Administration and an official from the Urban Mass Transit Administration, and then proceeded to ask them specific questions about federal regulations and their application to the West Side Highway. The officials' responses revealed the fundamental importance of arriving at a consensus on transportation priorities before approaching the federal funding agencies. For example, one participant asked if the Interstate were withdrawn, would the $550 million transfer money be designated for use only within the Westside corridor, or could it be diverted (against the wishes of the mediation group) to finance the Second Avenue Subway? The official replied that the money could be used anywhere within the urbanized area, and that there was no prohibition against using the money on the Second Avenue Subway--that guarantee would have to be negotiated with Mayor Beame. This comment also underscored the need for the mayor to be regularly briefed on the mediation group's discussions and concerns (Point 2). The federal speakers stressed that their agencies would be as flexible as possible, "if the local groups would just decide what they wanted"(17).

After the funding lesson, a plan for spending the mass transit transfer funds was proposed by Robert Rickels, Executive Director of the Institute for Public Transportation, and former Commissioner of Air Resources for the City of New

York. His plan included repairing the IRT subway cars, extending the Flushing subway line, air-conditioning existing subway stock, and repairing IND subway stations. Representatives of Combined Planning Boards 2, 7, and 9 responded to this proposal by demanding that all funds go exclusively to the West Side corridor.

The Regional Plan Association then presented a "talking plan" for a highway. The plan was received negatively by the group: they were not about to endorse a particular highway configuration.

This negative response was followed closely by a demand from the representative of the American Institute of Architects that the City Planning Commission conduct a comprehensive land-use study, as required by the 1971 Memorandum of Understanding(18). He invited the group to endorse his demand, and was greeted by groans. It was too late to start a land-use study--the decision would have to be made without it. Some sort of highway appeared to be inevitable.

Although the group was not prepared to endorse a particular highway plan it appeared to be receptive to negotiation, and a physicist, Michael Marmor, representing the Scientists' Committee for Public Information, formulated a list of goals which the group might wish to endorse:

-- Keep jobs within New York City.
-- Create a good physical and aesthetic environment.
-- Guarantee access to the waterfront.
-- Guarantee the stability of the impacted communities.

These four points could be included in a binding land-use plan, Marmor suggested. The group nodded: these were all important considerations. They then requested that the professional planners provide a draft plan which would meet these requirements, and they requested that Marmor poll the participants to determine the specific provisions which the group might endorse.

Fourth Session: Election Day Ennui

The fourth meeting opened with a remainder from the mediator that highway planning deadlines were approaching, and that these decisions would be made with or without advice from the group. He

221

wondered aloud if a coalition were possible, and suggested that the West Side Highway Project (not the mayor or governor, Point 2) was ready to accept a statement from the group.

The mediator's comments sparked a partisan response from anti-Interstate participants, who claimed that it was premature to compromise until the gubernatorial election was settled. If Hugh Carey, the Democratic candidate, were elected, their side might have greater influence, and an Interstate would not be inevitable.

It became obvious that both extremes were avoiding compromise until the election was over. This ploy angered the representative of the Chamber of Commerce, who appeared to resent sharing access to decisionmakers with citizen intervenors. It is interesting to note that such frustration is not restricted to New York's business community. A similar attitude was noted in Nashville, Tennessee, regarding public participation in environmental management(19):

> . . . Some of the leaders of the private sector are less sanguine about involving citizens in complex issues. Accustomed to handling such matters in small groups ("All it takes is an hour over lunch and a few of us can settle most any problem quickly and efficiently"). they are uncomfortable with time consuming public meetings and the rambling, often ill informed or confused remarks of citizens attending them.

However, the New Yorker's remarks were more intemperate; while pounding the table, he exclaimed "this is not a democracy, but a republic. We elect officials to make a decision." He then claimed that he had no interest in participating in the group's decision, but wanted to know what they were up to, in order to protect himself.

Ignoring this outburst, the participants called for the results of the poll conducted by Michael Marmor. They wanted to get on with working out a compromise plan. Table 9-3 below summarizes the results of the poll. If one combines mass transit and the mixed mode category, these results indicate a near split between the Interstate advocates and those interested in mass transit. This distribution of priorities indicated that a consensus position on transportation would have to

Table 9-3.   Tabulation of Groups' Transportation
Priorities

NUMBER OF INTEREST GROUP RESPONSES FOR
EACH PRIORITY

7.0   Interstate (mostly civic and business groups)
3.5   Transfer all Interstate funds to mass
        transit (environmental groups)
5.5   Partial transfer of Interstate funds to
        mass transit (civic and environmental
        groups)

16.0 Total*

*Responses had not been received from
six organizations at the time of the meeting.

encompass the need for both highways and mass transportation.

The "essay" replies to the questionnaire addressed issues which were not developed during the mediation sessions, e.g., why do businesses actually leave New York City? The respondents uniformly opposed continuous service lanes for the West Side highway because they would add excess vehicle capacity and lure more cars onto the highway.

After Michael Marmor discussed the patterns revealed by his analysis of the questionnaire responses, the group decided to vote on a statement which reflected their areas of agreement. Considerable time was spent rewording the statement, but it was unanimously approved by a show of hands. It was interesting to note that the participants were sympathetic with the specific requests of their fellow participants. For example, when one of the local planning board members objected to the section which described future uses of the waterfront, and requested that commercial uses be included, because his district contained commercial interests which would reject the statement unless it included provision for some portion of the waterfront to remain commercial. The mediation group accepted his amendment.

And so it went, until the pro-Interstate participants demanded a vote be taken to determine the desirability of an Interstate from Battery Tunnel to 72nd Street. This resolution was rejected by a vote of thirteen against, seven in favor.

In an effort to regain the consensus which was threatened by this "extremist" demand, the group agreed to request that the West Side Highway Project provide a no-build (no highway) evaluation, and an explanation of vehicle capacity forecasting. (The representative of Combined Planning Boards 2, 7, and 9 was adamant that the Project provide the land-use study of transportation systems and alternatives, including no new highway, and based his demand on the 1971 Memorandum of Understanding.) The next meeting was scheduled for November 13, 1974 a week after the election.

Fifth Session: Recapitulation and Termination

The West Side Highway Project Staff attempted to clarify the four land/six lane controversy, by

explaining positive aspects of a six lane road.
Perhaps more confused than before the West Side
Highway Project presentation, the mediation group
decided to review current economic and political
changes. Mayor Beame had placed a ban on all new
capital projects and had stopped work on the Second
Avenue Subway and the Third Water Tunnel. Hugh
Carey, the Democratic candidate for governor had
been elected and had appointed an advisory Task
Force on the West Side Highway which included
mediation participants Carolyn Konheim and John
Keith. These economic and political changes made
the inevitability of an Interstate highway
questionable.

During the previous mediation session the
pro-Interstate participants lost the vote on
endorsing an Interstate. Now, with the political
tables turned, (i.e, with a Democratic governor),
anti-Interstate advocates demanded a vote on a
resolution to transfer Interstate funds to public
transportation. The mediator felt that this was
not the appropriate time for such a vote--and with
hindsight, one can guess that it too would have
failed, since such an all-or-nothing approach left
the groups who favored some highway plan and mass
transit aid without a compromise package.

The group reviewed yet another highway plan
sketch, and began to compose a statement of
agreement which officially became a group press
release on November 20, 1974(20). It was hoped
that the release would precede the long-awaited
City Planning Commission land-use study, and not be
lost in the shuffle. However, it was not clear,
what the purpose of the press release was and who
was to be influenced by it. Essentially, this
document restated the goals and guidelines which
were developed during the fourth session. The day
following the press release the City Planning
Commission issued its own plan for an Interstate
West Side Highway(21).

Epilogue: Litigation

The press release, in effect, terminated the
experiment, although several participants met with
City Planning Commissioner John Zuccotti, to
discuss his "Westway" plan and to present their
goals.

On December 19, 1974, Action for Rational
Transit filed suit in federal court against Mayor
Beame, and other city, state and federal officials,

for declaratory injunctive relief, to block
I-478(22). They charged that the <u>Federal</u> <u>Clean</u> <u>Air</u>
<u>Act</u> and the <u>National</u> <u>Environmental</u> <u>Policy</u> <u>Act</u> had
been violated in the planning of the West Side
Highway Project. The defendants were charged with
"arbitrary and capricious action' and 'derogation
of duty' in executing federal and state
law(s). . ." and they ignored their "legal
obligation to improve air quality and mass transit
systems by taking advantage of the 'interstate
transfer.'" The plaintiff charged that the State
had "withheld a study of mass transit alternatives
for the West Side Corridor, and that there were
violations of the procedures governing the conduct
of public hearings." Finally, the socio-economic
concerns of the community were asserted by the
group(23):

> There is a strong conviction among West Side
> residents that construction of an interstate
> would literally destroy their communities and
> contribute to the continuing decline of
> Manhattan as a place to live and work.

The outcome of the judicial proceedings is
still to be determined. However, on February 11,
1975, Governor Carey's Task Force on the West Side
Highway terminated its deliberations in a split
decision: three favored an Interstate (including
John Keith), and two favored the mass transit
transfer (including Carolyn Konheim)(24).
On March 3, 1975, Manhattan Borough President
Percy Sutton announced his opposition to I-478, and
the remaining undecided state legislators have
started to announce their opposition. As of early
March 1975, all seven community planning boards
opposed I-478. And on March 8, 1975, Governor
Carey accepted the Mayor's plan(25). During this
hiatus the city has decided to resurface the
roadway below the elevated West Side Highway
structure, at a cost of $446,921(26).
Most recently (September 1979) distinguished
experts recommended against the Westway and
similar large projects, in favor of small.
Neighborhood rehabilitation projects(27).

CONCLUSIONS

Although it was only a minor episode in the
long saga of the West Side Highway dispute, it

would not be fair to classify the mediation
experiment as a total failure. For it was an
educational and socializing experience for the
participants, who had developed very strong
hostilities over the years. It provided an
opportunity for a dialogue, and eliminated the
harangues of public hearings which permit only
one-way communication.

On the other hand, the experiment did not
resolve the dispute. Our model was not the
approach employed by the mediator, but it is
difficult to predict if the experiment would have
succeeded had our model been utilized. The
document which the group produced might have been
developed three years earlier by the West Side
Highway Project's Steering Committee, particularly
since its charter required public
participation(28). However, as with other
attempts at citizen involvement, the Steering
Committee used its public members from the six
community planning boards as a buffer against
community opposition, to "promote management plans
and proposals and to discharge public animosity
toward the agency"(29).

It appears that the governor and mayor did not
perceive the anti-highway groups as a potentially
significant electoral threat. This seems to be
consistent with Reidel's claim that citizen
intervenors are unable to mobilize a major segment
of the electorate(30).

The mediation experiment was an attempt to
compensate for a faulty participatory process.
However, the agenda for the mediation group was
developed by the highway planners: it was an
agenda of highway designs developed by
"professional high priests"(31). It was not
surprising then, that the citizen intervenors were
unprepared to select a highway design, and instead
wanted to discuss The equity of the interstate plan
and social goals which required a binding land-use
plan. They found that in order to address those
goals they had to initiate litigation, for as
Dorothy Nelkin's study of the expansion of Boston's
Logan International Airport illustrated(32),

> left alone, public bureaucracies responsible
> for technological changes will not willingly
> incorporate . . .social costs into their
> calculations. Their self-perception does not
> depend on their accountability to those
> negatively affected by their policies.

(The lack of accountability in the Boston dispute was particularly acute because Massport is an independent agency which is financed through tax-exempt revenue bonds and is unaffected by public opinion.)(33) The West Side Highway Project staff were in theory, more accountable to public opinion because they depended upon the mayor and governor's consent.

We think that the West Side Highway Project's interest in the mediation experiment was probably founded on the hope that they would coopt the group and legitimize the highway in the mayor and governor's eyes. Instead, public participation at such a late stage alienated and mobilized the local community to fight the Interstate through the courts. If public agencies continue to view public participation and intervention as a last minute cooptation process to avoid litigation, they will continue to be frustrated(34).

Potential for consensus has been identified within the West Side Highway mediation group. From this analysis we have observed that for mediation to work no party should benefit from continued delay. Mediation also requires that the mediator be independent and be provided with sanctions by the executive official with the authority to implement the settlement.

Analysis of the West Side Highway dispute revealed a pattern of fragmented authority (see Table 3). However, it has been noted that(35)

> . . .fragmentation of authority does increase levels of visible conflict. But visible conflict may bring out information, clarify issues and encourage a search for mutually agreeable solutions . . . .

This is important because fragmentation of authority creates multiple sources of information which can be utilized in developing a range of policy options and determining marginal considerations which can be negotiated in order to reach a settlement. For example, the information generated by the various authorities associated with the West Side Highway (see Table 3) might not have been available if one jurisdiction had a monopoly over transportation policy implementation. In particular, the federal transportation officials provided the mediation participants with an understanding of the flexibility of funding mechanisms which they could use in their negotiations with the mayor.

228

Aside from generating relevant information, however, jurisdictional fragmentation was not a major factor in the West Side Highway dispute(35). Rather, we observed that the federal officials from the funding agencies offered to bend their regulations to please the local community, if the community could persuade the mayor. Their offer corroborated the statement of a federal official in Chicago, who stated that "if a community can't plan for its own development and growth, we can't do a damn thing for them"(37).

New York's inability to resolve the competing socio-economic priorities of business, residential, environmental and civic groups cannot be attributed to jurisdictional arrangements. For example, jurisdictional arrangements do not prevent New York City's compliance with the Federal Clean Air Act, since several major air pollution control strategies are already within the discretionary powers of the mayor. He can impose tolls on the East River bridges, ban taxi cruising in the Central Business District and restrict off-street parking in the Central Business District (this last strategy is considered to be the most effective)(38).

We must conclude that it was politically expedient for the mayor and the governor to permit the highway dispute to be resolved in the courts, and subsequently, to approve the Westway(39). Despite this negative outcome, I believe that if the mediator had established political support for the mediation project, both the governor and the mayor would have been willing to accept the mediation settlement, based on the common objectives identified through the mediation sessions.

REFERENCES

1. West Side Highway Project, Draft Environmental Impact Statement for Interstate 478 (New York: West Side Highway Project, April 26, 1974).
2. Ibid., p. 11.
3. Jeffrey L. Pressman and Aaron Wildavsky, Implementation: How Great Expectations in Washington are Dashed in Oakland (Berkeley: University of California Press, 1973), p. 125.
4. Ibid., p. 119.

5. The Interstate transfer for I-478 was $327 million in 1974 and was increased to $550 million in January 1975.

6. The two Task Force members were Carolyn Konheim of the Scientists' Committee for Public Information and John Keith of the Regional Plan Association.

7. Michael J. Lazar and John E. Zuccotti, Land Use and the West Side Highway: Recommendations (New York: New York City Planning Commission, November 21, 1974), 48 pp. John Dornton, "Zuccotti, Planning Unit Head, Ranks High With Beame," New York Times, November 29, 1974, p. 41. Steven R. Weisman, "City Plans a Tunnel for West Side Road South of 42nd Street," New York Times, November 28, 1974, p. 42.

8. American Arbitration Association, Twenty Community Public Interest Groups Define Principles for New West Side Highway (New York: American Arbitration Association, November 20, 1974), 3pp. (Mimeographed.)

9. Action for Rational Transit, Help Stop the West Side Interstate (New York: Action for Rational Transit, September 1974). (Mimeographed.) Steven R. Weisman, "City's West Side Highway Plan Criticized by Community Boards," New York Times, November 27, 1974, p. 1.

10. Emanuel Perlmutter, "Moses Has West Side Highway Plan," New York Times, November 25, 1974, p. 60.

11. The sessions were held on August 14, 26, September 16, October 24 and November 13, 1974.

12. George H. Hagevik, Decision-Making in Air Pollution Control (New York: Praeger, 1970), p. 36.

13. John G. Grumm and Russel D. Murphy, "Dillon's Rule Reconsidered," The Annals of the Am. Acad. of Pol. and Soc. Sci., November 1974, p. 130.

14. Mr. Keith made this statement at the meeting on alternatives to the West Side Highway, September 24, 1974.

15. Brevard Crihfield and H. Clyde Reeves, "Intergovernmental Relations: A View from the State," The Annals of the Am. Acad. of Pol. and Soc. Sci., November 1974, p. 104.

16. West Side Highway Project, op cit., p. 110.

17. Mr. Mertz, Associate Administrator, ~~ral Highway Administration, statement before ~~ion group, September 16, 1974.

18. West Side Highway Project, _op cit._, pp. 10, 11.

19. Ford Foundation, _The Art of Managing the Environment_ (New York: September 1974), p. 28.

20. See note _supra_.

21. See note _supra_.

22. Action for Rational Transit, press release, _Beame and Others Sued on West Side Highway: Groups Oppose Interstate in U.S. District Court_ (New York: Action for Rational Transit, December 19, 1974), 3 pp. (Mimeographed.) The legal responsibilities for Interstate planning are extensively discussed in John W. Vardaman, Jr., "Federal Environmental Statutes and Transportation," in Erica L. Dolgin and Thomas G.P. Guilbert, eds., _Federal Environmental Law_ (St. Paul Minn.: West Publishing Co., 1974), pp. 1316-1413.

23. Action for Rational Transit, _op cit._, p. 3.

24. "Carey Task Force, 3 to 2, Urges Interstate Plan for West Side," _New York Times_, February 12, 1975, p. 74.

25. Peter Freiberg and George Arzt, "Carey, Beame Set of OK Interstate," _New York Post_, March 7, 1975, pp. 1, 3. Edward Burks, "Interstate Highway Backed for West Side," _New York Times_, March 8, 1975, pp. 1, 52.

26. Edward Burks, "West Side Detour to be Built Soon," _New York Times_, February 23, 1975, p. 28.

27. Edward Schumacher "Panel Asks City to Drop Westway." _New York Times_, September 23, 1979, p. 41.

28. West Side Highway Project, _op cit._, p. 12.

29. Harvey Frauenglass, "Environmental Policy: Public Participation and the Open Information Syste," _Nat. Resources J._, July 1971, p. 492.

30. Reidel, _op cit._, p. 214.

31. Arnold Bolle, "Public Participation and Environmental Quality," _Nat. Resources J._, July 1971, p. 501.

32. Dorothy Nelkin, "Massport vs. Community," _Transaction/Society_ II, June 1974, pp. 27-39.

33. _Ibid._, p. 39.

34. Daniel Mazmanian, _Citizens and the Assessment of Technology: An Examination of the Participation Thesis_ (Chicago: American Political Science Association, Annual Meeting, September 1974), p. 47. (Mimeographed.)

35. Robert Bish and Vincent Ostrom, <u>op</u> <u>cit</u>., p. 93.

36. See Charles M. Hassett, "Enforcement Problems in the Air Quality Field: Some Intergovernmental Structural Aspects," <u>Ecology</u> <u>Law</u> <u>Quarterly</u> Vol. 4, Winter 1974, pp. 63-92.

37. Pressman and Wildavsky, <u>op</u> <u>cit</u>., p. 141.

38. Lazar and Zuccotti, <u>op</u> <u>cit</u>., p. 8.

39. Steven R. Weisman, "Koch Backs Westway; Carey Pledges to Save 50c Fare and Raise Aid," <u>New</u> <u>York</u> <u>Times</u>, April 20, 1978, p. 1, B11.

APPENDIX

WEST SIDE HIGHWAY MEDIATION EXPERIMENT
PARTICIPATING ORGANIZATIONS

*American Institute of Architects, New York
    Chapter
*Automobile Club of New York
*Citizens' Budget Commission
*Citizens for Clean Air
*Citizens' Housing and Planning Council
*Consultants to Community Planning Boards, 2, 4, 7,
    9, 12
*Community Planning Boards 2, 4, 7, 9, 12
**Community Service Society
*Council on the Environment of New York City
*Downtown Lower Manhattan Association
*Institute for Public Transportation
*Municipal Art Society
*National Audubon Society
**New York Chamber of Commerce and Industry
*Real Estate Board of New York
*Regional Plan Association
*Scientists' Committee for Public Information
*Women's City Club of New York

---

*Indicates group endorsed press release and
attended all sessions.
    **Indicates group attended at least one
session, but did not endorse press release.

233